Hands-On Financial Trading with Python

A practical guide to using Zipline and other Python libraries for backtesting trading strategies

Jiri Pik

Sourav Ghosh

Packt>

BIRMINGHAM—MUMBAI

Hands-On Financial Trading with Python

Group Product Manager: Kunal Parikh
Publishing Product Manager: Aditi Gour
Senior Editor: Mohammed Yusuf Imaratwale
Content Development Editor: Athikho Sapuni Rishana
Technical Editor: Manikandan Kurup
Copy Editor: Safis Editing
Project Coordinator: Aishwarya Mohan
Proofreader: Safis Editing
Indexer: Priyanka Dhadke
Production Designer: Nilesh Mohite

First published: April 2021
Production reference: 1290421

Published by Packt Publishing Ltd.
Livery Place
35 Livery Street
Birmingham
B3 2PB, UK.

ISBN 978-1-83898-288-1

`www.packt.com`

Contributors

About the authors

Jiri Pik is an artificial intelligence architect and strategist who works with major investment banks, hedge funds, and other players. He has architected and delivered breakthrough trading, portfolio, and risk management systems, as well as decision support systems, across numerous industries. His consulting firm, Jiri Pik—RocketEdge, provides its clients with certified expertise, judgment, and execution at lightspeed.

Sourav Ghosh has worked in several proprietary high-frequency algorithmic trading firms over the last decade. He has built and deployed extremely low-latency, high-throughput automated trading systems for trading exchanges around the world, across multiple asset classes. He specializes in statistical arbitrage market-making and pairs trading strategies for the most liquid global futures contracts. He works as a senior quantitative developer at a trading firm in Chicago. He holds a master's in computer science from the University of Southern California. His areas of interest include computer architecture, FinTech, probability theory and stochastic processes, statistical learning and inference methods, and natural language processing.

About the reviewer

Ratanlal Mahanta is currently working as a quantitative analyst at bittQsrv, a global quantitative research company offering quant models for its investors. He has several years of experience in the modeling and simulation of quantitative trading. He holds a master's degree in science in computational finance, and his research areas include quant trading, optimal execution, and high-frequency trading. He has over 9 years' experience in the finance industry and is gifted at solving difficult problems that lie at the intersection of markets, technology, research, and design.

Table of Contents

3

High-Speed Scientific Computing Using NumPy

4

Data Manipulation and Analysis with pandas

5

Data Visualization Using Matplotlib

6

Statistical Estimation, Inference, and Prediction

Section 3: Algorithmic Trading in Python

7

Financial Market Data Access in Python

8

Introduction to Zipline and PyFolio

9
Fundamental Algorithmic Trading Strategies

Appendix A
How to Setup a Python Environment

Other Books You May Enjoy

Index

Preface

Algorithmic trading helps you stay ahead of the market by devising strategies in quantitative analysis to gain profits and cut losses. This book will help you to understand financial theories and execute a range of algorithmic trading strategies confidently.

The book starts by introducing you to algorithmic trading, the pyfinance ecosystem, and Quantopian. You'll then cover algorithmic trading and quantitative analysis using Python, and learn how to build algorithmic trading strategies on Quantopian. As you advance, you'll gain an in-depth understanding of Python libraries such as NumPy and pandas for analyzing financial datasets, and also explore the matplotlib, statsmodels, and scikit-learn libraries for advanced analytics. Moving on, you'll explore useful financial concepts and theories such as financial statistics, leveraging and hedging, and short selling, which will help you understand how financial markets operate. Finally, you will discover mathematical models and approaches for analyzing and understanding financial time series data.

By the end of this trading book, you will be able to build predictive trading signals, adopt basic and advanced algorithmic trading strategies, and perform portfolio optimization on the Quantopian platform.

Who this book is for

This book is for data analysts and financial traders who want to explore algorithmic trading using Python core libraries. If you are looking for a practical guide to execute various algorithmic trading strategies, then this book is for you. Basic working knowledge of Python programming and statistics will be helpful.

What this book covers

Chapter 1, Introduction to Algorithmic Trading and Python, introduces the key financial trading concepts and explains why Python is best suited for algorithmic trading.

Chapter 2, Exploratory Data Analysis in Python, provides an overview of the first step in processing any dataset, exploratory data analysis.

Chapter 3, High-Speed Scientific Computing Using NumPy, takes a detailed look at NumPy, a library for fast and scalable structured arrays and vectorized computations.

Chapter 4, Data Manipulation and Analysis with pandas, introduces the pandas library, built on top of NumPy, which provides data manipulation and analysis methods to structured DataFrames.

Chapter 5, Data Visualization Using Matplotlib, focuses on one of the primary visualization libraries in Python, Matplotlib.

Chapter 6, Statistical Estimation, Inference, and Prediction, discusses the statsmodels and scikit-learn libraries for advanced statistical analysis techniques, time series analysis techniques, as well as training and validating machine learning models.

Chapter 7, Financial Market Data Access in Python, describes alternative ways to retrieve market data in Python.

Chapter 8, Introduction to Zipline and PyFolio, covers Zipline and PyFolio, which are Python libraries that abstract away the complexities of actual backtesting and performance/risk analysis of algorithmic trading strategies. They allow you to entirely focus on the trading logic.

Chapter 9, Fundamental Algorithmic Trading Strategies, introduces the concept of an algorithmic strategy, and eight different trading algorithms representing the most used algorithms.

To get the most out of this book

Follow the instructions in the *Appendix* section on how to recreate the `conda` virtual environment using the `environment.yml` file stored in the book's GitHub's repository. One command restores the entire environment.

Software/Hardware covered in the book	OS Requirements
Anaconda, Python 3.6, JupyterLab	Windows, Mac OS X, and Linux (Any)
List of packages can be found in the `environment.yml` file in the GitHub repo	

If you are using the digital version of this book, we advise you to type the code yourself or access the code via the GitHub repository (link available in the next section). Doing so will help you avoid any potential errors related to the copying and pasting of code.

Download the example code files

You can download the example code files for this book from GitHub at `https://github.com/PacktPublishing/Hands-On-Financial-Trading-with-Python`. In case there's an update to the code, it will be updated on the existing GitHub repository.

We also have other code bundles from our rich catalog of books and videos available at `https://github.com/PacktPublishing/`. Check them out!

Download the color images

We also provide a PDF file that has color images of the screenshots/diagrams used in this book. You can download it here: `https://static.packt-cdn.com/downloads/9781838982881_ColorImages.pdf`.

Conventions used

There are a number of text conventions used throughout this book.

`Code in text`: Indicates code words in text, database table names, folder names, filenames, file extensions, pathnames, dummy URLs, user input, and Twitter handles. Here is an example: "Let's create a `zipline_env` virtual environment with Python 3.6."

A block of code is set as follows:

```
from zipline import run_algorithm
from zipline.api import order_target_percent, symbol
from datetime import datetime
import pytz
```

When we wish to draw your attention to a particular part of a code block, the relevant lines or items are set in bold:

```
from . import quandl  # noqa
from . import csvdir  # noqa
from . import quandl_eod  # noqa
```

Bold: Indicates a new term, an important word, or words that you see onscreen. For example, words in menus or dialog boxes appear in the text like this. Here is an example: "Then, specify the variable in the **Environment Variables...** dialog."

> **Tips or important notes**
> Appear like this.

Get in touch

Feedback from our readers is always welcome.

General feedback: If you have questions about any aspect of this book, mention the book title in the subject of your message and email us at `customercare@packtpub.com`.

Errata: Although we have taken every care to ensure the accuracy of our content, mistakes do happen. If you have found a mistake in this book, we would be grateful if you would report this to us. Please visit `www.packtpub.com/support/errata`, selecting your book, clicking on the Errata Submission Form link, and entering the details.

Piracy: If you come across any illegal copies of our works in any form on the Internet, we would be grateful if you would provide us with the location address or website name. Please contact us at `copyright@packt.com` with a link to the material.

If you are interested in becoming an author: If there is a topic that you have expertise in and you are interested in either writing or contributing to a book, please visit `authors.packtpub.com`.

Reviews

Please leave a review. Once you have read and used this book, why not leave a review on the site that you purchased it from? Potential readers can then see and use your unbiased opinion to make purchase decisions, we at Packt can understand what you think about our products, and our authors can see your feedback on their book. Thank you!

For more information about Packt, please visit `packt.com`.

Section 1: Introduction to Algorithmic Trading

This section will introduce you to important concepts in algorithmic trading and Python.

This section comprises the following chapter:

- *Chapter 1, Introduction to Algorithmic Trading and Python*

1
Introduction to Algorithmic Trading

In this chapter, we will take you through a brief history of trading and explain in which situations manual and algorithmic trading each make sense. Additionally, we will discuss financial asset classes, which are a categorization of the different types of financial assets. You will learn about the components of the modern electronic trading exchange, and, finally, we will outline the key components of an algorithmic trading system.

In this chapter, we will cover the following topics:

- Walking through the evolution of algorithmic trading
- Understanding financial asset classes
- Going through the modern electronic trading exchange
- Understanding the components of an algorithmic trading system

Walking through the evolution of algorithmic trading

The concept of trading one possession for another has been around since the beginning of time. In its earliest form, trading was useful for exchanging a less desirable possession for a more desirable possession. Eventually, with the passage of time, trading has evolved into participants trying to find a way to buy and hold trading instruments (that is, products) at prices perceived as lower than fair value in the hopes of being able to sell them in the future at a price higher than the purchase price. This **buy-low-and-sell-high principle** serves as the basis for all profitable trading to date; of course, how to achieve this is where the complexity and competition lies.

Markets are driven by the **fundamental economic forces of supply and demand**. As demand increases without a commensurate increase in supply, or supply decreases without a decrease in demand, a commodity becomes scarce and increases in value (that is, its market price). Conversely, if demand drops without a decrease in supply, or supply increases without an increase in demand, a commodity becomes more easily available and less valuable (a lower market price). Therefore, the market price of a commodity should reflect the equilibrium price based on available supply (sellers) and available demand (buyers).

There are many drawbacks to the **manual trading approach**, as follows:

- Human traders are inherently slow at processing new market information, making them likely to miss information or to make errors in interpreting updated market data. This leads to bad trading decisions.
- Humans, in general, are also prone to distractions and biases that reduce profits and/or generate losses. For example, the fear of losing money and the joy of making money also causes us to deviate from the optimal systematic trading approach, which we understand in theory but fail to execute in practice. In addition, people are also naturally and non-uniformly biased against profitable trades versus losing trades; for instance, human traders are quick to increase the amount of risk after profitable trades and slow down to decrease the amount of risk after losing trades.
- Human traders learn by experiencing market conditions, for example, by being present and trading live markets. So, they cannot learn from and **backtest** over historical market data conditions – an important advantage of automated strategies, as we will see later.

With the advent of technology, trading has evolved from pit trading carried out by yelling and signaling buy and sell orders all the way to using sophisticated, efficient, and fast computer hardware and software to execute trades, often without much human intervention. Sophisticated algorithmic trading software systems have replaced human traders and engineers, and mathematicians who build, operate, and improve these systems, known as **quants**, have risen to power.

In particular, the key advantages of an **automated, computer-driven systematic/ algorithmic trading approach** are as follows:

- Computers are extremely good at performing clearly defined and repetitive rule-based tasks. They can perform these tasks extremely quickly and can handle massive throughputs.
- Additionally, computers do not get distracted, tired, or make mistakes (unless there is a software bug, which, technically, counts as a software developer error).
- Algorithmic trading strategies also have no emotions as far as trading through losses or profits; therefore, they can stick to a systematic trading plan no matter what.

All of these advantages make systematic algorithmic trading the perfect candidate to set up low-latency, high-throughput, scalable, and robust trading businesses.

However, algorithmic trading is not always better than manual trading:

- Manual trading is better at dealing with significantly complex ideas and the complexities of real-world trading operations that are, sometimes, difficult to express as an automated software solution.
- Automated trading systems require significant investments in time and R&D costs, while manual trading strategies are often significantly faster to get to market.
- Algorithmic trading strategies are also prone to software development/operation bugs, which can have a significant impact on a trading business. Entire automated trading operations being wiped out in a matter of a few minutes is not unheard of.
- Often, automated quantitative trading systems are not good at dealing with extremely unlikely events termed as **black swan** events, such as the LTCM crash, the 2010 flash crash, the Knight Capital crash, and more.

In this section, we learned about the history of trading and when automated/algorithmic is better than manual trading. Now, let's proceed toward the next section, where we will learn about the actual subject of trading categorized into financial asset classes.

Understanding financial asset classes

Algorithmic trading deals with the trading of financial assets. A financial asset is a non-physical asset whose value arises from contractual agreements.

The major financial asset classes are as follows:

- **Equities** (**stocks**): These allow market participants to invest directly in the company and become owners of the company.
- **Fixed income** (**bonds**): These represent a loan made by the investor to a borrower (for instance, a government or a firm). Each bond has its end date when the principal of the loan is due to be paid back and, usually, either fixed or variable interest payments made by the borrower over the lifetime of the bond.
- **Real Estate Investment Trusts** (**REITs**): These are publicly traded companies that own or operate or finance income-producing real estate. These can be used as a proxy to directly invest in the housing market, say, by purchasing a property.
- **Commodities**: Examples include metals (silver, gold, copper, and more) and agricultural produce (wheat, corn, milk, and more). They are financial assets tracking the price of the underlying commodities.
- **Exchange-Traded Funds** (**ETFs**): An EFT is an exchange-listed security that tracks a collection of other securities. ETFs, such as SPY, DIA, and QQQ, hold equity stocks to track the larger well-known S&P 500, Dow Jones Industrial Average, and Nasdaq stock indices. ETFs such as **United States Oil Fund** (**USO**) track oil prices by investing in short-term WTI crude oil futures. ETFs are a convenient investment vehicle for investors to invest in a wide range of asset classes at relatively lower costs.
- **Foreign Exchange** (**FX**) between different currency pairs, the major ones being the **US Dollar** (**USD**), **Euro** (**EUR**), **Pound Sterling** (**GBP**), **Japanese Yen** (**JPY**), **Australian Dollar** (**AUD**), **New Zealand Dollar** (**NZD**), **Canadian Dollar** (**CAD**), **Swiss Franc** (**CHF**), **Norwegian Krone** (**NOK**), and **Swedish Krona** (**SEK**). These are often referred to as the G10 currencies.
- The key **Financial derivatives** are options and futures – these are complex leveraged derivative products that can magnify the risk as well as the reward:

  a) **Futures** are financial contracts to buy or sell an asset at a predetermined future date and price.

  b) **Options** are financial contracts giving their owner the right, but not the obligation, to buy or sell an underlying asset at a stated price (strike price) prior to or on a specified date.

In this section, we learned about the financial asset classes and their unique properties. Now, let's discuss the order types and exchange matching algorithms of modern electronic trading exchanges.

Going through the modern electronic trading exchange

The first trading exchange was the Amsterdam Stock Exchange, which began in 1602. Here, the trading happened in person. The applications of technology to trading included using pigeons, telegraph systems, Morse code, telephones, computer terminals, and nowadays, high-speed computer networks and state-of-the-art computers. With the passage of time, the trading microstructure has evolved into the order types and matching algorithms that we are used to today.

Knowledge of the modern electronic trading exchange microstructure is important for the design of algorithmic strategies.

Order types

Financial trading strategies employ a variety of different order types, and some of the most common ones include Market orders, Market with Price Protection orders, **Immediate-Or-Cancel** (**IOC**) orders, **Fill and Kill** (**FAK**) orders, **Good-'Till-Day** (**GTD**) orders, **Good-'Till-Canceled** (**GTC**) orders, Stop orders, and Iceberg orders.

For the strategies that we will be exploring in this book, we will focus on Market orders, IOC, and GTC.

Market orders

Market orders are buy-or-sell orders that need to be executed instantly at the current market price and are used when the immediacy of execution is preferred to the execution price.

These orders will execute against all available orders on the opposite side at the order's price until all the quantity asked for is executed. If it runs out of available liquidity to match against, it can be configured to **sit in the order book** or **expire**. Sitting in the book means the order becomes a resting order that is added to the book for other participants to trade against. To expire means that the remaining order quantity is canceled instead of being added to the book so that new orders cannot match against the remaining quantity.

So, for instance, a buy market order will match against all sell orders sitting in the book from the best price to the worst price until the entire market order is executed.

These orders may suffer from extreme **slippage**, which is defined as the difference in the executed order's price and the market price at the time the order was sent.

IOC orders

IOC orders cannot execute at prices worse than what they were sent for, which means buy orders cannot execute higher than the order's price, and sell orders cannot execute lower than the order's price. This concept is known as **limit price** since that price is limited to the worst price the order can execute at.

An IOC order will continue matching against orders on the order side until one of the following happens:

- The entire quantity on the IOC order is executed.
- The price of the passive order on the other side is worse than the IOC order's price.
- The IOC order is partially executed, and the remaining quantity expires.

An IOC order that is sent at a price better than the best available order on the other side (that is, the buy order is lower than the best offer price, or the sell order is higher than the best bid price) does not execute at all and just expires.

GTC orders

GTC orders can persist indefinitely and require a specific cancellation order.

Limit order books

The exchange accepts order requests from all market participants and maintains them in a **limit order book**. Limit order books are a view into all the market participant's visible orders available at the exchange at any point in time.

Buy orders (or **bids**) are arranged from the highest price (that is, the best price) to the lowest price (that is, the worst price), and **Ask orders** (that is, **asks** or **offers**) are arranged from the lowest price (that is, the best price) to the highest price (that is, the lowest price).

The highest bid prices are considered the best bid prices because buy orders with the highest buy prices are the first to be matched, and the reverse is true for ask prices, that is, sell orders with the lowest sell prices match first.

Orders on the same side and at the same price level are arranged in the **First-In-First-Out (FIFO)** order, which is also known as priority order – orders with better priority are ahead of orders with lower priority because the better priority orders have reached the exchange before the others. All else being equal (that is, the same order side, price, and quantity), orders with better priority will execute before orders with worse priority.

The exchange matching engine

The matching engine at the electronic trading exchange performs the **matching of orders** using **exchange matching algorithms**. The process of matching entails checking all active orders entered by market participants and matching the orders that cross each other in price until there are no unmatched orders that could be matched – so, buy orders with prices at or above other sell orders match against them, and the converse is true as well, that is, sell orders with prices at or below other buy orders match against them. The remaining orders remain in the exchange matching book until a new order flow comes in, leading to new matches if possible.

In the FIFO matching algorithm, orders are matched first – from the best price to the worst price. So, an incoming buy order tries to match against resting sell orders (that is, asks/offers) from the lowest price to the highest price, and an incoming sell order tries to match against resting buy orders (that is, bids) from the highest price to the lowest price. New incoming orders are matched with a specific sequence of rules. For incoming aggressive orders (orders with prices better than the best price level on the other side), they are matched on a first-come-first-serve basis, that is, orders that show up first, take out liquidity and, therefore, match first. For passive resting orders that sit in the book, since they do not execute immediately, they are assigned based on priority on a first-come-first-serve basis. That means orders on the same side and at the same price are arranged based on the time it takes them to reach the matching engine; orders with earlier times are assigned better priority and, therefore, are eligible to be matched first.

In this section, we learned about the order types and exchange matching engine of the modern electronic trading exchange. Now, let's proceed toward the next section, where we will learn about the components of an algorithmic trading system.

Understanding the components of an algorithmic trading system

A client-side algorithmic trading infrastructure can be broken down broadly into two categories: **core infrastructure** and **quantitative infrastructure**.

The core infrastructure of an algorithmic trading system

A core infrastructure handles communication with the exchange using market data and order entry protocols. It is responsible for relaying information between the exchange and the algorithmic trading strategy.

Its components are also responsible for capturing, timestamping, and recording historical market data, which is one of the top priorities for algorithmic trading strategy research and development.

The core infrastructure also includes a layer of risk management components to guard the trading system against erroneous or runaway trading strategies to prevent catastrophic outcomes.

Finally, some of the less glamorous tasks involved in the algorithmic trading business, such as back-office reconciliation tasks, compliance, and more, are also addressed by the core infrastructure.

Trading servers

The trading server involves one or more computers receiving and processing market and other relevant data, and trading exchange information (for example, an order book), and issuing trading orders.

From the limit order book, updates to the exchange matching book are disseminated to all market participants over **market data protocols**.

Market participants have **trading servers** that receive these market data updates. While, technically, these trading servers can be anywhere in the world, modern algorithmic trading participants have their trading servers placed in a data center very close to the exchange matching engine. This is called a **colocated** or **Direct Market Access (DMA)** setup, which guarantees that participants receive market data updates as fast as possible by being as close to the matching engine as possible.

Once the market data update, which is communicated via exchange-provided market data protocols, is received by each market participant, they use software applications known as **market data feed handlers** to decode the market data updates and feed it to the algorithmic trading strategy on the client side.

Once the algorithmic trading strategy has digested the market data update, based on the intelligence developed in the strategy, it generates outgoing order flow. This can be the addition, modification, or cancellation of orders at specific prices and quantities.

The order requests are picked up by an, often, separate client component known as the **order entry gateway**. The order entry gateway component communicates with the exchange using **order entry protocols** to translate this request from the strategy to the exchange. Notifications in response to these order requests are sent by the electronic exchange back to the order entry gateway. Again, in response to this order flow by a specific market participant, the matching engine generates market data updates, therefore going back to the beginning of this information flow loop.

The quantitative infrastructure of an algorithmic trading system

A quantitative infrastructure builds on top of the platform provided by the core infrastructure and, essentially, tries to build components on top to research, develop, and effectively leverage the platform to generate revenue.

The research framework includes components such as backtesting, **Post-Trade Analytics (PTA)**, and signal research components.

Other components that are used in research as well as deployed to live markets would be limit order books, predictive signals, and signal aggregators, which combine individual signals into a composite signal.

Execution logic components use trading signals and do the heavy lifting of managing live orders, positions, and **Profit And Loss (PnL)** across different strategies and trading instruments.

Finally, trading strategies themselves have a risk management component to manage and mitigate risk across different strategies and instruments.

Trading strategies

Profitable trading ideas have always been driven by human intuition developed from observing the patterns of market conditions and the outcomes of various strategies under different market conditions.

For example, historically, it has been observed that large market rallies generate investor confidence, causing more market participants to jump in and buy more; therefore, recursively causing larger rallies. Conversely, large drops in market prices scare off participants invested in the trading instrument, causing them to sell their holdings and exacerbate the drop in prices. These intuitive ideas backed by observations in markets led to the idea of **trend-following strategies**.

It has also been observed that short-term volatile moves in either direction often tend to revert to their previous market price, leading to **mean reversion-based speculators and trading strategies**. Similarly, historical observations that similar product prices move together, which also makes intuitive sense have led to the generation of correlation and collinearity-based trading strategies such as **statistical arbitrage** and **pairs trading** strategies.

Since every market participant uses different trading strategies, the final market prices reflect the majority of market participants. Trading strategies whose views align with the majority of market participants are profitable under those conditions. A single trading strategy generally cannot be profitable 100 percent of the time, so sophisticated participants have a portfolio of trading strategies.

Trading signals

Trading signals are also referred to as features, calculators, indicators, predictors, or alpha.

Trading signals are what drive algorithmic trading strategy decisions. Signals are well-defined pieces of intelligence derived from market data, alternative data (such as news, social media feeds, and more), and even our own order flow, which is designed to predict certain market conditions in the future.

Signals almost always originate from some intuitive idea and observation of certain market conditions and/or strategy performance. Often, most quantitative developers spend most of their time researching and developing new trading signals to improve profitability under different market conditions and to improve the algorithmic trading strategy overall.

The trading signal research framework

A lot of man-hours are invested in researching and discovering new signals to improve trading performance. To do that in a systematic, efficient, scalable, and scientific manner, often, the first step is to build a good **signal research framework**.

This framework has subcomponents for the following:

- Data generation is based on the signal we are trying to build and the market conditions/objectives we are trying to capture/predict. In most real-world algorithmic trading, we use tick data, which is data that represents every single event in the market. As you might imagine, there are a lot of events every day and this leads to massive amounts of data, so you also need to think about subsampling the data received. **Subsampling** has several advantages, such as reducing the scale of data, eliminating the noise/spurious patches of data, and highlighting interesting/important data.

- The evaluation of the predictive power or usefulness of features concerning the market objective that they are trying to capture/predict.
- The maintenance of historical results of signals under different market conditions along with tuning existing signals to changing market conditions.

Signal aggregators

Signal aggregators are optional components that take inputs from individual signals and aggregate them in different ways to generate a new composite signal.

A very simple aggregation method would be to take the average of all the input signals and output the average as the composite signal value.

Readers familiar with statistical learning concepts of ensemble learning – bagging and boosting – might be able to spot a similarity between those learning models and signal aggregators. Oftentimes signal aggregators are just statistical models (regression/classification) where the input signals are just features used to predict the same final market objective.

The execution of strategies

The execution of strategies deals with efficiently managing and executing orders based on the outputs of the trading signals to minimize trading fees and slippage.

Slippage is the difference between market prices and execution prices and is caused due to the latency experienced by an order to get to the market before prices change as well as the size of an order causing a change in price once it hits the market.

The quality of execution strategies employed in an algorithmic trading strategy can significantly improve/degrade the performance of profitable trading signals.

Limit order books

Limit order books are built both in the exchange match engine and during the algorithmic trading strategies, although not necessarily all algorithmic trading signals/strategies require the entire limit order book.

Sophisticated algorithmic trading strategies can build a lot more intelligence into their limit order books. We can detect and track our own orders in the limit book and understand, given our priority, what our probability of getting our orders executed is. We can also use this information to execute our own orders even before the order entry gateway gets the execution notification from the exchange and leverage that ability to our advantage. Other more complex microstructure features such as detecting icebergs, detecting stop orders, detecting large in-flow or out-flow of buy/sell orders, and more are all possible with limit order books and market data updates at a lot of electronic trading exchanges.

Position and PnL management

Let's explore how positions and PnLs evolve as a trading strategy opens and closes long and short positions by executing trades.

When a strategy does not have a position in the market, that is, price changes do not affect the trading account's value, it is referred to as having a flat position.

From a flat position, if a buy order executes, then it is referred to as having a long position. If a strategy has a long position and prices increase, the position profits from the price increase. PnL also increases in this scenario, that is, profit increases (or loss decreases). Conversely, if a strategy has a long position and prices decrease, the position loses from the price decrease. PnL decreases in this scenario, for example, the profit decreases (or the loss increases).

From a flat position, if a sell order is executed then it is referred to as having a short position. If a strategy has a short position and prices decrease, the position profits from the price decrease. PnL increases in this scenario. Conversely, if a strategy has a short position and prices increase, then PnL decreases. PnL for a position that is still open is referred to as **unrealized PnL** since PnL changes with price changes as long as the position remains open.

A long position is closed by selling an amount of the instrument equivalent to the position size. This is referred to as closing or flattening a position, and, at this point, PnL is referred to as **realized PnL** since it no longer changes as price changes since the position is closed.

Similarly, short positions are closed by buying the same amount as the position size.

At any point, the **total PnL** is the sum of realized PnLs on all closed positions and unrealized PnLs on all open positions.

When a long or short position is composed of buys or sells at multiple prices with different sizes, then the average price of the position is computed by computing the **Volume Weighted Average Price (VWAP)**, which is the price of each execution weighted by the quantity executed at each price. Marking to market refers to taking the VWAP of a position and comparing that to the current market price to get a sense of how profitable or lossy a certain long/short position is.

Backtesting

A backtester uses historically recorded market data and simulation components to simulate the behavior and performance of an algorithmic trading strategy as if it were deployed to live markets in the past. Algorithmic trading strategies are developed and optimized using a backtester until the strategy performance is in line with expectations.

Backtesters are complex components that need to model market data flow, client-side and exchange-side latencies in software and network components, accurate FIFO priorities, slippage, fees, and market impact from strategy order flow (that is, how would other market participants react to a strategy's order flow being added to the market data flow) to generate accurate strategy and portfolio performance statistics.

PTA

PTA is performed on trades generated by an algorithmic trading strategy run in simulation or live markets.

PTA systems are used to generate performance statistics from historically backtested strategies with the objective to understand historical strategy performance expectations.

When applied to trades generated from live trading strategies, PTA can be used to understand strategy performance in live markets as well as compare and assert that live trading performance is in line with simulated strategy performance expectations.

Risk management

Good risk management principles ensure that strategies are run for optimal PnL performance and safeguards are put in place against runaway/errant strategies.

Bad risk management cannot only turn a profitable trading strategy into a non-profitable one but can also put the investor's entire capital at risk due to uncontrolled strategy losses, malfunctioning strategies, and possible regulatory repercussions.

Summary

In this chapter, we have learned when algorithmic trading has an advantage over manual trading, what the financial asset classes are, the most used order types, what the limit order book is, and how the orders are matched by the financial exchange.

We have also discussed the key components of an algorithmic trading system – the core infrastructure and the quantitative infrastructure which consists of trading strategies, their execution, limit order book, position, PnL management, backtesting, post-trade analytics, and risk management.

In the next chapter, we will discuss the value of Python when it comes to algorithmic trading.

Section 2: In-Depth Look at Python Libraries for the Analysis of Financial Datasets

This section will deep dive into the core Python libraries NumPy and pandas, which are used for the analysis and manipulation of large DataFrames. We will also cover the visualization library Matplotlib, which is closely linked to pandas. Finally, we will look at the statsmodels and scikit-learn libraries, which allow more advanced analysis of financial datasets.

This section comprises the following chapters:

- *Chapter 2, Exploratory Data Analysis in Python*
- *Chapter 3, High-Speed Scientific Computing Using NumPy*
- *Chapter 4, Data Manipulation and Analysis with Pandas*
- *Chapter 5, Data Visualization Using Matplotlib*
- *Chapter 6, Statistical Estimation, Inference, and Prediction*

2
Exploratory Data Analysis in Python

This chapter focuses on **exploratory data analysis** (**EDA**), which is the first step in processing any dataset. The objective of EDA is to load data into data structures most suitable for further analysis to identify and rectify any wrong/bad data and get basic insight into the data—the types of fields there are; whether they are categorical or not; how many missing values there are; how the fields are related; and so on.

These are the main topics discussed in this chapter:

- Introduction to EDA
- Special Python libraries for EDA

Technical requirements

The Python code used in this chapter is available in the `Chapter02/eda.ipynb` notebook in the book's code repository.

Introduction to EDA

EDA is the process of procuring, understanding, and deriving meaningful statistical insights from structured/unstructured data of interest. It is the first step before a more complex analysis, such as predicting future expectations from the data. In the case of financial data, EDA helps obtain insights used later for building profitable trading signals and strategies.

EDA guides later decisions of which features/signals to use or avoid and which predictive models to use or avoid, and invalidates incorrect hypotheses while validating and introducing correct hypotheses about the nature of variables and the relationships between them.

EDA is also important in understanding how sample (a smaller dataset representative of a complete dataset) statistics differ from population (a complete dataset or an ultimate truth) statistics and keeping that in mind when drawing conclusions about the population, based on observations of samples. Thus, EDA helps cut down possible search spaces down the road; otherwise, we would waste a lot more time later on building incorrect/insignificant models or strategies.

EDA must be approached with a scientific mindset. Sometimes, we might reach inadequately validated conclusions based on anecdotal evidence rather than statistical evidence.

Hypotheses based on anecdotal evidence suffer from issues stemming from the following:

- Not being statistically significant—too low number of observations.
- Selection bias—the hypothesis is only created because it was first observed.
- Confirmation bias—our inherent belief in the hypothesis biases our results.
- Inaccuracies in observations.

Let's explore the different steps and techniques involved in EDA, using real datasets.

Steps in EDA

Here is a list of steps involved in EDA (we'll be going through each of them in the subsections that follow):

1. Loading the necessary libraries and setting them up
2. Data collection
3. Data wrangling/munging

4. Data cleaning
5. Obtaining descriptive statistics
6. Visual inspection of the data
7. Data cleaning
8. Advanced visualization techniques

Loading the necessary libraries and setting them up

We will be using `numpy`, `pandas`, and `matplotlib`, and these libraries can be loaded with the help of the following code:

```
%matplotlib inline

import numpy as np
import pandas as pd
from scipy import stats
import seaborn as sn
import matplotlib.pyplot as plt

import mpld3
mpld3.enable_notebook()

import warnings
warnings.filterwarnings('ignore')

pd.set_option('display.max_rows', 2)
```

We use the `mpld3` library for enabling zooming within Jupyter's `matplotlib` charts. The last line of the preceding code block specifies that only a maximum of two rows of `pandas` DataFrames should be displayed.

Data collection

Data collection is usually the first step for EDA. Data may come from many different sources (**comma-separated values** (**CSV**) files, Excel files, web scrapes, binary files, and so on) and will often need to be standardized and first formatted together correctly.

For this exercise, we will use data for three different trading instruments for a period of 5 years, stored in `.csv` format. The identity of these instruments is deliberately not revealed since that might give away their expected behavior/relationships, but we will reveal their identity at the end of this exercise to evaluate intuitively how well we performed EDA on them.

Let's start by loading up our available datasets into three DataFrames (`A`, `B`, and `C`), as follows:

```
A = pd.read_csv('A.csv', parse_dates=True, index_col=0);
A
```

DataFrame `A` has the following structure:

	Open	High	Low	Close	Adj Close	Volume
Date						
2015-05-15	18251.970703	18272.720703	18215.070313	18272.560547	18272.560547	108220000
...	...	...	...	...	...	...
2020-05-14	23049.060547	23630.859375	22789.619141	23625.339844	23625.339844	472700000

1211 rows × 6 columns

Figure 2.1 – DataFrame constructed from the A.csv file

Similarly, let's load DataFrame `B`, as follows:

```
B = pd.read_csv('B.csv', parse_dates=True, index_col=0);
B
```

DataFrame `B` has the following structure:

	Open	High	Low	Close	Adj Close	Volume
Date						
2015-05-15	2122.070068	2123.889893	2116.810059	2122.72998	2122.72998	3092080000
...	...	...	...	...	...	...
2020-05-14	2794.540039	2852.800049	2766.639893	2852.50000	2852.50000	5641920000

1209 rows × 6 columns

Figure 2.2 – DataFrame constructed from the B.csv file

Finally, let's load the C data into a DataFrame, as follows:

```
C = pd.read_csv('C.csv', parse_dates=True, index_col=0);
C
```

And we see C has the following fields:

	Open	High	Low	Close	Adj Close	Volume
Date						
2015-05-15	12.46	13.090000	12.350000	12.380000	12.380000	0
...	...	...	...	...	...	...
2020-05-14	35.16	39.279999	32.330002	32.610001	32.610001	0

1206 rows × 6 columns

Figure 2.3 – DataFrame constructed from the C.csv file

As we can observe, all three data sources have the same format with **Open**, **High**, **Low**, **Close**, and **Adj Close** prices and **Volume** information between approximately `2015-05-15` and `2020-05-14`.

Data wrangling/munging

Data rarely comes in a ready-to-use format. Data wrangling/munging refers to the process of manipulating and transforming data from its initial raw source into structured, formatted, and easily usable datasets.

Let's use `pandas.DataFrame.join(...)` to merge the DataFrames and align them to have the same `DateTimeIndex` format. Using the `lsuffix=` and `rsuffix=` parameters, we assign the `_A`, `_B`, and `_C` suffixes to the columns coming from the three DataFrames, as follows:

```
merged_df = A.join(B, how='outer', lsuffix='_A', sort=True).
join(C, how='outer', lsuffix='_B', rsuffix='_C', sort=True)
merged_df
```

We will inspect the `merged_df` DataFrame we just created and make sure it has all the fields we expected from all three DataFrames (displaying only the first seven columns). The DataFrame can be seen here:

	Open_A	High_A	Low_A	Close_A	Adj Close_A	Volume_A	Open_B
Date							
2015-05-15	18251.970703	18272.720703	18215.070313	18272.560547	18272.560547	108220000.0	2122.070068
...	...	...	...	...	...	...	...
2020-05-14	23049.060547	23630.859375	22789.619141	23625.339844	23625.339844	472700000.0	2794.540039

1259 rows × 18 columns

Figure 2.4 – DataFrame constructed by joining the DataFrames A, B, and C

Notice that the original three DataFrames (`A`, `B`, and `C`) had 1,211, 1,209 and 1,206 rows respectively, but the combined DataFrame has 1,259 rows. This is because we used an outer join, which uses the union of dates across all three DataFrames. When it cannot find values for a specific DataFrame for a specific date, it places a `NaN` value there for that DataFrame's fields.

Data cleaning

Data cleaning refers to the process of addressing data errors coming from missing data, incorrect data values, and outliers.

In our example, `merged_df` has missing values for many fields coming from the original datasets and coming from merging DataFrames with different sets of dates.

Let's first check if there are any rows where all values are missing (`NaN`), as follows:

```
merged_df[merged_df.isnull().all(axis=1)]
```

The result shows that we do not have any row with all fields missing, as we can see here:

	Open_A	High_A	Low_A	Close_A	Adj Close_A	Volume_A	Open_B
Date							

Figure 2.5 – DataFrame showing that there are no rows with all fields missing

Now, let's find out how many rows exist that have at least one field that is missing/`NaN`, as follows:

```
merged_df[['Close_A', 'Close_B', 'Close_C']].isnull().
any(axis=1).sum()
```

So, it turns out 148 rows out of our 1,259 rows have one or more fields with missing values, as shown here:

```
148
```

For our further analysis, we need to have valid `Close` prices. Thus, we can drop all rows where the `Close` price for any of the three instruments is missing, by running the following code:

```
valid_close_df = merged_df.dropna(subset=['Close_A', 'Close_B',
'Close_C'], how='any')
```

After dropping the missing `Close` prices, we should have no more missing `Close` price fields, as illustrated in the following code snippet:

```
valid_close_df[['Close_A', 'Close_B', 'Close_C']].isnull().
any(axis=1).sum()
```

The result confirms there are no rows left where any of the `Close_A`, `Close_B`, or `Close_C` fields are `NaN` values, as we can see here:

```
0
```

Let's inspect the new DataFrame, as follows:

```
valid_close_df
```

Here is the result (displaying only the first seven columns):

	Open_A	High_A	Low_A	Close_A	Adj Close_A	Volume_A	Open_B
Date							
2015-05-15	18251.970703	18272.720703	18215.070313	18272.560547	18272.560547	108220000.0	2122.070068
...	...	...	...	...	...	...	...
2020-05-14	23049.060547	23630.859375	22789.619141	23625.339844	23625.339844	472700000.0	2794.540039

1111 rows × 18 columns

Figure 2.6 – Resulting DataFrame with no missing/NaN values for any close prices

As expected, we dropped the 148 rows that had missing/`NaN` values for any of the close prices.

Next, let's deal with rows that have `NaN` values for any of the other fields, starting with getting a sense of how many such rows exist. We can do this by running the following code:

```
valid_close_df.isnull().any(axis=1).sum()
```

Here is the output of that query:

```
165
```

So, there exist 165 rows that have at least some fields with a missing value.

Let's quickly inspect a few of the rows with at least some fields with a missing value, as follows:

```
valid_close_df[valid_close_df.isnull().any(axis=1)]
```

Some of the rows with some missing values are displayed (displaying only the first seven columns), as shown here:

	Open_A	High_A	Low_A	Close_A	Adj Close_A	Volume_A	Open_B
Date							
2015-05-18	18267.250000	18325.539063	18244.259766	18298.880859	18298.880859	79080000.0	2121.300049
...	...	...	...	...	...	...	...
2020-05-01	24120.779297	24120.779297	23645.300781	23723.689453	23723.689453	418160000.0	NaN

165 rows × 18 columns

Figure 2.7 – DataFrame showing there are still some rows with some missing values

So, we can see that the `Low_C` field on `2015-05-18` (not visible in the preceding screenshot) and the `Open_B` field on `2020-05-01` have `NaN` values (among 163 others, of course).

Let's use the `pandas.DataFrame.fillna(...)` method with a method called `backfill`—this uses the next valid value after the missing value to fill in the missing value. The code is illustrated in the following snippet:

```
valid_close_complete = valid_close_df.fillna(method='backfill')
```

Let's see the impact of the backfilling, as follows:

```
valid_close_complete.isnull().any(axis=1).sum()
```

Now, this is the output for the query:

```
0
```

As we can see, after the `backfill` operation, there are no more missing/`NaN` values left for any field in any row.

Obtaining descriptive statistics

The next step is to generate the key basic statistics on data to build familiarity with each field, with the `DataFrame.describe(...)` method. The code is illustrated in the following snippet:

```
pd.set_option('display.max_rows', None)
valid_close_complete.describe()
```

Notice that we have increased the number of rows of a `pandas` DataFrame to display.

Here is the output of running `pandas.DataFrame.describe(...)`, displaying only the first seven columns:

	Open_A	High_A	Low_A	Close_A	Adj Close_A	Volume_A	Open_B
count	1111.000000	1111.000000	1111.000000	1111.000000	1111.000000	1.111000e+03	1111.000000
mean	22291.125036	22402.395046	22168.922744	22292.881128	22292.531416	2.614436e+08	2517.857235
std	3771.056417	3784.558787	3755.740756	3769.395516	3767.906829	1.537677e+08	374.081451
min	15676.259766	15897.820313	15370.330078	15660.179688	15660.179688	4.589000e+07	1833.400024
25%	18232.280274	18285.384766	18156.614258	18230.160156	18227.615235	1.233350e+08	2144.320069
50%	22762.029297	22872.890625	22634.449219	22773.669922	22773.669922	2.631800e+08	2521.199951
75%	25516.320312	25659.810547	25382.705078	25518.895508	25518.895508	3.328450e+08	2815.010010
max	29440.470703	29568.570313	29406.750000	29551.419922	29551.419922	2.190810e+09	3380.449951

Figure 2.8 – Descriptive statistics of the valid_close_complete DataFrame

The preceding output provides quick summary statistics for every field in our DataFrame.

Key observations from *Figure 2.8* are outlined here:

- `Volume_C` has all statistics values to be `0`, implying every row has the `Volume_C` value set to `0`. Therefore, we need to remove this column.

- `Open_C` has a minimum value of `-400`, which is unlikely to be true for the following reasons:

  a) The other price fields—`High_C`, `Low_C`, `Close_C`, and `Adj Close_C`—all have minimum values around `9`, so it doesn't make sense for `Open_C` to have a minimum value of `-400`.

  b) Given that the 25th percentile for `Open_C` is `12.4`, it is unlikely that the minimum value would be so much lower than that.

  c) The price of an asset should be non-negative.

- `Low_C` has a maximum value of `330`, which is again unlikely because of the following reasons:

  a) For the same reasons given previously to those outlined previously, as `Open_C` is not correct.

  b) In addition, considering that `Low_C` should always be lower than `High_C`, by definition, the lowest price in a day has to be lower than the highest price on a day.

Let's put back the output of all the `pandas` DataFrames to be just two rows, as follows:

```
pd.set_option('display.max_rows', 2)
```

Now, let's remove the `Volume` fields for all three instruments, with the following code:

```
prices_only = valid_close_complete.drop(['Volume_A',
'Volume_B', 'Volume_C'], axis=1)
prices_only
```

And the `prices_only` DataFrame has the following data (displaying only the first seven columns):

	Open_A	High_A	Low_A	Close_A	Adj Close_A	Open_B
Date						
2015-05-15	18251.970703	18272.720703	18215.070313	18272.560547	18272.560547	2122.070068
...	...	...	...	...	...	...
2020-05-14	23049.060547	23630.859375	22789.619141	23625.339844	23625.339844	2794.540039

1111 rows × 15 columns

Figure 2.9 – The prices_only DataFrame

As expected, after we removed the three volume columns, we reduced the DataFrame dimensions to `1111 × 15`—these were previously `1111 × 18`.

Visual inspection of the data

There do not seem to be any obvious errors or discrepancies with the other fields, so let's plot a quick visualization of the prices to see if that sits in line with what we learned from the descriptive statistics.

First, we will start with the prices of `A`, since we expect those to be correct based on the descriptive statistics summary. The code is illustrated in the following snippet:

```
valid_close_complete['Open_A'].plot(figsize=(12,6),
linestyle='--', color='black', legend='Open_A')
valid_close_complete['Close_A'].plot(figsize=(12,6),
linestyle='-', color='grey', legend='Close_A')
valid_close_complete['Low_A'].plot(figsize=(12,6),
linestyle=':', color='black', legend='Low_A')
valid_close_complete['High_A'].plot(figsize=(12,6),
linestyle='-.', color='grey', legend='High_A')
```

The output is consistent with our expectations, and we can conclude that the prices of `A` are valid based on the statistics and the plot shown in the following screenshot:

Figure 2.10 – Plot showing Open, Close, High, and Low prices for trading instrument A over 5 years

Now, let's plot the prices of C to see if the plot provides further evidence regarding our suspicions about some prices being incorrect. The code can be seen in the following snippet:

```
valid_close_complete['Open_C'].plot(figsize=(12,6),
linestyle='--', color='black', legend='Open_C')
valid_close_complete['Close_C'].plot(figsize=(12,6),
linestyle='-', color='grey', legend='Close_C')
valid_close_complete['Low_C'].plot(figsize=(12,6),
linestyle=':', color='black', legend='Low_C')
valid_close_complete['High_C'].plot(figsize=(12,6),
linestyle='-.', color='grey', legend='High_C')
```

The output confirms that `Open_C` and `Low_C` have some erroneous values extremely far away from other values—these are the outliers. The following screenshot shows a plot illustrating this:

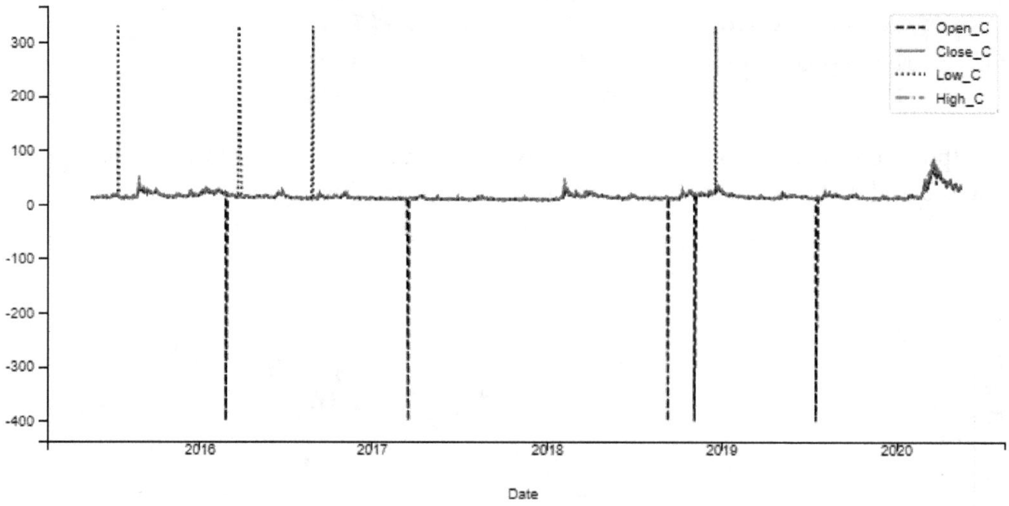

Figure 2.11 – Plot showing large outliers in the prices of C in both positive and negative directions

We will need to perform some further data cleaning to eliminate these outlier values so that we do not derive incorrect statistical insights from our data.

The two most commonly used methods to detect and remove outliers are the **interquartile range** (**IQR**) and the Z-score.

IQR

The IQR method uses a percentile/quantile range of values over the entire dataset to identify and remove outliers.

When applying the IQR method, we usually use extreme percentile values, such as 5% to 95%, to minimize the risk of removing correct data points.

In our example of `Open_C`, let's use the 25th percentile and 75th percentile and remove all data points with values outside that range. The 25th-to-75th percentile range is `(12.4, 17.68)`, so we would remove the outlier value of `-400`.

Z-score

The Z-score (or standard score) is obtained by subtracting the mean of the dataset from each data point and normalizing the result by dividing by the standard deviation of the dataset.

In other words, the Z-score of a data point represents the distance in the number of standard deviations that the data point is away from the mean of all the data points.

For a normal distribution (applicable for large enough datasets) there is a distribution rule of **68-95-99**, summarized as follows:

- 68% of all data will lie in a range of one standard deviation from the mean.
- 95% of all data will lie in a range of two standard deviations from the mean.
- 99% of all data will lie within a range of three standard deviations from the mean.

So, after computing Z-scores of all data points in our dataset (which is large enough), there is an approximately 1% chance of a data point having a Z-score larger than or equal to `3`.

Therefore, we can use this information to filter out all observations with Z-scores of `3` or higher to detect and remove outliers.

In our example, we will remove all rows with values whose Z-score is less than `-6` or greater than `6`—that is, six standard deviations away from the mean.

First, we use `scipy.stats.zscore(...)` to compute Z-scores of each column in the `prices_only` DataFrame, and then we use `numpy.abs(...)` to get the magnitude of the Z-scores. Finally, we select rows where all fields have Z-scores lower than 6, and save that in a `no_outlier_prices` DataFrame. The code is illustrated in the following snippet:

```
no_outlier_prices = prices_only[(np.abs(stats.zscore(prices_
only)) < 6).all(axis=1)]
```

Let's see what impact this Z-score outlier removal code had on the price fields for instrument `C` by plotting its prices again and comparing to the earlier plot, as follows:

```
no_outlier_prices['Open_C'].plot(figsize=(12,6),
linestyle='--', color='black', legend='Open_C')
no_outlier_prices['Close_C'].plot(figsize=(12,6),
linestyle='-', color='grey', legend='Close_C')
no_outlier_prices['Low_C'].plot(figsize=(12,6), linestyle=':',
color='black', legend='Low_C')
no_outlier_prices['High_C'].plot(figsize=(12,6),
linestyle='-.', color='grey', legend='High_C')
```

Here's the output:

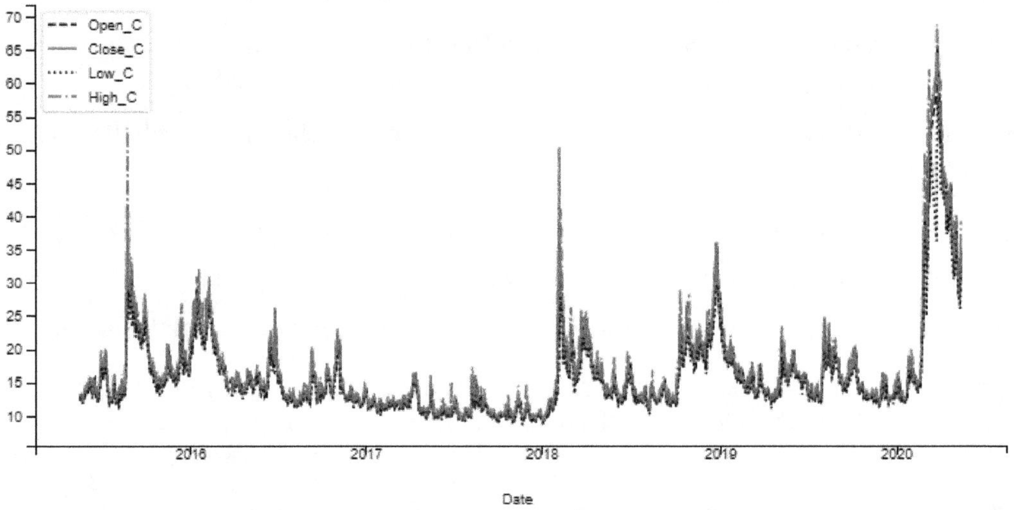

Figure 2.12 – Plot showing the prices of C after removing outliers by applying data cleaning

The plot clearly shows that the earlier observation of extreme values for `Open_C` and `Low_C` has been discarded; there is no longer the dip of `-400`.

Note that while we removed the extreme outliers, we were still able to preserve the sharp spikes in prices during 2015, 2018, and 2020, thus not leading to a lot of data losses.

Let's also check the impact of our outlier removal work by re-inspecting the descriptive statistics, as follows:

```
pd.set_option('display.max_rows', None)
no_outlier_prices[['Open_C', 'Close_C', 'Low_C', 'High_C']].
describe()
```

These statistics look significantly better—as we can see in the following screenshot, the `min` and `max` values for all prices now look in line with expectations and do not have extreme values, so we succeeded in our data cleaning task:

	Open_C	Close_C	Low_C	High_C
count	1095.000000	1095.000000	1095.000000	1095.000000
mean	16.147571	16.072648	15.223635	17.214539
std	6.764147	6.773569	5.995822	7.588690
min	9.010000	9.140000	8.560000	9.310000
25%	12.420000	12.285000	11.865000	12.890000
50%	14.160000	14.060000	13.440000	14.940000
75%	17.625000	17.500000	16.550000	18.929999
max	65.669998	63.950001	58.029999	68.860001

Figure 2.13 – Descriptive statistics for the no_outlier_prices selected columns

Let's reset back the number of rows to display for a `pandas` DataFrame, as follows:

```
pd.set_option('display.max_rows', 5)
```

Advanced visualization techniques

In this section, we will explore univariate and multivariate statistics visualization techniques.

First, let's collect the close prices for the three instruments, as follows:

```
close_prices = no_outlier_prices[['Close_A', 'Close_B',
'Close_C']]
```

Next, let's compute the daily close price changes to evaluate if there is a relationship between daily price changes between the three instruments.

Daily close price changes

We will use the `pandas.DataFrame.shift(...)` method to shift the original DataFrame one period forward so that we can compute the price changes. The `pandas.DataFrame.fillna(...)` method here fixes the one missing value generated in the first row as a result of the `shift` operation. Finally, we will rename the columns to `Delta_Close_A`, `Delta_Close_B`, and `Delta_Close_C` to reflect the fact that these values are price differences and not actual prices. The code is illustrated in the following snippet:

```
delta_close_prices = (close_prices.shift(-1) - close_prices).
fillna(0)
delta_close_prices.columns = ['Delta_Close_A', 'Delta_Close_B',
'Delta_Close_C']
delta_close_prices
```

The content of the newly generated `delta_close_prices` DataFrame is shown in the following screenshot:

	Delta_Close_A	Delta_Close_B	Delta_Close_C
Date			
2015-05-15	26.320312	6.469971	0.350000
2015-05-18	13.509766	-1.369873	0.120000
...	...	...	...
2020-05-13	377.369141	32.500000	-2.669998
2020-05-14	0.000000	0.000000	0.000000

1095 rows × 3 columns

Figure 2.14 – The delta_close_prices DataFrame

These values look correct, judging from the first few actual prices and the calculated price differences.

Now, let's quickly inspect the summary statistics for this new DataFrame to get a sense of how the delta price values are distributed, as follows:

```
pd.set_option('display.max_rows', None)
delta_close_prices.describe()
```

The descriptive statistics on this DataFrame are shown in the following screenshot:

	Delta_Close_A	Delta_Close_B	Delta_Close_C
count	1095.000000	1095.000000	1095.000000
mean	4.888383	0.666457	0.018475
std	268.137091	29.218995	1.938761
min	-2848.310547	-294.049805	-9.120001
25%	-70.894532	-7.140076	-0.760000
50%	15.539063	1.770020	-0.080000
75%	113.290039	12.255005	0.540001
max	1351.619141	154.510009	20.010001

Figure 2.15 – Descriptive statistics for the delta_close_prices DataFrame

We can observe from these statistics that all three delta values' means are close to 0, with instrument `A` experiencing large price swings and instrument `C` experiencing significantly smaller price moves (from the `std` field).

Histogram plot

Let's observe the distribution of `Delta_Close_A` to get more familiar with it, using a histogram plot. The code for this is shown in the following snippet:

```
delta_close_prices['Delta_Close_A'].plot(kind='hist', bins=100,
figsize=(12,6), color='black', grid=True)
```

In the following screenshot, we can see that the distribution is approximately normally distributed:

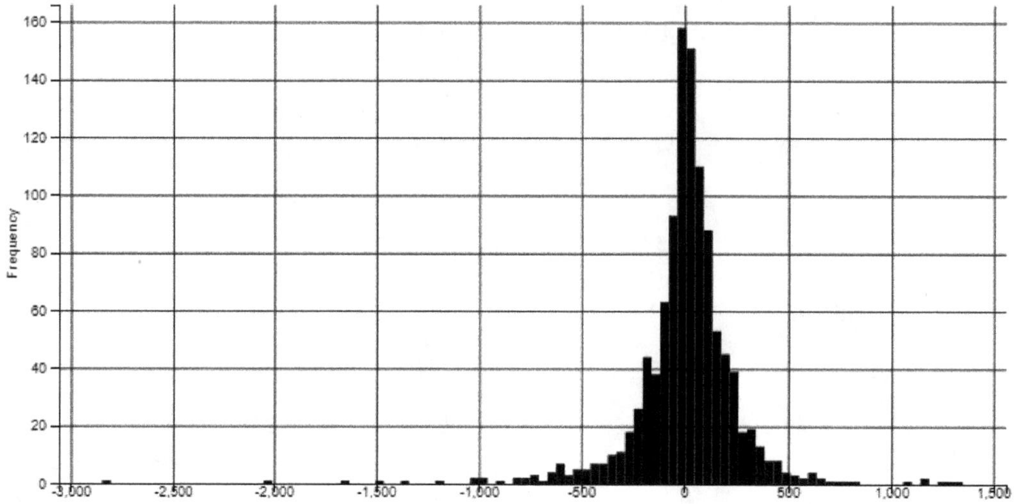

Figure 2.16 – Histogram of Delta_Close_A values roughly normally distributed around the 0 value

Box plot

Let's draw a box plot, which also helps in assessing the values' distribution. The code for this is shown in the following snippet:

```
delta_close_prices['Delta_Close_B'].plot(kind='box',
figsize=(12,6), color='black', grid=True)
```

The output can be seen in the following screenshot:

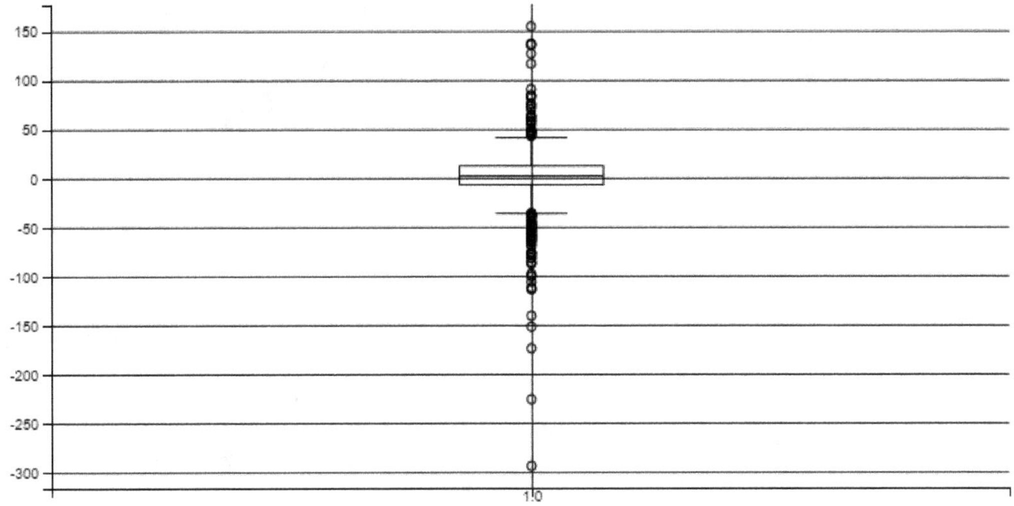

Figure 2.17 – Box plot showing mean, median, IQR (25th to 75th percentile), and outliers

Correlation charts

The first step in multivariate data statistics is to assess the correlations between `Delta_Close_A`, `Delta_Close_B`, and `Delta_Close_C`.

The most convenient way to do that is to plot a correlation scatter matrix that shows the pairwise relationship between the three variables, as well as the distribution of each individual variable.

In our example, we demonstrate the option of using **kernel density estimation** (**KDE**), which is closely related to histograms but provides a smoother distribution surface across the plots on the diagonals. The code for this is shown in the following snippet:

```
pd.plotting.scatter_matrix(delta_close_prices, figsize=(10,10),
color='black', alpha=0.75, diagonal='kde', grid=True)
```

This plot indicates that there is a strong positive correlation between `Delta_Close_A` and `Delta_Close_B` and a strong negative correlation between `Delta_Close_C` and the other two variables. The diagonals also display the distribution of each individual variable, using KDE.

A scatter plot of the fields can be seen in the following screenshot:

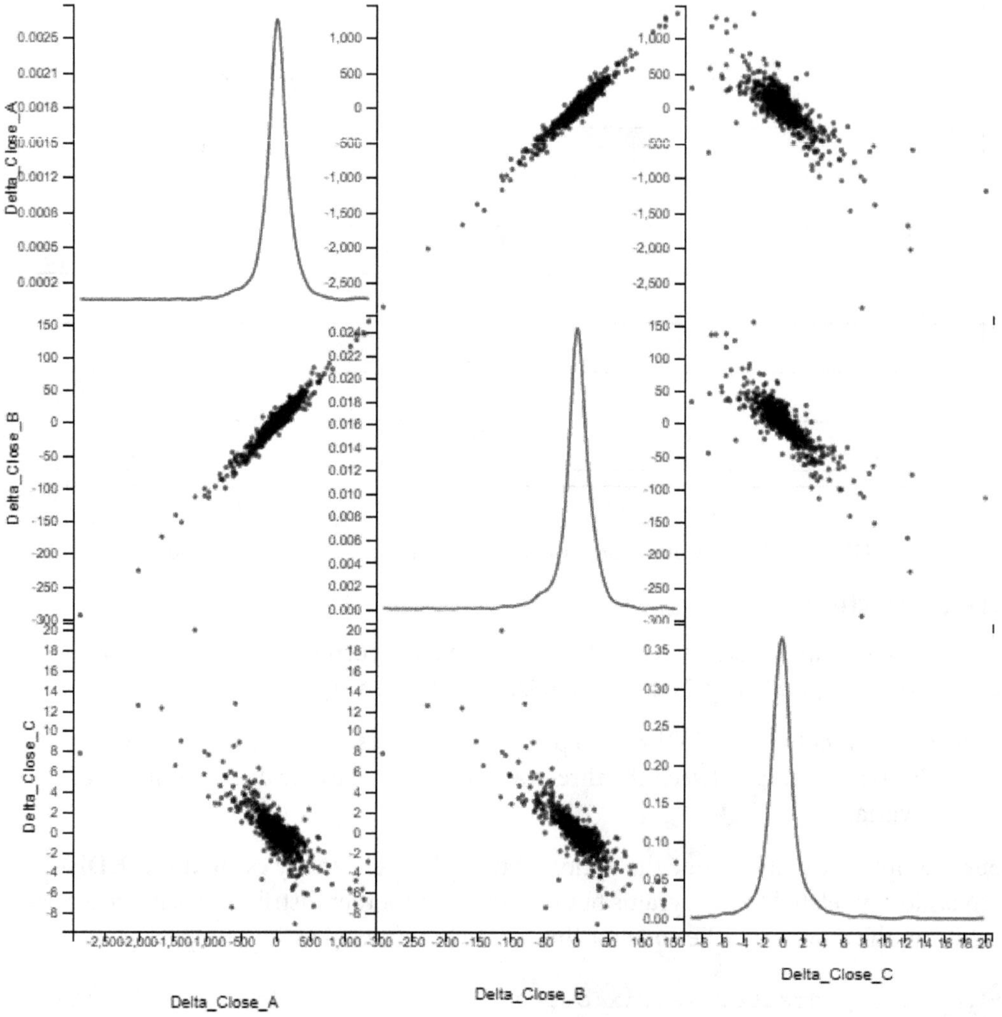

Figure 2.18 – Scatter plot of Delta_Close fields with KDE histogram on the diagonals

Next, let's look at some statistics that provide the relationship between the variables. `DataFrame.corr(...)` does that for us and also displays linear correlations. This can be seen in the following code snippet:

```
delta_close_prices.corr()
```

The correlation matrix confirms that `Delta_Close_A` and `Delta_Close_B` have a strong positive correlation (very close to 1.0, which is the maximum), as we expected based on the scatter plot. Also, `Delta_Close_C` is negatively correlated (closer to -1.0 than 0.0) to the other two variables.

You can see the correlation matrix in the following screenshot:

	Delta_Close_A	Delta_Close_B	Delta_Close_C
Delta_Close_A	1.000000	0.976104	-0.785566
Delta_Close_B	0.976104	1.000000	-0.817788
Delta_Close_C	-0.785566	-0.817788	1.000000

Figure 2.19 – Correlation matrix for Delta_Close_A, Delta_Close_B, and Delta_Close_C

Pairwise correlation heatmap

An alternative visualization technique known as a **heatmap** is available in `seaborn.heatmap(...)`, as illustrated in the following code snippet:

```
plt.figure(figsize=(6,6))
sn.heatmap(delta_close_prices.corr(), annot=True, square=True,
linewidths=2)
```

In the plot shown in the following screenshot, the rightmost scale shows a legend where the darkest values represent the strongest negative correlation and the lightest values represent the strongest positive correlations:

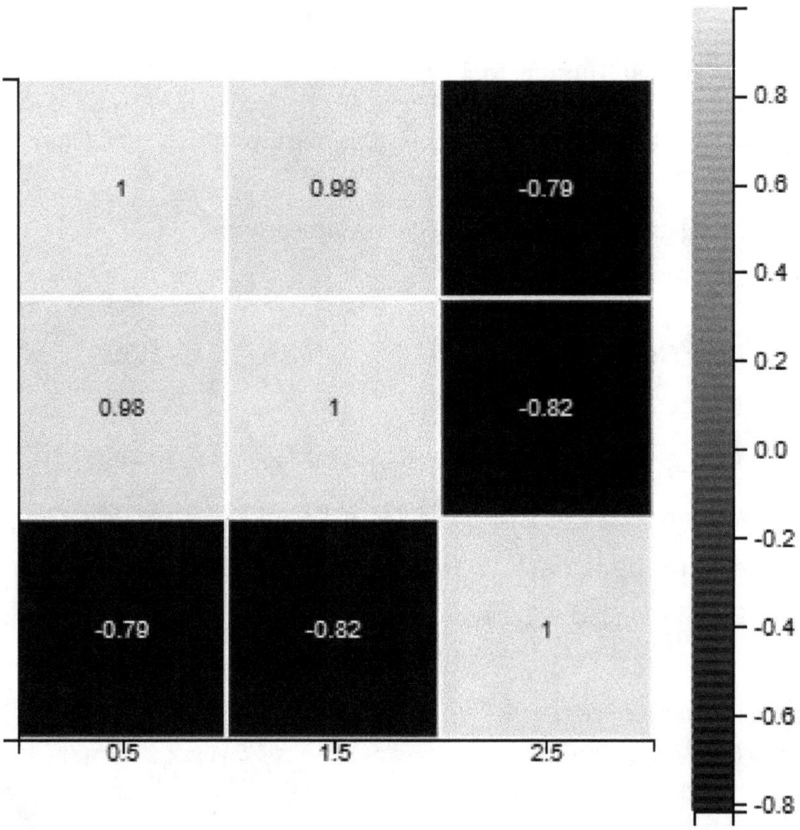

Figure 2.20 – Seaborn heatmap visualizing pairwise correlations between Delta_Close fields

The heatmap shows graphically the same message as the table in the previous section— there is a very high correlation between `Delta_Close_A` and `Delta_Close_B` and a very high negative correlation between `Delta_Close_A` and `Delta_Close_C`. There is also a very high negative correlation between `Delta_Close_B` and `Delta_Close_C`.

Revelation of the identity of A, B, and C and EDA's conclusions

The A instrument is the **Dow Jones Industrial Average (DJIA)**, a large cap equity index **exchange traded fund (ETF)**. The B instrument is the **S&P 500 (SPY)**, another large cap equity index ETF. The C instrument is the **Chicago Board Options Exchange (CBOE) Volatility Index (VIX)**, which basically tracks how volatile markets are at any given time (basically, a function of equity index price swings).

From our EDA on the mystery instruments, we drew the following conclusions:

- C (VIX) cannot have negative prices or prices above 90, which has historically been true.
- A (DJIA) and B (SPY) had huge drops in 2008 and 2020, corresponding to the stock market crash and the COVID-19 pandemic, respectively. Also, the price of C (VIX) spiked at the same time, indicating heightened market turmoil.
- A (DJIA) has largest daily price swings, followed by B (SPY), and finally C (VIX), with very low daily price swings. These are also correct observations considering the underlying instruments that they were hiding.

A (DJIA) and B (SPY) have very strong positive correlations, which makes sense since both are large cap equity indices. C (VIX) has strong negative correlations with both A (DJIA) and B (SPY), which also makes sense since during periods of prosperity, volatility remains low and markets rise, and during periods of crisis, volatility spikes and markets drop.

In the next section, we introduce one special Python library that generates the most common EDA charts and tables automatically.

Special Python libraries for EDA

There are multiple Python libraries that provide EDA in a single line of code. One of the most advanced of them is `dtale`, shown in the following code snippet:

```
import dtale
dtale.show(valid_close_df)
```

The preceding command produces a table with all the data (displaying only the first seven columns), as follows:

► 19 / 1111	Date	Open_A	High_A	Low_A	Close_A	Adj Close_A	Volume_A	Open_B
0	2015-05-15	18251.97	18272.72	18215.07	18272.56	18272.56	108220000.00	2122.07
1	2015-05-18	18267.25	18325.54	18244.26	18298.88	18298.88	79080000.00	2121.30
2	2015-05-19	18300.48	18351.36	18261.35	18312.39	18312.39	87200000.00	2129.45
3	2015-05-21	18285.87	18314.89	18249.90	18285.74	18285.74	84270000.00	2125.55
4	2015-05-22	18286.87	18286.87	18217.14	18232.02	18232.02	78890000.00	2130.36
5	2015-05-26	18229.75	18229.75	17990.02	18041.54	18041.54	109440000.00	2125.34
6	2015-05-27	18045.08	18190.35	18045.08	18162.99	18162.99	96400000.00	2105.13
7	2015-05-28	18154.14	18154.14	18066.40	18126.12	18126.12	67510000.00	2122.27
8	2015-05-29	18128.12	18128.12	17967.74	18010.68	18010.68	139810000.00	2120.66
9	2015-06-01	18017.82	18105.83	17982.06	18040.37	18040.37	85640000.00	2108.64
10	2015-06-02	18033.33	18091.87	17925.33	18011.94	18011.94	77550000.00	2110.41
11	2015-06-03	18018.42	18168.09	18010.42	18076.27	18076.27	73120000.00	2110.64
12	2015-06-05	17905.38	17940.78	17822.90	17849.46	17849.46	89140000.00	2095.09
13	2015-06-08	17849.46	17852.35	17760.61	17766.55	17766.55	86300000.00	nan
14	2015-06-09	17766.95	17817.83	17714.97	17764.04	17764.04	90550000.00	2079.07
15	2015-06-10	17765.38	18045.14	17765.38	18000.40	18000.40	96980000.00	2081.12
16	2015-06-11	18001.27	18109.77	18001.27	18039.37	18039.37	89490000.00	2106.24

Figure 2.21 – The dtale component showing spreadsheet-like control over the valid_close_df DataFrame

Clicking on the arrow at the top displays a menu with all the functionality, as illustrated in the following screenshot:

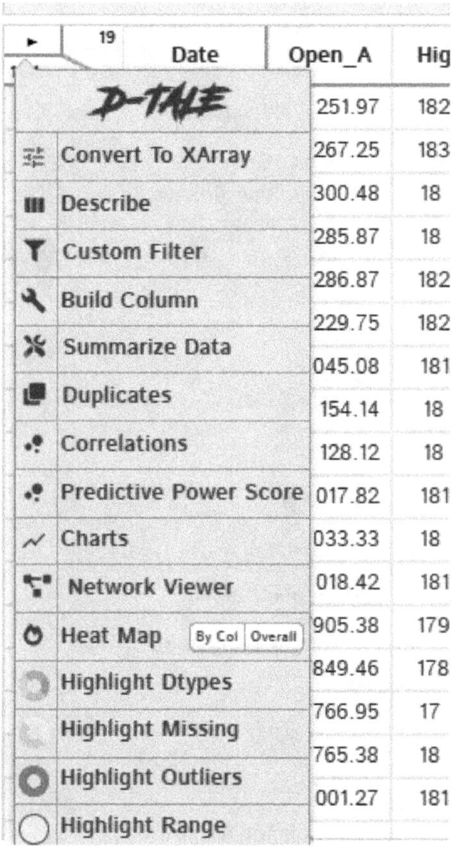

Figure 2.22 – The dtale global menu showing its functionality

Clicking on the column header displays each feature's individual commands, as illustrated in the following screenshot:

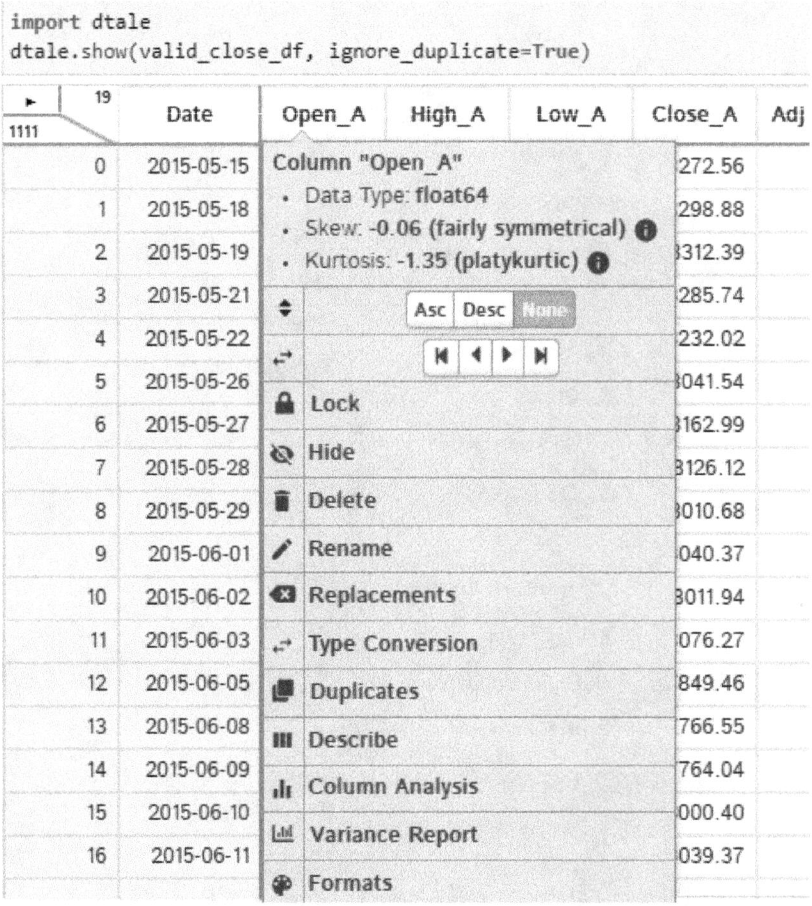

Figure 2.23 – The dtale column menu showing column functionality

Interactive EDA, rather than command-driven EDA, has its advantages—it is intuitive, it promotes visual creativity, and it can be faster.

Summary

The objective of EDA is to get a feel for the dataset we work with, and to correct basic data errors such as unlikely outliers. We have described both an EDA built by running individual Python commands and an automated EDA using a special Python EDA library.

The next chapter introduces us to one of the most important Python libraries: `numpy`.

3
High-Speed Scientific Computing Using NumPy

This chapter introduces us to NumPy, a high-speed Python library for matrix calculations. Most data science/algorithmic trading libraries are built upon NumPy's functionality and conventions.

In this chapter, we are going to cover the following key topics:

- Introduction to NumPy
- Creating NumPy n-dimensional arrays (ndarrays)
- Data types used with NumPy arrays
- Indexing of ndarrays
- Basic ndarray operations
- File operations on ndarrays

Technical requirements

The Python code used in this chapter is available in the `Chapter03/numpy.ipynb` notebook in the book's code repository.

Introduction to NumPy

Multidimensional heterogeneous arrays can be represented in Python using lists. A list is a 1D array, a list of lists is a 2D array, a list of lists of lists is a 3D array, and so on. However, this solution is complex, difficult to use, and extremely slow.

One of the primary design goals of the NumPy Python library was to introduce high-performant and scalable structured arrays and vectorized computations.

Most data structures and operations in NumPy are implemented in C/C++, which guarantees their superior speed.

Creating NumPy ndarrays

An **ndarray** is an extremely high-performant and space-efficient data structure for multidimensional arrays.

First, we need to import the NumPy library, as follows:

```
import numpy as np
```

Next, we will start creating a 1D ndarray.

Creating 1D ndarrays

The following line of code creates a 1D ndarray:

```
arr1D = np.array([1.1, 2.2, 3.3, 4.4, 5.5]);
arr1D
```

This will give the following output:

```
array([1.1, 2.2, 3.3, 4.4, 5.5])
```

Let's inspect the type of the array with the following code:

```
type(arr1D)
```

This shows that the array is a NumPy ndarray, as can be seen here:

```
numpy.ndarray
```

We can easily create ndarrays of two dimensions or more.

Creating 2D ndarrays

To create a 2D ndarray, use the following code:

```
arr2D = np.array([[1, 2], [3, 4]]);
arr2D
```

The result has two rows and each row has two values, so it is a 2 x 2 ndarray, as illustrated in the following code snippet:

```
array([[1, 2],
       [3, 4]])
```

Creating any-dimension ndarrays

An ndarray can construct arrays with arbitrary dimensions. The following code creates an ndarray of 2 x 2 x 2 x 2 dimensions:

```
arr4D = np.array(range(16)).reshape((2, 2, 2, 2));
arr4D
```

The representation of the array is shown here:

```
array([[[[ 0,  1],
         [ 2,  3]],
        [[ 4,  5],
         [ 6,  7]]],
       [[[ 8,  9],
         [10, 11]],
        [[12, 13],
         [14, 15]]]])
```

NumPy ndarrays have a `shape` attribute that describes the ndarray's dimensions, as shown in the following code snippet:

```
arr1D.shape
```

The following snippet shows that `arr1D` is a one-dimensional array with five elements:

```
(5,)
```

We can inspect the `shape` attribute on `arr2D` with the following code:

```
arr2D.shape
```

As expected, the output describes it as being a 2 x 2 ndarray, as we can see here:

```
(2, 2)
```

In practice, there are certain matrices that are more frequently used, such as a matrix of 0s, a matrix of 1s, an identity matrix, a matrix containing a range of numbers, or a random matrix. NumPy provides support for generating these frequently used ndarrays with one command.

Creating an ndarray with np.zeros(...)

The `np.zeros(...)` method creates an ndarray populated with all 0s, as illustrated in the following code snippet:

```
np.zeros(shape=(2,5))
```

The output is all 0s, with dimensions being 2 x 5, as illustrated in the following code snippet:

```
array([[0., 0., 0., 0., 0.],
       [0., 0., 0., 0., 0.]])
```

Creating an ndarray with np.ones(...)

`np.ones(...)` is similar, but each value is assigned a value of 1 instead of 0. The method is shown in the following code snippet:

```
np.ones(shape=(2,2))
```

The result is a 2 x 2 ndarray with every value set to 1, as illustrated in the following code snippet:

```
array([[1., 1.],
       [1., 1.]])
```

Creating an ndarray with np.identity(...)

Often in matrix operations we need to create an identity matrix, which is available in the `np.identity(...)` method, as illustrated in the following code snippet:

```
np.identity(3)
```

This creates a 3 x 3 identity matrix with 1s on the diagonals and 0s everywhere else, as illustrated in the following code snippet:

```
array([[1., 0., 0.],
       [0., 1., 0.],
       [0., 0., 1.]])
```

Creating an ndarray with np.arange(...)

`np.arange(...)` is the NumPy equivalent of the Python `range(...)` method. This generates values with a start value, end value, and increment, except this returns NumPy ndarrays instead, as shown here:

```
np.arange(5)
```

The ndarray returned is shown here:

```
array([0, 1, 2, 3, 4])
```

By default, values start at 0 and increment by 1.

Creating an ndarray with np.random.randn(...)

`np.random.randn(…)` generates an ndarray of specified dimensions, with each element populated with random values drawn from a standard normal distribution (`mean=0`, `std=1`), as illustrated here:

```
np.random.randn(2,2)
```

The output is a 2 x 2 ndarray with random values, as illustrated in the following code snippet:

```
array([[ 0.57370365, -1.22229931],
       [-1.25539335,  1.11372387]])
```

Data types used with NumPy ndarrays

NumPy ndarrays are homogenous—that is, each element in an ndarray has the same data type. This is different from Python lists, which can have elements with different data types (heterogenous).

The `np.array(...)` method accepts an explicit `dtype=` parameter that lets us specify the data type that the ndarray should use. Common data types used are `np.int32`, `np.float64`, `np.float128`, and `np.bool`. Note that `np.float128` is not supported on Windows.

The primary reason why you should be conscious about the various numeric types for ndarrays is the memory usage—the more precision the data type provides, the larger memory requirements it has. For certain operations, a smaller data type may be just enough.

Creating a numpy.float64 array

To create a 128-bit floating-values array, use the following code:

```
np.array([-1, 0, 1], dtype=np.float64)
```

The output is shown here:

```
array([-1.,  0.,  1.], dtype=float64)
```

Creating a numpy.bool array

We can create an ndarray by converting specified values to the target type. In the following code example, we see that even though integer data values were provided, the resulting ndarray has `dtype` as `bool`, since the data type was specified to be `np.bool`:

```
np.array([-1, 0, 1], dtype=np.bool)
```

The values are shown here:

```
array([ True, False,  True])
```

We observe that the integer values (`-1, 0, 1`) were converted to `bool` values (`True, False, True`). `0` gets converted to `False`, and all other values get converted to `True`.

ndarrays' dtype attribute

ndarrays have a `dtype` attribute to inspect the data type, as shown here:

```
arr1D.dtype
```

The output is a NumPy `dtype` object with a `float64` value, as illustrated here:

```
dtype('float64')
```

Converting underlying data types of ndarray with numpy.ndarrays.astype(...)

We can easily convert the underlying data type of an ndarray to any other compatible data type with the `numpy.ndarrays.astype(...)` method. For example, to convert `arr1D` from `np.float64` to `np.int64`, we use the following code:

```
arr1D.astype(np.int64).dtype
```

This reflects the new data type, as follows:

```
dtype('int64')
```

When `numpy.ndarray.astype(...)` converts to a narrower data type, it will truncate the values, as follows:

```
arr1D.astype(np.int64)
```

This converts `arr1D` to the following integer-valued ndarray:

```
array([1, 2, 3, 4, 5])
```

The original floating values (1.1, 2.2, …) are converted to their truncated integer values (1, 2, …).

Indexing of ndarrays

Array indexing refers to the way of accessing a particular array element or elements. In NumPy, all ndarray indices are zero-based—that is, the first item of an array has index `0`. Negative indices are understood as counting from the end of the array.

Direct access to an ndarray's element

Direct access to a single ndarray's element is one of the most used forms of access.

The following code builds a 3 x 3 random-valued ndarray for our use:

```
arr = np.random.randn(3,3);
arr
```

The `arr` ndarray has the following elements:

```
array([[-0.04113926, -0.273338  , -1.05294723],
       [ 1.65004669, -0.09589629,  0.15586867],
       [ 0.39533427,  1.47193681,  0.32148741]])
```

We can index the first element with integer index `0`, as follows:

```
arr[0]
```

This gives us the first row of the `arr` ndarray, as follows:

```
array([-0.04113926, -0.273338  , -1.05294723])
```

We can access the element at the second column of the first row by using the following code:

```
arr[0][1]
```

The result is shown here:

```
-0.2733379996693689
```

ndarrays also support an alternative notation to perform the same operation, as illustrated here:

```
arr[0, 1]
```

It accesses the same element as before, as can be seen here:

```
-0.2733379996693689
```

The `numpy.ndarray[index_0, index_1, … index_n]` notation is especially more concise and useful when accessing ndarrays with very large dimensions.

Negative indices start from the end of the ndarray, as illustrated here:

```
arr[-1]
```

This returns the last row of the ndarray, as follows:

```
array([0.39533427, 1.47193681, 0.32148741])
```

ndarray slicing

While single ndarray access is useful, for bulk processing we require access to multiple elements of the array at once (for example, if the ndarray contains all daily prices of an asset, we might want to process only all Mondays' prices).

Slicing allows access to multiple ndarray records in one command. Slicing ndarrays also works similarly to slicing of Python lists.

The basic slice syntax is *i:j:k*, where *i* is the index of the first record we want to include, *j* is the stopping index, and *k* is the step.

Accessing all ndarray elements after the first one

To access all elements after the first one, we can use the following code:

```
arr[1:]
```

This returns all the rows after the first one, as illustrated in the following code snippet:

```
array([[ 1.65004669, -0.09589629,  0.15586867],
       [ 0.39533427,  1.47193681,  0.32148741]])
```

Fetching all rows, starting from row 2 and columns 1 and 2

Similarly, to fetch all rows starting from the second one, and columns up to but not including the third one, run the following code:

```
arr[1:, :2]
```

This is a 2 x 2 ndarray as expected, as can be seen here:

```
array([[ 1.65004669, -0.09589629],
       [ 0.39533427,  1.47193681]])
```

Slicing with negative indices

More complex slicing notation that mixes positive and negative index ranges is also possible, as follows:

```
arr[1:2, -2:-1]
```

This is a less intuitive way of finding the slice of an element at the second row and at the second column, as illustrated here:

```
array([[-0.09589629]])
```

Slicing with no indices

Slicing with no indices yields the entire row/column. The following code generates a slice containing all elements on the third row:

```
arr[:][2]
```

The output is shown here:

```
array([0.39533427, 1.47193681, 0.32148741])
```

The following code generates a slice of the original `arr` ndarray:

```
arr[:][:]
```

The output is shown here:

```
array([[-0.04113926, -0.273338  , -1.05294723],
       [ 1.65004669, -0.09589629,  0.15586867],
       [ 0.39533427,  1.47193681,  0.32148741]])
```

Setting values of a slice to 0

Frequently, we will need to set certain values of an ndarray to a given value.

Let's generate a slice containing the second row of `arr` and assign it to a new variable, `arr1`, as follows:

```
arr1 = arr[1:2];
arr1
```

`arr1` now contains the last row, as shown in the following code snippet:

```
array([[ 1.65004669, -0.09589629,  0.15586867]])
```

Now, let's set every element of `arr1` to the value `0`, as follows:

```
arr1[:] = 0;
arr1
```

As expected, `arr1` now contains all 0s, as illustrated here:

```
array([[0., 0., 0.]])
```

Now, let's re-inspect our original `arr` ndarray, as follows:

```
arr
```

The output is shown here:

```
array([[-0.04113926, -0.273338  , -1.05294723],
       [ 0.        ,  0.        ,  0.        ],
       [ 0.39533427,  1.47193681,  0.32148741]])
```

We see that our operation on the `arr1` slice also changed the original `arr` ndarray. This brings us to the most important point: ndarray slices are views into the original ndarrays, not copies.

It is important to remember this when working with ndarrays so that we do not inadvertently change something we did not mean to. This design is purely for efficiency reasons, since copying large ndarrays incurs large overheads.

To create a copy of an ndarray, we explicitly call the `numpy.ndarray.copy(...)` method, as follows:

```
arr_copy = arr.copy()
```

Now, let's change some values in the `arr_copy` ndarray, as follows:

```
arr_copy[1:2] = 1;
arr_copy
```

We can see the change in `arr_copy` in the following code snippet:

```
array([[-0.04113926, -0.273338  , -1.05294723],
       [ 1.        ,  1.        ,  1.        ],
       [ 0.39533427,  1.47193681,  0.32148741]])
```

Let's inspect the original `arr` ndarray as well, as follows:

```
arr
```

The output is shown here:

```
array([[-0.04113926, -0.273338  , -1.05294723],
       [ 0.        ,  0.        ,  0.        ],
       [ 0.39533427,  1.47193681,  0.32148741]])
```

We see that the original ndarray is unchanged since `arr_copy` is a copy of `arr` and not a reference/view to it.

Boolean indexing

NumPy provides multiple ways of indexing ndarrays. NumPy arrays can be indexed by using conditions that evaluate to `True` or `False`. Let's start by regenerating an `arr` ndarray, as follows:

```
arr = np.random.randn(3,3);
arr
```

This is a 3 x 3 ndarray with random values, as can be seen in the following code snippet:

```
array([[-0.50566069, -0.52115534,  0.0757591 ],
       [ 1.67500165, -0.99280199,  0.80878346],
       [ 0.56937775,  0.36614928, -0.02532004]])
```

Let's revisit the output of running the following code, which is really just calling the `np.less(...)` **universal function (ufunc)**—that is, the result of the following code is identical to calling the `np.less(arr, 0))` method:

```
arr < 0
```

This generates another ndarray of `True` and `False` values, where `True` means the corresponding element in `arr` was negative and `False` means the corresponding element in `arr` was not negative, as illustrated in the following code snippet:

```
array([[ True,  True, False],
       [False,  True, False],
       [False, False,  True]])
```

We can use that array as an index to `arr` to find the actual negative elements, as follows:

```
arr[(arr < 0)]
```

As expected, this fetches the following negative values:

```
array([-0.50566069, -0.52115534, -0.99280199, -0.02532004])
```

We can combine multiple conditions with `&` (and) and | (or) operators. Python's `&` and | Boolean operators do not work on ndarrays since they are for scalars. An example of a `&` operator is shown here:

```
(arr > -1) & (arr < 1)
```

This generates an ndarray with the value `True`, where the elements are between `-1` and `1` and `False` otherwise, as illustrated in the following code snippet:

```
array([[ True,  True,  True],
       [False,  True,  True],
       [ True,  True,  True]])
```

As we saw before, we can use that Boolean array to index `arr` and find the actual elements, as follows:

```
arr[((arr > -1) & (arr < 1))]
```

The following output is an array of elements that satisfied the condition:

```
array([-0.50566069, -0.52115534,  0.0757591 , -0.99280199,
0.80878346,
        0.56937775,  0.36614928, -0.02532004])
```

Indexing with arrays

ndarray indexing also allows us to directly pass lists of indices of interest. Let's first generate an ndarray of random values to use, as follows:

```
arr
```

The output is shown here:

```
array([[-0.50566069, -0.52115534,  0.0757591 ],
       [ 1.67500165, -0.99280199,  0.80878346],
       [ 0.56937775,  0.36614928, -0.02532004]])
```

We can select the first and third rows, using the following code:

```
arr[[0, 2]]
```

The output is a 2 x 3 ndarray containing the two rows, as illustrated here:

```
array([[-0.50566069, -0.52115534,  0.0757591 ],
       [ 0.56937775,  0.36614928, -0.02532004]])
```

We can combine row and column indexing using arrays, as follows:

```
arr[[0, 2], [1]]
```

The preceding code gives us the second column of the first and third rows, as follows:

```
array([-0.52115534,  0.36614928])
```

We can also change the order of the indices passed, and this is reflected in the output. The following code picks out the third row followed by the first row, in that order:

```
arr[[2, 0]]
```

The output reflects the two rows in the order we expected (third row first; first row second), as illustrated in the following code snippet:

```
array([[ 0.56937775,  0.36614928, -0.02532004],
       [-0.50566069, -0.52115534,  0.0757591 ]])
```

Now that we have learned how to create ndarrays and about the various ways to retrieve the values of their elements, let's discuss the most common ndarray operations.

Basic ndarray operations

In the following examples, we will use an `arr2D` ndarray, as illustrated here:

```
arr2D
```

This is a 2 x 2 ndarray with values from `1` to `4`, as shown here:

```
array([[1, 2],
       [3, 4]])
```

Scalar multiplication with an ndarray

Scalar multiplication with an ndarray has the effect of multiplying each element of the ndarray, as illustrated here:

```
arr2D * 4
```

The output is shown here:

```
array([[ 4,  8],
       [12, 16]])
```

Linear combinations of ndarrays

The following operation is a combination of scalar and ndarray operations, as well as operations between ndarrays:

```
2*arr2D + 3*arr2D
```

The output is what we would expect, as can be seen here:

```
array([[ 5, 10],
       [15, 20]])
```

Exponentiation of ndarrays

We can raise each element of the ndarray to a certain power, as illustrated here:

```
arr2D ** 2
```

The output is shown here:

```
array([[ 1,  4],
       [ 9, 16]])
```

Addition of an ndarray with a scalar

Addition of an ndarray with a scalar works similarly, as illustrated here:

```
arr2D + 10
```

The output is shown here:

```
array([[11, 12],
       [13, 14]])
```

Transposing a matrix

Finding the transpose of a matrix, which is a common operation, is possible in NumPy with the `numpy.ndarray.transpose(...)` method, as illustrated in the following code snippet:

```
arr2D.transpose()
```

This transposes the ndarray and outputs it, as follows:

```
array([[1, 3],
       [2, 4]])
```

Changing the layout of an ndarray

The `np.ndarray.reshape(...)` method allows us to change the layout (shape) of the ndarray without changing its data to a compatible shape.

For instance, to reshape `arr2D` from 2 x 2 to 4 x 1, we use the following code:

```
arr2D.reshape((4, 1))
```

The new reshaped 4 x 1 ndarray is displayed here:

```
array([[1],
       [2],
       [3],
       [4]])
```

The following code example combines `np.random.randn(...)` and `np.ndarray.reshape(...)` to create a 3 x 3 ndarray of random values:

```
arr = np.random.randn(9).reshape((3,3));
arr
```

The generated 3 x 3 ndarray is shown here:

```
array([[ 0.24344963, -0.53183761,  1.08906941],
       [-1.71144547, -0.03195253,  0.82675183],
       [-2.24987291,  2.60439882, -0.09449784]])
```

Finding the minimum value in an ndarray

To find the minimum value in an ndarray, we use the following command:

```
np.min(arr)
```

The result is shown here:

```
-2.249872908111852
```

Calculating the absolute value

The `np.abs(...)` method, shown here, calculates the absolute value of an ndarray:

```
np.abs(arr)
```

The output ndarray is shown here:

```
array([[0.24344963, 0.53183761, 1.08906941],
       [1.71144547, 0.03195253, 0.82675183],
       [2.24987291, 2.60439882, 0.09449784]])
```

Calculating the mean of an ndarray

The `np.mean(...)` method, shown here, calculates the mean of all elements in the ndarray:

```
np.mean(arr)
```

The mean of the elements of `arr` is shown here:

```
0.01600703714906236
```

We can find the mean along the columns by specifying the `axis=` parameter, as follows:

```
np.mean(arr, axis=0)
```

This returns the following array, containing the mean for each column:

```
array([-1.23928958,  0.68020289,  0.6071078 ])
```

Similarly, we can find the mean along the rows by running the following code:

```
np.mean(arr, axis=1)
```

That returns the following array, containing the mean for each row:

```
array([ 0.26689381, -0.30554872,  0.08667602])
```

Finding the index of the maximum value in an ndarray

Often, we're interested in finding where in an array its largest value is. The `np.argmax(...)` method finds the location of the maximum value in the ndarray, as follows:

```
np.argmax(arr)
```

This returns the following value, to represent the location of the maximum value (`2.60439882`):

```
7
```

The `np.argmax(...)` method also accepts the `axis=` parameter to perform the operation row-wise or column-wise, as illustrated here:

```
np.argmax(arr, axis=1)
```

This finds the location of the maximum value on each row, as follows:

```
array([2, 2, 1], dtype=int64)
```

Calculating the cumulative sum of elements of an ndarray

To calculate the running total, NumPy provides the `np.cumsum(...)` method. The `np.cumsum(...)` method, illustrated here, finds the cumulative sum of elements in the ndarray:

```
np.cumsum(arr)
```

The output provides the cumulative sum after each additional element, as follows:

```
array([ 0.24344963, -0.28838798,  0.80068144, -0.91076403,
-0.94271656,
       -0.11596474, -2.36583764,  0.23856117,  0.14406333])
```

Notice the difference between a cumulative sum and a sum. A cumulative sum is an array of a running total, whereas a sum is a single number.

Applying the `axis=` parameter to the `cumsum` method works similarly, as illustrated in the following code snippet:

```
np.cumsum(arr, axis=1)
```

This goes row-wise and generates the following array output:

```
array([[ 0.24344963, -0.28838798,  0.80068144],
       [-1.71144547, -1.743398  , -0.91664617],
       [-2.24987291,  0.35452591,  0.26002807]])
```

Finding NaNs in an ndarray

Missing or unknown values are often represented in NumPy using a **Not a Number** (**NaN**) value. For many numerical methods, these must be removed or replaced with an interpolation.

First, let's set the second row to `np.nan`, as follows:

```
arr[1, :] = np.nan;
arr
```

The new ndarray has the NaN values, as illustrated in the following code snippet:

```
array([[ 0.64296696, -1.35386668, -0.63063743],
       [        nan,         nan,         nan],
       [-0.19093967, -0.93260398, -1.58520989]])
```

The `np.isnan(...)` ufunc finds if values in an ndarray are NaNs, as follows:

```
np.isnan(arr)
```

The output is an ndarray with a `True` value where NaNs exist and a `False` value where NaNs do not exist, as illustrated in the following code snippet:

```
array([[False, False, False],
       [ True,  True,  True],
       [False, False, False]])
```

Finding the truth values of x1>x2 of two ndarrays

Boolean ndarrays are an efficient way of obtaining indices for values of interest. Using Boolean ndarrays is far more performant than looping over the matrix elements one by one.

Let's build another `arr1` ndarray with random values, as follows:

```
arr1 = np.random.randn(9).reshape((3,3));
arr1
```

The result is a 3 x 3 ndarray, as illustrated in the following code snippet:

```
array([[ 0.32102068, -0.51877544, -1.28267292],
       [-1.34842617,  0.61170993, -0.5561239 ],
       [ 1.41138027, -2.4951374 ,  1.30766648]])
```

Similarly, let's build another `arr2` ndarray, as follows:

```
arr2 = np.random.randn(9).reshape((3,3));
arr2
```

The output is shown here:

```
array([[ 0.33189432,  0.82416396, -0.17453351],
       [-1.59689203, -0.42352094,  0.22643589],
       [-1.80766151,  0.26201455, -0.08469759]])
```

The `np.greater(...)` function is a binary ufunc that generates a `True` value when the left-hand-side value in the ndarray is greater than the right-hand-side value in the ndarray. This function can be seen here:

```
np.greater(arr1, arr2)
```

The output is an ndarray of `True` and `False` values as described previously, as we can see here:

```
array([[False, False, False],
       [ True,  True, False],
       [ True, False,  True]])
```

The > infix operator, shown in the following snippet, is a shorthand of `numpy.greater(...)`:

```
arr1 > arr2
```

The output is the same, as we can see here:

```
array([[False, False, False],
       [ True,  True, False],
       [ True, False,  True]])
```

any and all Boolean operations on ndarrays

In addition to relational operators, NumPy supports additional methods for testing conditions on matrices' values.

The following code generates an ndarray containing `True` for elements that satisfy the condition, and `False` otherwise:

```
arr_bool = (arr > -0.5) & (arr < 0.5);
arr_bool
```

The output is shown here:

```
array([[False, False,  True],
       [False, False, False],
       [False,  True,  True]])
```

The following `numpy.ndarray.any(...)` method returns `True` if any element is `True` and otherwise returns `False`:

```
arr_bool.any()
```

Here, we have at least one element that is `True`, so the output is `True`, as shown here:

```
True
```

Again, it accepts the common `axis=` parameter and behaves as expected, as we can see here:

```
arr_bool.any(axis=1)
```

And the operation performed row-wise yields, as follows:

```
array([True, False, True])
```

The following `numpy.ndarray.all(...)` method returns `True` when all elements are `True`, and `False` otherwise:

```
arr_bool.all()
```

This returns the following, since not all elements are `True`:

```
False
```

It also accepts the `axis=` parameter, as follows:

```
arr_bool.all(axis=1)
```

Again, each row has at least one `False` value, so the output is `False`, as shown here:

```
array([False, False, False])
```

Sorting ndarrays

Finding an element in a sorted ndarray is faster than processing all elements of the ndarray.

Let's generate a 1D random array, as follows:

```
arr1D = np.random.randn(10);
arr1D
```

The ndarray contains the following data:

```
array([ 1.14322028,  1.61792721, -1.01446969,  1.26988026,
-0.20110113,
        -0.28283051,  0.73009565, -0.68766388,  0.27276319,
-0.7135162 ])
```

The `np.sort(...)` method is pretty straightforward, as can be seen here:

```
np.sort(arr1D)
```

The output is shown here:

```
array([-1.01446969, -0.7135162 , -0.68766388, -0.28283051,
-0.20110113,
         0.27276319,  0.73009565,  1.14322028,  1.26988026,
1.61792721])
```

Let's inspect the original ndarray to see if it was modified by the `numpy.sort(...)` operation, as follows:

```
arr1D
```

The following output shows that the original array is unchanged:

```
array([ 1.14322028,  1.61792721, -1.01446969,  1.26988026,
-0.20110113,
        -0.28283051,  0.73009565, -0.68766388,  0.27276319,
-0.7135162 ])
```

The following `np.argsort(...)` method creates an array of indices that represent the location of each element in a sorted array:

```
np.argsort(arr1D)
```

The output of this operation generates the following array:

```
array([2, 9, 7, 5, 4, 8, 6, 0, 3, 1])
```

NumPy ndarrays have the `numpy.ndarray.sort(...)` method as well, which sorts arrays in place. This method is illustrated in the following code snippet:

```
arr1D.sort()
np.argsort(arr1D)
```

After the call to `sort()`, we call `numpy.argsort(...)` to make sure the array was sorted, and this yields the following array that confirms that behavior:

```
array([0, 1, 2, 3, 4, 5, 6, 7, 8, 9])
```

Searching within ndarrays

Finding indices of elements where a certain condition is met is a fundamental operation on an ndarray.

First, we start with an ndarray with consecutive values, as illustrated here:

```
arr1 = np.array(range(1, 11));
arr1
```

This creates the following ndarray:

```
array([ 1,  2,  3,  4,  5,  6,  7,  8,  9, 10])
```

We create a second ndarray based on the first one, except this time the values in the second one are multiplied by `1000`, as illustrated in the following code snippet:

```
arr2 = arr1 * 1000;
arr2
```

Then, we know `arr2` contains the following data:

```
array([ 1000,  2000,  3000,  4000,  5000,  6000,  7000,  8000,
9000,
        10000])
```

We define another ndarray that contains 10 `True` and `False` values randomly, as follows:

```
cond = np.random.randn(10) > 0;
cond
```

The values in the `cond` ndarray are shown here:

```
array([False, False,  True, False, False,  True,  True,  True,
False,  True])
```

The `np.where(...)` method allows us to select values from one ndarray or another, depending on the condition being `True` or `False`. The following code will generate an ndarray with a value picked from `arr1` when the corresponding element in the `cond` array is `True`; otherwise, the value is picked from `arr2`:

```
np.where(cond, arr1, arr2)
```

The returned array is shown here:

```
array([1000, 2000,    3, 4000, 5000,    6,    7,    8, 9000,
10])
```

File operations on ndarrays

Most NumPy arrays are read in from files and, after processing, written out back to files.

File operations with text files

The key advantages of text files are that they are human-readable and compatible with any custom software.

Let's start with the following random array:

```
arr
```

This array contains the following data:

```
array([[-0.50566069, -0.52115534,  0.0757591 ],
       [ 1.67500165, -0.99280199,  0.80878346],
       [ 0.56937775,  0.36614928, -0.02532004]])
```

The `numpy.savetxt(...)` method saves the ndarray to disk in text format.

The following example uses a `fmt='%0.21f'` format string and specifies a comma delimiter:

```
np.savetxt('arr.csv', arr, fmt='%0.21f', delimiter=',')
```

Let's inspect the `arr.csv` file written out to disk in the current directory, as follows:

```
!cat arr.csv
```

The **comma-separated values** (**CSV**) file contains the following data:

```
-0.51,-0.52,0.08
1.68,-0.99,0.81
0.57,0.37,-0.03
```

The `numpy.loadtxt(...)` method loads an ndarray from text file to memory. Here, we explicitly specify the `delimiter=','` parameter, as follows:

```
arr_new = np.loadtxt('arr.csv', delimiter=',');
arr_new
```

And the ndarray read in from the text file contains the following data:

```
array([[-0.51, -0.52,  0.08],
       [ 1.68, -0.99,  0.81],
       [ 0.57,  0.37, -0.03]])
```

File operations with binary files

Binary files are far more efficient for computer processing—they save and load more quickly and are smaller than text files. However, their format may not be supported by other software.

The `numpy.save(...)` method stores ndarrays in a binary format, as illustrated in the following code snippet:

```
np.save('arr', arr)
!cat arr.npy
```

The output of the `arr.npy` file is shown here:

```
�NUMPY�v{'descr': '<f8', 'fortran_order': False, 'shape': (3, 3), }
�:*��?�?     ��{f��w������ � � Q��'[/g������4
```

The `numpy.save(...)` method automatically assigns the `.npy` extension to binary files it creates.

The `numpy.load(...)` method, shown in the following code snippet, is used for reading binary files:

```
arr_new = np.load('arr.npy');
arr_new
```

The newly read-in ndarray is shown here:

```
array([[-0.50566069, -0.52115534,  0.0757591 ],
       [ 1.67500165, -0.99280199,  0.80878346],
       [ 0.56937775,  0.36614928, -0.02532004]])
```

Another advantage of having binary file formats is that data can be stored with extreme precision, especially when dealing with floating values, which is not always possible with text files since there is some loss of precision in certain cases.

Let's check if the old `arr` ndarray and the newly read-in `arr_new` array match exactly, by running the following code:

```
arr == arr_new
```

This will generate the following array, containing `True` if the elements are equal and `False` otherwise:

```
array([[ True,  True,  True],
       [ True,  True,  True],
       [ True,  True,  True]])
```

So, we see that each element matches exactly.

Summary

In this chapter, we have learned how to create matrices of any dimension in Python, how to access the matrices' elements, how to calculate basic linear algebra operations on matrices, and how to save and load matrices.

Working with NumPy matrices is a principal operation for any data analysis since vector operations are machine-optimized and thus are much faster than operations on Python lists—usually between 5 and 100 times faster. Backtesting any algorithmic strategy typically consists of processing enormous matrices, and then the speed difference can translate to hours or days of saved time.

In the next chapter, we introduce the second most important library for data analysis: Pandas, built upon NumPy. NumPy provides support for data manipulations based upon DataFrames (a DataFrame is the Python version of an Excel worksheet—that is, a two-dimensional data structure where each column has its own type).

4
Data Manipulation and Analysis with pandas

In this chapter, you will learn about the Python `pandas` library built upon NumPy, which provides data manipulation and analysis methods for structured data frames. The name **pandas** is derived from **panel data**, an econometrics term for multidimensional structured datasets, according to the Wikipedia page on pandas.

The `pandas` library contains two fundamental data structures to represent and manipulate structured rectangular datasets with a variety of indexing options: Series and DataFrames. Both use the index data structure.

Most operations in the processing of financial data in Python are based upon DataFrames. A DataFrame is like an Excel worksheet – a two-dimensional table that may contain multiple time series stored in columns. Therefore, we recommend you execute all the examples in this chapter yourself in your environment to get practice with the syntax and to better know what is possible.

In this chapter, we are going to cover the following topics:

- Introducing pandas Series, pandas DataFrames, and pandas Indexes
- Learning essential operations on pandas DataFrames
- Exploring file operations with pandas DataFrames

Technical requirements

The Python code used in this chapter is available in the `Chapter04/pandas.ipynb` notebook in the book's code repository.

Introducing pandas Series, pandas DataFrames, and pandas Indexes

pandas Series, pandas DataFrames, and pandas Indexes are the fundamental pandas data structures.

pandas.Series

The `pandas.Series` data structure represents a one-dimensional series of homogenous values (integer values, string values, double values, and so on). Series are a type of list and can contain only a single list with an index. A Data Frame, on the other hand, is a collection of one or more series.

Let's create a `pandas.Series` data structure:

```
import pandas as pd
ser1 = pd.Series(range(1, 6));
ser1
```

That series contains the index in the first column, and in the second column, the index's corresponding values:

```
0    1
1    2
2    3
3    4
4    5
dtype: int64
```

We can specify custom index names by specifying the `index` parameter:

```
ser2 = pd.Series(range(1, 6),
                 index=['a', 'b', 'c', 'd', 'e']);
ser2
```

The output will look like the following:

```
a    1
b    2
c    3
d    4
e    5
dtype: int64
```

We can also create a series by specifying the `index -> value` mapping via a dictionary:

```
ser3 = pd.Series({ 'a': 1.0, 'b': 2.0, 'c': 3.0,
                   'd': 4.0, 'e': 5.0 });
ser3
```

The output is as follows:

```
a    1.0
b    2.0
c    3.0
d    4.0
e    5.0
dtype: float64
```

The `pandas.Series.index` attribute lets us access the index:

```
ser3.index
```

The index is of type `pandas.Index`:

```
Index(['a', 'b', 'c', 'd', 'e'], dtype='object')
```

The values of the series can be accessed using the `pandas.Series.values` attribute:

```
ser3.values
```

The values are as follows:

```
array([ 1.,  2.,  3.,  4.,  5.])
```

We can assign the series a name by modifying the `pandas.Series.name` attribute:

```
ser3.name = 'Alphanumeric'; ser3
```

The output is as follows:

```
a    1.0
b    2.0
c    3.0
d    4.0
e    5.0
Name: Alphanumeric, dtype: float64
```

The preceding examples demonstrated numerous ways how to construct a pandas Series. Let's learn about DataFrames, a data structure that may contain multiple Series.

pandas.DataFrame

The `pandas.DataFrame` data structure is a collection of multiple `pandas.Series` objects of possibly different types indexed by the same common Index object.

The majority of all statistical time series operations are performed on DataFrames and `pandas.DataFrame` is optimized for parallel super-fast processing of DataFrames, much faster than if the processing was done on separate series.

We can create a DataFrame from a dictionary, where the key is the column name and the value of that key contains the data for the corresponding series/column:

```
df1 = pd.DataFrame({'A': range(1,5,1),
                    'B': range(10,50,10),
                    'C': range(100, 500, 100)});
df1
```

The output is as follows:

```
   A  B   C
0  1  10  100
1  2  20  200
```

```
2    3    30    300
3    4    40    400
```

We can also pass the `index=` parameter here to label the indices:

```
df2 = pd.DataFrame({'A': range(1,5,1),
                    'B': range(10,50,10),
                    'C': range(100, 500, 100)},
                    index=['a', 'b', 'c', 'd']);
df2
```

This constructs the following DataFrame:

```
     A    B    C
a    1    10   100
b    2    20   200
c    3    30   300
d    4    40   400
```

The `pandas.DataFrame.columns` attribute returns the names of the different columns:

```
df2.columns
```

The result is an `Index` object:

```
Index(['A', 'B', 'C'], dtype='object')
```

The indices can be accessed from the `pandas.DataFrame.index` attribute:

```
df2.index
```

That gives us this:

```
Index(['a', 'b', 'c', 'd'], dtype='object')
```

The DataFrame also contains the `pandas.DataFrame.values` attribute, which returns the values contained in the columns:

```
df2.values
```

The result is the following 2D array:

```
array([[   1,   10,  100],
       [   2,   20,  200],
       [   3,   30,  300],
       [   4,   40,  400]])
```

We can add a new column to the DataFrame with specified values and the same index with the following:

```
df2['D'] = range(1000,5000,1000);
df2
```

The updated DataFrame is as follows:

```
    A   B    C    D
a   1   10   100  1000
b   2   20   200  2000
c   3   30   300  3000
d   4   40   400  4000
```

We can assign names to the DataFrame's index and columns.

We can name the index by modifying the `pandas.DataFrame.index.name` attribute:

```
df2.index.name = 'lowercase'; df2
```

And that yields the following updated DataFrame:

```
           A   B    C    D
lowercase
a          1   10   100  1000
b          2   20   200  2000
c          3   30   300  3000
d          4   40   400  4000
```

The columns can be renamed using the `pandas.DataFrame.columns.name` attribute:

```
df2.columns.name = 'uppercase'; df2
```

The new DataFrame is as follows:

```
uppercase  A    B     C      D
lowercase
a          1    10    100    1000
b          2    20    200    2000
c          3    30    300    3000
d          4    40    400    4000
```

The preceding examples demonstrated how a DataFrame can be constructed.

pandas.Index

Both the `pandas.Series` and `pandas.DataFrame` data structures utilize the `pandas.Index` data structure.

There are many special types of `Index` objects:

- `Int64Index`: `Int64Index` contains integer index values.
- `MultiIndex`: `MultiIndex` contains indices that are tuples used in hierarchical indexing, which we will explore in this chapter.
- `DatetimeIndex`: `DatetimeIndex`, which we have seen before, contains datetime index values for time series datasets.

We can create a `pandas.Index` object by doing the following:

```
ind2 = pd.Index(list(range(5))); ind2
```

The result is this:

```
Int64Index([0, 1, 2, 3, 4], dtype='int64')
```

> **Note**
>
> `Index` objects are immutable and thus cannot be modified in place.

Let's see what happens if we try to modify an element in an `Index` object:

```
ind2[0] = -1
```

We get the following output:

```
------------------------------------------------------------------
------------
TypeError                                 Traceback (most
recent call last)
<ipython-input-34-20c233f961b2> in <module>()
----> 1 ind2[0] = -1
...
TypeError: Index does not support mutable operations
```

Python warns us that we cannot manually modify the index object.

We have now learned how to construct series and DataFrames. Let's explore the essential operations done on DataFrames.

Learning essential pandas.DataFrame operations

This section describes the essential operations done on DataFrames. Knowing they exist and how to use them will save you an enormous amount of time.

Indexing, selection, and filtering of DataFrames

pandas data structures are indexed by special `Index` objects (while `numpy.ndarrays` and Python list objects are only indexable by integers). The steps for this lesson are as follows:

1. Let's inspect the contents of the `df2` DataFrame created earlier in the chapter:

   ```
   df2
   ```

   The output is as follows:

   ```
   uppercase A  B   C    D
   lowercase
   a         1  10  100  1000
   b         2  20  200  2000
   c         3  30  300  3000
   d         4  40  400  4000
   ```

2. We can select the Series of values in column `B` by performing the following operation:

```
df2['B']
```

This yields the following Series:

```
lowercase
a      10
b      20
c      30
d      40
Name: B, dtype: int64
```

3. We can select multiple columns by passing a list of column names (somewhat similar to what we saw with `numpy.ndarrays`):

```
df2[['A', 'C']]
```

This yields the following DataFrame with two columns:

```
uppercase  A    C
lowercase
a          1    100
b          2    200
c          3    300
d          4    400
```

4. We can use Boolean selection with DataFrames by doing the following:

```
df2[(df2['D'] > 1000) & (df2['D'] <= 3000)]
```

This selects the following rows, which satisfy the provided condition:

```
uppercase    A    B     C      D
lowercase
b            2    20    200    2000
c            3    30    300    3000
```

5. The `pandas.DataFrame.loc[...]` attribute lets us index rows instead of columns. The following selects the two rows `c` and `d`:

```
df2.loc[['c', 'd']]
```

This yields the following subset DataFrame:

```
uppercase    A    B    C    D
lowercase
c            3    30   300  3000
d            4    40   400  4000
```

6. pandas DataFrames still support standard integer indexing through the `pandas.DataFrame.iloc[...]` attribute. We can select the first row by doing this:

```
df2.iloc[[0]]
```

This selects the following single-row DataFrame:

```
uppercase    A    B    C    D
lowercase
a            1    10   100  1000
```

We can modify the DataFrame with an operation like this:

```
df2[df2['D'] == 2000] = 0; df2
```

This updates the DataFrame to this new DataFrame:

```
uppercase    A    B    C    D
lowercase
a            1    10   100  1000
b            0    0    0    0
c            3    30   300  3000
d            4    40   400  4000
```

In this section, we have learned how to index, select, and filter DataFrames. In the next section, we will learn how to drop rows and columns.

Dropping rows and columns from a DataFrame

Dropping rows and columns from a DataFrame is a critical operation – it not only helps save the computer's memory but also ensures that the DataFrame contains only logically needed information. The steps are as follows:

1. Let's display the current DataFrame:

```
df2
```

This DataFrame contains the following:

uppercase	A	B	C	D
lowercase				
a	1	10	100	1000
b	0	0	0	0
c	3	30	300	3000
d	4	40	400	4000

2. To drop the row at index `b`, we use the `pandas.DataFrame.drop(...)` method:

```
df2.drop('b')
```

This yields a new DataFrame without the row at index `b`:

uppercase	A	B	C	D
lowercase				
a	1	10	100	1000
c	3	30	300	3000
d	4	40	400	4000

Let's check whether the original DataFrame was changed:

```
df2
```

The output shows that it was not, that is, `pandas.DataFrame.drop(...)` is not in place by default:

uppercase	A	B	C	D
lowercase				
a	1	10	100	1000
b	0	0	0	0
c	3	30	300	3000
d	4	40	400	4000

3. To modify the original DataFrame, we use the `inplace=` parameter:

```
df2.drop('b', inplace=True);
df2
```

The new in-place modified DataFrame is as follows:

uppercase	A	B	C	D
lowercase				

```
a            1    10    100    1000
c            3    30    300    3000
d            4    40    400    4000
```

4. We can drop multiple rows as well:

```
df2.drop(['a', 'd'])
```

This returns the following new DataFrame:

```
uppercase    A    B     C      D
lowercase
c            3    30    300    3000
```

5. To drop columns instead of rows, we specify the additional `axis=` parameter:

```
df2.drop(['A', 'B'], axis=1)
```

This gives us this new DataFrame with two dropped columns:

```
uppercase   C      D
lowercase
a           100    1000
c           300    3000
d           400    4000
```

We have learned how to drop rows and columns in this section. In the next section, we will learn how to sort values and rand them.

Sorting values and ranking the values' order within a DataFrame

First, let's create a DataFrame with integer row indices, integer column names, and random values:

```
import numpy as np
df = pd.DataFrame(np.random.randn(5,5),
                  index=np.random.randint(0, 100, size=5),
                  columns=np.random.randint(0,100,size=5));
df
```

The DataFrame contains the following data:

87	79	74	3	61	
7	0.355482	-0.246812	-1.147618	-0.293973	-0.560168
52	1.748274	0.304760	-1.346894	-0.548461	0.457927
80	-0.043787	-0.680384	1.918261	1.080733	1.346146
29	0.237049	0.020492	1.212589	-0.462218	1.284134
0	-0.153209	0.995779	0.100585	-0.350576	0.776116

`pandas.DataFrame.sort_index(...)` sorts the DataFrame by index values:

```
df.sort_index()
```

The result is as follows:

87	79	74	3	61	
0	-0.153209	0.995779	0.100585	-0.350576	0.776116
7	0.355482	-0.246812	-1.147618	-0.293973	-0.560168
29	0.237049	0.020492	1.212589	-0.462218	1.284134
52	1.748274	0.304760	-1.346894	-0.548461	0.457927
80	-0.043787	-0.680384	1.918261	1.080733	1.346146

We can also sort by column name values by specifying the `axis` parameter:

```
df.sort_index(axis=1)
```

This yields the following DataFrame with the columns arranged in order:

	3	61	74	79	87
7	-0.293973	-0.560168	-1.147618	-0.246812	0.355482
52	-0.548461	0.457927	-1.346894	0.304760	1.748274
80	1.080733	1.346146	1.918261	-0.680384	-0.043787
29	-0.462218	1.284134	1.212589	0.020492	0.237049
0	-0.350576	0.776116	0.100585	0.995779	-0.153209

To sort the values in the DataFrame, we use the `pandas.DataFrame.sort_values(...)` method, which takes a `by=` parameter specifying which column(s) to sort by:

```
df.sort_values(by=df.columns[0])
```

This yields the following DataFrame sorted by the values in the first column:

	87	79	74	3	61
0	-0.153209	0.995779	0.100585	-0.350576	0.776116
80	-0.043787	-0.680384	1.918261	1.080733	1.346146
29	0.237049	0.020492	1.212589	-0.462218	1.284134
7	0.355482	-0.246812	-1.147618	-0.293973	-0.560168
52	1.748274	0.304760	-1.346894	-0.548461	0.457927

The `pandas.DataFrame.rank(...)` method yields a DataFrame containing the rank/order of values in each column:

```
df.rank()
```

The output contains the rank (in ascending order) of values:

	87	79	74	3	61
7	4.0	2.0	2.0	4.0	1.0
52	5.0	4.0	1.0	1.0	2.0
80	2.0	1.0	5.0	5.0	5.0
29	3.0	3.0	4.0	2.0	4.0
0	1.0	5.0	3.0	3.0	3.0

With this lesson completed, in the next section we will perform arithmetic operations on DataFrames.

Arithmetic operations on DataFrames

First, let's create two DataFrames for our examples:

```
df1 = pd.DataFrame(np.random.randn(3,2),
                   index=['A', 'C', 'E'],
                   columns=['colA', 'colB']);
df1
```

The `df1` DataFrame contains the following:

	colA	colB
A	0.519105	-0.127284
C	-0.840984	-0.495306
E	-0.137020	0.987424

Now we create the `df2` DataFrame:

```
df2 = pd.DataFrame(np.random.randn(4,3),
                   index=['A', 'B', 'C', 'D'],
                   columns=['colA', 'colB', 'colC']);
df2
```

This contains the following:

	colA	colB	colC
A	-0.718550	1.938035	0.220391
B	-0.475095	0.238654	0.405642
C	0.299659	0.691165	-1.905837
D	0.282044	-2.287640	-0.551474

We can add the two DataFrames together. Note that they have different index values as well as different columns:

```
df1 + df2
```

The output is a summation of elements if the index and column exists in both DataFrames, otherwise it is NaN:

	colA	colB	colC
A	-0.199445	1.810751	NaN
B	NaN	NaN	NaN
C	-0.541325	0.195859	NaN
D	NaN	NaN	NaN
E	NaN	NaN	NaN

We can use the `pandas.DataFrame.add(...)` method with `fill_value=` to a value to be used instead of `NaN` (in this case `0`):

```
df1.add(df2, fill_value=0)
```

The output is as follows:

	colA	colB	colC
A	-0.199445	1.810751	0.220391
B	-0.475095	0.238654	0.405642

```
C    -0.541325    0.195859    -1.905837
D     0.282044   -2.287640    -0.551474
E    -0.137020    0.987424     NaN
```

We can perform arithmetic operations between DataFrames and Series as well:

```
df1 - df2[['colB']]
```

The output of this operation is the following (since the right-hand-side only had `colB`):

```
     colA    colB
A    NaN     -2.065319
B    NaN     NaN
C    NaN     -1.186471
D    NaN     NaN
E    NaN     NaN
```

Let's now learn how to merge and combine multiple DataFrames into a single Dataframe.

Merging and combining multiple DataFrames into a single DataFrame

Let's start by creating two DataFrames, `df1` and `df2`:

```
df1.index.name = 'Index'; df1.columns.name = 'Columns'; df1
```

The `df1` DataFrame has the following data:

```
Columns     colA         colB
Index
A            0.519105    -0.127284
C           -0.840984    -0.495306
E           -0.137020     0.987424
```

Now we create `df2`:

```
df2.index.name = 'Index'; df2.columns.name = 'Columns'; df2
```

The `df2` DataFrame has the following data:

```
Columns     colA        colB        colC
Index
```

```
A         -0.718550     1.938035     0.220391
B         -0.475095     0.238654     0.405642
C          0.299659     0.691165    -1.905837
D          0.282044    -2.287640    -0.551474
```

The `pandas.merge(...)` method joins/merges two DataFrames. The `left_index=` and `right_index=` parameters indicate that the merge should be performed on Index values in both DataFrames:

```
pd.merge(df1, df2, left_index=True, right_index=True)
```

That yields the following merged DataFrame. The _x and _y suffixes are added to differentiate between left and right DataFrame columns with the same name:

```
Columns colA_x    colB_x     colA_y     colB_y     colC
Index
A         0.519105  -0.127284  -0.718550  1.938035   0.220391
C        -0.840984  -0.495306   0.299659  0.691165  -1.905837
```

We can specify custom suffixes with the `suffixes=` parameter:

```
pd.merge(df1, df2, left_index=True, right_index=True,
         suffixes=('_1', '_2'))
```

The result is the following DataFrame with the suffixes we provided:

```
Columns   colA_1    colB_1     colA_2     colB_2    colC
Index
A           0.519105  -0.127284  -0.718550  1.938035  0.220391
C          -0.840984  -0.495306   0.299659  0.691165 -1.905837
```

We can specify the behavior of the join (outer, inner, left, or right join) using the `how=` parameter:

```
pd.merge(df1, df2, left_index=True, right_index=True,
         suffixes=('_1', '_2'), how='outer')
```

This yields the following DataFrame with `NaNs` for missing values:

```
Columns   colA_1    colB_1    colA_2    colB_2    colC
Index
A         0.519105  -0.127284  -0.718550  1.938035  0.220391
```

B	NaN	NaN	-0.475095	0.238654	0.405642
C	-0.840984	-0.495306	0.299659	0.691165	-1.905837
D	NaN	NaN	0.282044	-2.287640	-0.551474
E	-0.137020	0.987424	NaN	NaN	NaN

pandas DataFrames themselves have a `pandas.DataFrame.merge(...)` method that behaves the same way:

```
df1.merge(df2, left_index=True, right_index=True,
          suffixes=('_1', '_2'), how='outer')
```

This yields the following:

Columns	colA_1	colB_1	colA_2	colB_2	colC
Index					
A	0.519105	-0.127284	-0.718550	1.938035	0.220391
B	NaN	NaN	-0.475095	0.238654	0.405642
C	-0.840984	-0.495306	0.299659	0.691165	-1.905837
D	NaN	NaN	0.282044	-2.287640	-0.551474
E	-0.137020	0.987424	NaN	NaN	NaN

Another alternative is the `pandas.DataFrame.join(...)` method:

```
df1.join(df2, lsuffix='_1', rsuffix='_2')
```

And the output of the join (left join by default) is as follows:

Columns	colA_1	colB_1	colA_2	colB_2	colC
Index					
A	0.519105	-0.127284	-0.718550	1.938035	0.220391
C	-0.840984	-0.495306	0.299659	0.691165	-1.905837
E	-0.137020	0.987424	NaN	NaN	NaN

The `pandas.concat(...)` method combines DataFrames by concatenating rows together:

```
pd.concat([df1, df2])
```

This yields the following concatenated DataFrame with `NaNs` for missing values:

	colA	colB	colC
Index			

A	0.519105	-0.127284	NaN
C	-0.840984	-0.495306	NaN
E	-0.137020	0.987424	NaN
A	-0.718550	1.938035	0.220391
B	-0.475095	0.238654	0.405642
C	0.299659	0.691165	-1.905837
D	0.282044	-2.287640	-0.551474

We can concatenate across columns by specifying the `axis=` parameter:

```
pd.concat([df1, df2], axis=1)
```

This yields the following DataFrame with additional columns from `df2`:

Columns	colA	colB	colA	colB	colC
A	0.519105	-0.127284	-0.718550	1.938035	0.220391
B	NaN	NaN	-0.475095	0.238654	0.405642
C	-0.840984	-0.495306	0.299659	0.691165	-1.905837
D	NaN	NaN	0.282044	-2.287640	-0.551474
E	-0.137020	0.987424	NaN	NaN	NaN

We will now look at hierarchical indexing.

Hierarchical indexing

So far, we have been dealing with Index objects that were a simple single value. Hierarchical indexing uses `MultiIndex` objects, which are tuples of multiple values per Index. This lets us create sub-DataFrames inside a single DataFrame.

Let's create a `MultiIndex` DataFrame:

```
df = pd.DataFrame(np.random.randn(10, 2),
                  index=[list('aaabbbccdd'),
                  [1, 2, 3, 1, 2, 3, 1, 2, 1, 2]],
                  columns=['A', 'B']);
df
```

This is the layout of the `MultiIndex` DataFrame that uses hierarchical indexing:

		A	B
a	1	0.289379	-0.157919

```
        2   -0.409463   -1.103412
        3    0.812444   -1.950786
b       1   -1.549981    0.947575
        2    0.344725   -0.709320
        3    1.384979   -0.716733
c       1   -0.319983    0.887631
        2   -1.763973    1.601361
d       1    0.171177   -1.285323
        2   -0.143279    0.020981
```

We can assign names to the `MultiIndex` object with the `pandas.MultiIndex.names` attribute – it requires a list of names with the same dimension as the dimensions of the `MultiIndex` DataFrame (in this case, two elements):

```
df.index.names = ['alpha', 'numeric']; df
```

This yields the following:

```
                         A            B
alpha    numeric
a        1            0.289379    -0.157919
         2           -0.409463    -1.103412
         3            0.812444    -1.950786
...
```

The `pandas.DataFrame.reset_index(...)` method removes all indexing levels from a `MultiIndex` DataFrame by default, but can be used to remove one or more levels:

```
df.reset_index()
```

This leads to the following integer indexed DataFrame and the `MultiIndex` values are added as columns in this DataFrame:

```
      alpha     numeric        A            B
0     a         1            0.289379    -0.157919
1     a         2           -0.409463    -1.103412
2     a         3            0.812444    -1.950786
...
```

The `pandas.DataFrame.unstack(...)` method has similar behavior and pivots the inner level of indexing and converts them to columns:

```
df.unstack()
```

Let's inspect the new DataFrame where the innermost indexing level `[1, 2, 3]` becomes columns:

```
                A                                      B
numeric         1              2             3
                1              2             3
alpha
a               0.289379      -0.409463      0.812444
     -0.157919      -1.103412      -1.950786
b              -1.549981       0.344725      1.384979
     0.947575      -0.709320      -0.716733
c              -0.319983      -1.763973       NaN
              0.887631       1.601361          NaN
d               0.171177      -0.143279      NaN
              -1.285323      0.020981            NaN
```

The `pandas.DataFrame.stack(...)` method does the opposite of `unstack(...)`:

```
df.stack()
```

The output DataFrame is the original DataFrame with hierarchical indexing:

```
alpha  numeric
a      1         A    0.289379
                 B   -0.157919
       2         A   -0.409463
                 B   -1.103412
       3         A    0.812444
                 B   -1.950786
...
dtype: float64
```

Let's examine the structure of the `MultiIndex` DataFrame. Note that we first call `pandas.DataFrame.stack(...)` to convert the columns `[A, B]` into a third level of indexing in the `MultiIndex` DataFrame:

```
df.stack().index
```

This gives us a `MultiIndex` object with three levels of indexing:

```
MultiIndex(levels=[['a', 'b', 'c', 'd'],
                   [1, 2, 3], ['A', 'B']],
           labels=[[0, 0, 0, 0, 0, 0, 1, 1, 1, 1, 1, 1, 2, 2,
2, 2, 3, 3, 3, 3], [0, 0, 1, 1, 2, 2, 0, 0, 1, 1, 2, 2, 0, 0,
1, 1, 0, 0, 1, 1], [0, 1, 0, 1, 0, 1, 0, 1, 0, 1, 0, 1, 0, 1,
0, 1, 0, 1, 0, 1]],
           names=['alpha', 'numeric', None])
```

Now we will learn how to group operations in DataFrames.

Grouping operations in DataFrames

Grouping operations in pandas generally follow the split-apply-combine process of operations:

1. First, the data is split into groups based on one or more keys.
2. Then we apply necessary functions to these groups to compute the desired results.
3. Finally, we combine them to build the transformed dataset.

Thus, grouping a single indexed DataFrame builds a hierarchical DataFrame. The steps are as follows:

1. Let's use the `pandas.DataFrame.reset_index(...)` method to remove all hierarchical indexing from our previous `df` DataFrame:

   ```
   df = df.reset_index(); df
   ```

   This returns the following DataFrame with integer indexing:

	alpha	numeric	A	B
0	a	1	-0.807285	0.170242
1	a	2	0.704596	1.568901
2	a	3	-1.417366	0.573896
3	b	1	1.110121	0.366712
...				

2. Let's use the `pandas.DataFrame.groupby(...)` method to group the `A` and `B` columns by the `alpha` column:

```
grouped = df[['A','B']].groupby(df['alpha']); grouped
```

This yields the following `DataFrameGroupBy` object, which we can subsequently operate on:

```
<pandas.core.groupby.DataFrameGroupBy object at
0x7fd21f24cc18>
```

3. We can use the `DataFrameGroupBy.describe(...)` method to collect summary descriptive statistics:

```
grouped.describe()
```

This yields the following output where statistics for `A` and `B` are generated but grouped by the `alpha` column:

```
            A          B
alpha
a           count      3.000000     3.000000
mean    -0.506685      0.771013
std      1.092452      0.719863
min     -1.417366      0.170242
25%     -1.112325      0.372069
50%     -0.807285      0.573896
75%     -0.051344      1.071398
max      0.704596      1.568901
...
```

4. We can apply the `pandas.DataFrame.unstack(...)` method using the `DataFrameGroupBy.apply(...)` method, which accepts different functions and applies them to each group of the `grouped` object:

```
grouped.apply(pd.DataFrame.unstack)
```

This generates the following hierarchical DataFrame:

```
alpha
a        A  0    -0.807285
            1     0.704596
            2    -1.417366
```

```
        B  0     0.170242
           1     1.568901
           2     0.573896
...
dtype: float64
```

5. There also exists the `DataFrameGroupBy.agg(...)` method, which accepts functions and aggregates each column for each group using that method. The next example aggregates using the `mean` method:

```
grouped[['A', 'B']].agg('mean')
```

The output contains the mean for columns `A` and `B` grouped by values in `alpha`:

```
                A            B
alpha
     a   -0.506685     0.771013
     b    0.670435     0.868550
     c    0.455688    -0.497468
     d   -0.786246     0.107246
```

6. A similar method is the `DataFrameGroupBy.transform(...)` method, with the only difference being that transform works on one column at a time and returns a sequence of values of the same length as the series, while apply can return any type of result:

```
from scipy import stats
grouped[['A', 'B']].transform(stats.zscore)
```

This generates the Z score for columns `A` and `B`, which we explained in *Chapter 2, Exploratory Data Analysis*:

```
          A           B
0  -0.337002   -1.022126
1   1.357964    1.357493
2  -1.020962   -0.335367
3   0.610613   -0.567813
4  -1.410007    1.405598
5   0.799394   -0.837785
6  -1.000000    1.000000
7   1.000000   -1.000000
```

```
8     -1.000000     -1.000000
9      1.000000      1.000000
```

We will now learn how to transform values in DataFrames' axis indices.

Transforming values in DataFrames' axis indices

Let's first reinspect the `df2` DataFrame that we will be using in these examples:

```
df2
```

This contains the following data:

Columns	colA	colB	colC
Index			
A	-2.071652	0.742857	0.632307
B	0.113046	-0.384360	0.414585
C	0.690674	1.511816	2.220732
D	0.184174	-1.069291	-0.994885

We can rename the Index labels using the `pandas.DataFrame.index` attribute as we saw before:

```
df2.index = ['Alpha', 'Beta', 'Gamma', 'Delta'];
df2
```

This generates the following transformed DataFrame:

Columns	colA	colB	colC
Alpha	-2.071652	0.742857	0.632307
Beta	0.113046	-0.384360	0.414585
Gamma	0.690674	1.511816	2.220732
Delta	0.184174	-1.069291	-0.994885

The `pandas.Index.map(...)` method applies functions to transform the Index.

In the following example, the `map` function takes the first three characters of the name and sets that as the new name:

```
df2.index = df2.index.map(lambda x : x[:3]); df2
```

The output is as follows:

Columns	colA	colB	colC
Alp	-2.071652	0.742857	0.632307
Bet	0.113046	-0.384360	0.414585
Gam	0.690674	1.511816	2.220732
Del	0.184174	-1.069291	-0.994885

The `pandas.DataFrame.rename(...)` method lets us transform both Index names and column names and accepts a dictionary mapping from the old name to the new name:

```
df2.rename(index={'Alp': 0, 'Bet': 1, 'Gam': 2, 'Del': 3},
           columns={'colA': 'A', 'colB': 'B', 'colC': 'C'})
```

The resulting DataFrame has new labels on both axes:

Columns	A	B	C
0	-2.071652	0.742857	0.632307
1	0.113046	-0.384360	0.414585
2	0.690674	1.511816	2.220732
3	0.184174	-1.069291	-0.994885

With this lesson learned, we will learn how to handle missing data in DataFrames.

Handling missing data in DataFrames

Missing data is a common phenomenon in data science and can happen for multiple reasons – for example, technical error, human error, market holiday.

Filtering out missing data

When dealing with missing data, the first option is to remove all observations with any missing data.

This code block modifies the `df2` DataFrame using the `pandas.DataFrame.at[...]` attribute and sets some values to `NaN`:

```
for row, col in [('Bet', 'colA'), ('Bet', 'colB'),
  ('Bet', 'colC'), ('Del', 'colB'), ('Gam', 'colC')]:
    df2.at[row, col] = np.NaN

df2
```

The modified DataFrame is as follows:

Columns	colA	colB	colC
Alp	-1.721523	-0.425150	1.425227
Bet	NaN	NaN	NaN
Gam	-0.408566	-1.121813	NaN
Del	0.361053	NaN	0.580435

The `pandas.DataFrame.isnull(...)` method finds missing values in a DataFrame:

```
df2.isnull()
```

The result is a DataFrame with `True` where values are missing and `False` otherwise:

Columns	colA	colB	colC
Alp	False	False	False
Bet	True	True	True
Gam	False	False	True
Del	False	True	False

The `pandas.DataFrame.notnull(...)` method does the opposite (detects non-missing values):

```
df2.notnull()
```

The output is the following DataFrame:

Columns	colA	colB	colC
Alp	True	True	True
Bet	False	False	False
Gam	True	True	False
Del	True	False	True

The `pandas.DataFrame.dropna(...)` method allows us to drop rows with missing values. The additional `how=` parameter controls which rows get dropped. To drop rows that have `NaN` for all fields, we do the following:

```
df2.dropna(how='all')
```

The result is the following modified DataFrame with the `Bet` row removed since that was the only one with all `NaN`:

Columns	colA	colB	colC
Alp	-1.721523	-0.425150	1.425227
Gam	-0.408566	-1.121813	NaN
Del	0.361053	NaN	0.580435

Setting `how=` to `any` removes rows with any NaN values:

```
df2.dropna(how='any')
```

This gives us the following DataFrame with all non-NaN values:

Columns	colA	colB	colC
Alp	-1.721523	-0.42515	1.425227

We will now look at how to fill in missing data.

Filling in missing data

The second option when dealing with missing data is to fill in the missing values either with a value of our choice or using other valid values in the same column to duplicate/extrapolate the missing values.

Let's start by re-inspecting the `df2` DataFrame:

```
df2
```

This yields the following DataFrame with some missing values:

Columns	colA	colB	colC
Alp	-1.721523	-0.425150	1.425227
Bet	NaN	NaN	NaN
Gam	-0.408566	-1.121813	NaN
Del	0.361053	NaN	0.580435

Now, let's use the `pandas.DataFrame.fillna(...)` method with the `method='backfill'` and `inplace=True` arguments to use the `backfill` method to backward fill the missing values from the other values and change the DataFrame in place:

```
df2.fillna(method='backfill', inplace=True);
df2
```

The new DataFrame contains the following:

Columns	colA	colB	colC
Alp	-1.721523	-0.425150	1.425227
Bet	-0.408566	-1.121813	0.580435
Gam	-0.408566	-1.121813	0.580435
Del	0.361053	NaN	0.580435

The `NaN` value at `(Del,colB)` is because there were no observations after that row, so backfill could not be performed. That can be fixed instead with forward fill.

The transformation of DataFrames with functions and mappings

pandas DataFrame values can also be modified by passing functions and dictionary mappings that operate on one or more data values and generate new transformed values.

Let's modify the `df2` DataFrame by adding a new column, `Category`, containing discrete text data:

```
df2['Category'] = ['HIGH', 'LOW', 'LOW', 'HIGH']; df2
```

The new DataFrame contains the following:

Columns	colA	colB	colC	Category
Alp	1.017961	1.450681	-0.328989	HIGH
Bet	-0.079838	-0.519025	1.460911	LOW
Gam	-0.079838	-0.519025	1.460911	LOW
Del	0.359516	NaN	1.460911	HIGH

The `pandas.Series.map(...)` method accepts a dictionary containing a mapping from the old value to the new value and transforms the values. The following snippet changes the text values in `Category` to single characters:

```
df2['Category'] = df2['Category'].map({'HIGH': 'H',
                                        'LOW': 'L'});
df2
```

The updated DataFrame is as follows:

Columns	colA	colB	colC	Category
Alp	1.017961	1.450681	-0.328989	H

```
Bet        -0.079838    -0.519025    1.460911    L
Gam        -0.079838    -0.519025    1.460911    L
Del         0.359516     NaN         1.460911    H
```

The `pandas.DataFrame.applymap(...)` method allows us to apply functions to data values in a DataFrame.

The following code applies the `numpy.exp(...)` method, which calculates the exponential:

```
df2.drop('Category', axis=1).applymap(np.exp)
```

The result is a DataFrame containing exponential values of the original DataFrame's values (except the `NaN` value):

```
Columns    colA        colB        colC
Alp        2.767545    4.266020    0.719651
Bet        0.923266    0.595101    4.309883
Gam        0.923266    0.595101    4.309883
Del        1.432636    NaN         4.309883
```

Now that we've learned how to transform DataFrames, we will see how to discretize and bucket values in DataFrames.

Discretization/bucketing of DataFrame values

The simplest way to achieve discretization is to create ranges of values and assign a single discrete label to all values that fall within a certain bucket.

First, let's generate a random valued ndarray for our use:

```
arr = np.random.randn(10);
arr
```

This contains the following:

```
array([ 1.88087339e-01,  7.94570445e-01,  -5.97384701e-01,
       -3.01897668e+00, -5.42185315e-01,   1.10094663e+00,
        1.16002554e+00,  1.51491444e-03,  -2.21981570e+00,
        1.11903929e+00])
```

The `pandas.cut(...)` method can be used to discretize these values. The following code uses the `bins=` and `labels=[...]` arguments to bin the values into five discrete values with the labels provided:

```
cat = pd.cut(arr, bins=5, labels=['Very Low', 'Low', 'Med',
                                  'High', 'Very High']);
cat
```

We get the discrete values after the transformation:

```
 [High, Very High, Med, Very Low, Med, Very High, Very High,
High, Very Low, Very High]
Categories (5, object): [Very Low < Low < Med < High < Very
High]
```

The `pandas.qcut(...)` method is similar but uses quartiles to bin the continuous values to discrete values so that each category has the same amount of observations.

The following builds five discrete bins using the `q=` parameter:

```
qcat = pd.qcut(arr, q=5, labels=['Very Low', 'Low', 'Med',
                                 'High', 'Very High']);
qcat
```

And the quartile discretization yields the following categories:

```
[Med, High, Low, Very Low, Low, High, Very High, Med, Very Low,
Very High]
Categories (5, object): [Very Low < Low < Med < High < Very
High]
```

The following code block builds a pandas DataFrame consisting of the original continuous values as well as the categories generated from `cut` and `qcut`:

```
pd.DataFrame({'Value': arr, 'Category': cat,
              'Quartile Category': qcat})
```

This DataFrame allows side-by-side comparison:

```
Category    Quartile     Category    Value
0           High         Med         0.188087
1           Very High    High        0.794570
2           Med          Low         -0.597385
```

```
3          Very Low     Very Low    -3.018977
4          Med          Low         -0.542185
5          Very High    High         1.100947
6          Very High    Very High    1.160026
7          High         Med          0.001515
8          Very Low     Very Low    -2.219816
9          Very High    Very High    1.119039
```

The `pandas.Categorical.categories` attribute provides us with the bucket ranges:

```
pd.cut(arr, bins=5).categories
```

In this case, the buckets/range of values are as follows:

```
Index(['(-3.0232, -2.183]', '(-2.183, -1.347]',
       '(-1.347, -0.512]', '(-0.512, 0.324]',
       '(0.324, 1.16]'],
      dtype='object')
```

We can inspect the buckets for `qcut` as well:

```
pd.qcut(arr, q=5).categories
```

They are slightly different from the previous buckets and they are shown as follows:

```
Index(['[-3.019, -0.922]', '(-0.922, -0.216]',
       '(-0.216, 0.431]', '(0.431, 1.105]',
       '(1.105, 1.16]'],
      dtype='object')
```

We will now look at permuting and sampling DataFrame values to generate new DataFrames.

Permuting and sampling DataFrame values to generate new DataFrames

Permuting available datasets to generate new datasets and sampling datasets to either sub-sample (reduce the number of observations) or super-sample (increase the number of observations) are common operations in statistical analysis.

First, let's generate a DataFrame of random values to work with:

```
df = pd.DataFrame(np.random.randn(10,5),
                  index=np.sort(np.random.randint(0, 100,
                                                  size=10)),
                  columns=list('ABCDE'));
df
```

The result is the following:

```
            A          B          C          D          E
 0  -0.564568  -0.188190  -1.678637  -0.128102  -1.880633
 0  -0.465880   0.266342   0.950357  -0.867568   1.504719
29   0.589315  -0.968324  -0.432725   0.856653  -0.683398
...
```

The `numpy.random.permutation(...)` method, when applied to a DataFrame, randomly shuffles along the Index axis and can be used to permute the rows in the dataset:

```
df.loc[np.random.permutation(df.index)]
```

This yields the following DataFrame with the rows randomly shuffled:

```
            A          B          C          D          E
42   0.214554   1.108811   1.352568   0.238083  -1.090455
 0  -0.564568  -0.188190  -1.678637  -0.128102  -1.880633
 0  -0.465880   0.266342   0.950357  -0.867568   1.504719
62  -0.266102   0.831051  -0.164629   0.349047   1.874955
...
```

We can use the `numpy.random.randint(...)` method to generate random integers within a certain range and then use the `pandas.DataFrame.iloc[...]` attribute to randomly sample with replacement (the same observation can be picked more than once) from our DataFrame.

The following code block picks out five rows randomly sampled with replacement:

```
df.iloc[np.random.randint(0, len(df), size=5)]
```

This yields the following randomly sub-sampled DataFrame:

	A	B	C	D	E
54	0.692757	-0.584690	-0.176656	0.728395	-0.434987
98	-0.517141	0.109758	-0.132029	0.614610	-0.235801
29	0.589315	-0.968324	-0.432725	0.856653	-0.683398
35	0.520140	0.143652	0.973510	0.440253	1.307126
62	-0.266102	0.831051	-0.164629	0.349047	1.874955

In the following section, we will look at exploring file operations with `pandas.DataFrames`.

Exploring file operations with pandas.DataFrames

pandas supports the persistence of DataFrames in both plain-text and binary formats. The common text formats are CSV and JSON files, the most used binary formats are Excel XLSX, HDF5, and pickle.

In this book, we focus on plain-text persistence.

CSV files

CSV files (**comma-separated values** files) are data-exchange standard files.

Writing CSV files

Writing a pandas DataFrame to a CSV file is easily achievable using the `pandas.DataFrame.to_csv(...)` method. The `header=` parameter controls whether a header is written to the top of the file or not and the `index=` parameter controls whether the Index axis values are written to the file or not:

```
df.to_csv('df.csv', sep=',', header=True, index=True)
```

We can inspect the file written to disk using the following Linux command typed into the notebook. The `!` character instructs the notebook to run a shell command:

```
!head -n 4 df.csv
```

The file contains the following lines:

```
,A,B,C,D,E
4,-0.6329164608486778,0.3733235944037599,0.8225354680198685,-
0.5171618315489593,0.5492241692404063
17,0.7664860447792711,0.8427366352142621,0.9621402130525599,-
0.41134468872009666,-0.9704305306626816
24,-0.22976016405853183,0.38081314413811984,-
1.526376189972014,0.07229102135441286,-0.3297356221604555
```

Reading CSV files

Reading a CSV file and building a pandas DataFrame from the data in it can be achieved using the `pandas.read_csv(...)` method. Here we will specify the character (although that is the default for `read_csv`), the `index_col=` parameter to specify which column to treat as the Index of the DataFrame, and the `nrows=` parameter to specify how many rows to read in:

```
pd.read_csv('df.csv', sep=',', index_col=0, nrows=5)
```

This builds the following DataFrame, which is the same DataFrame that was written to disk:

	A	B	C	D	E
4	-0.632916	0.373324	0.822535	-0.517162	0.549224
17	0.766486	0.842737	0.962140	-0.411345	-0.970431
24	-0.229760	0.380813	-1.526376	0.072291	-0.329736
33	0.662259	-1.457732	-2.268573	0.332456	0.496143
33	0.335710	0.452842	-0.977736	0.677470	1.164602

We can also specify the `chunksize=` parameter, which reads in the specified number of lines at a time, which can help when exploring very large datasets contained in very large files:

```
pd.read_csv('df.csv', sep=',', index_col=0, chunksize=2)
```

That returns a pandas `TextFileReader` generator, which we can iterate through as needed instead of loading the entire file at once:

```
<pandas.io.parsers.TextFileReader at 0x7fb4e9933a90>
```

We can force the generator to finish evaluation by wrapping it in a list and observe the entire DataFrame loaded in chunks of two lines:

```
list(pd.read_csv('df.csv', sep=',', index_col=0,
                 chunksize=2))
```

That gives us the following list of two-line blocks:

```
[           A         B         C         D         E
 4  -0.632916  0.373324  0.822535 -0.517162  0.549224
 17  0.766486  0.842737  0.962140 -0.411345 -0.970431,
            A         B         C         D         E
 24 -0.229760  0.380813 -1.526376  0.072291 -0.329736
 33  0.662259 -1.457732 -2.268573  0.332456  0.496143,
...
```

We will now look at how to explore file operations in JSON files.

JSON files

JSON files are based upon data structures identical to Python dictionaries. This makes JSON files very convenient for many purposes including representing DataFrames as well as representing configuration files.

The `pandas.DataFrame.to_json(...)` method conveniently writes a DataFrame to a JSON file on disk. Here we write only the first four rows:

```
df.iloc[:4].to_json('df.json')
```

Let's check out the JSON file written to disk:

```
!cat df.json
```

This gives us the following dictionary-style JSON file written to disk:

```
{"A":{"4":-0.6329164608,"17":0.7664860448,"24":-
0.2297601641,"33":0.6622594878},"B":{"4":0.3733235944,
"17":0.8427366352,"24":0.3808131441,"33":-1.4577321521},
"C":{"4":0.822535468,"17":0.9621402131,"24":-1.52637619,"33":-
2.2685732447},"D":{"4":-0.5171618315,"17":-0.4113446887
,"24":0.0722910214,"33":0.3324557226},"E":{"4":0.5492241692
,"17":-0.9704305307,"24":-0.3297356222,"33":0.4961425281}}
```

Reading JSON files back into Pandas DataFrames is just as easy with the `pandas.read_json(...)` method:

```
pd.read_json('df.json')
```

This gives us back the original four-row DataFrame that was written to disk:

	A	B	C	D	E
4	-0.632916	0.373324	0.822535	-0.517162	0.549224
17	0.766486	0.842737	0.962140	-0.411345	-0.970431
24	-0.229760	0.380813	-1.526376	0.072291	-0.329736
33	0.662259	-1.457732	-2.268573	0.332456	0.496143

Congrats on successfully completing this lesson!

Summary

This chapter introduced us to the pandas library, upon which the majority, if not all, time-series operations in Python are done. We have learned how to create a DataFrame, how to alter it, and how to persist it.

Pandas DataFrames are principally for high-performance bulk data manipulation, selecting and reshaping data. They are the Python version of Excel worksheets.

In the next chapter, we will investigate visualization in Python using Matplotlib.

5
Data Visualization Using Matplotlib

Data visualization allows comprehending numerical data significantly more easily than reading pure tables of numbers. Getting instant insight into data and the identification of patterns, trends, and outliers are the primary uses of charting libraries.

When deciding which stock may be suitable for which algorithmic trading strategy, creating a chart of the stock price is the first step – some strategies are suitable only for trending stocks, some for mean-reversion stocks, and so on. While numerical statistics are critical, there is no substitute for a well-designed chart.

This chapter introduces us to Matplotlib, a static, animated, and interactive Python visualization library extending the capabilities of NumPy. The `pandas` library allows direct charting of DataFrames using Matplotlib.

This chapter covers the following main topics:

- Creating figures and subplots
- Enriching plots with colors, markers, and line styles
- Enriching axes with ticks, labels, and legends
- Enriching data points with annotations
- Saving plots to files
- Charting a `pandas` DataFrame with Matplotlib

Technical requirements

The Python code used in this chapter is available in the `Chapter05/matplotlib.ipynb` notebook in the book's code repository.

Creating figures and subplots

Matplotlib supports plotting multiple charts (subplots) on a single figure, which is Matplotlib's term for the drawing canvas.

Defining figures' subplots

To create a `matplotlib.pyplot.figure` object, use the following method:

```
import matplotlib.pyplot as plt
fig = plt.figure(figsize=(12, 6), dpi=200)
```

This yields an empty figure object (`0 Axes`):

```
<Figure size 2400x1200 with 0 Axes>
```

Before we plot anything on this figure, we need to add subplots to create space for them. The `matplotlib.pyplot.figure.add_subplot(...)` method lets us do that by specifying the size of the subplot and the location.

The following code block adds a subplot of size 1x2 grids on the left, then a subplot of 2x2 on the top right, and finally, a subplot of 2x2 on the bottom right:

```
ax1 = fig.add_subplot(1, 2, 1)
ax2 = fig.add_subplot(2, 2, 2)
ax3 = fig.add_subplot(2, 2, 4)
fig
```

The result is the following figure object containing the subplots we just added:

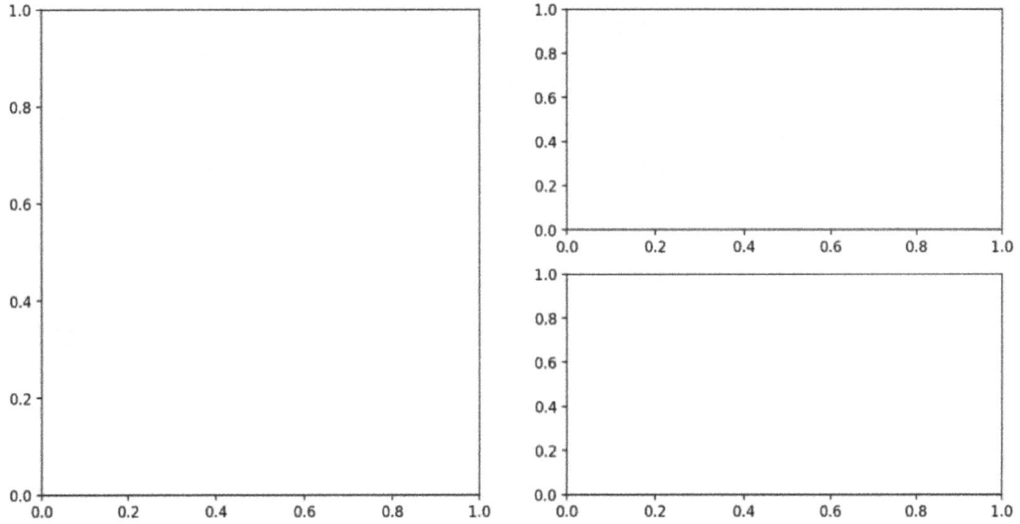

Figure 5.1 – Figure containing three empty subplots

Now, once we have created the space for the charts (`"plots"/"subplots"`), we can populate them with visualizations. In all reports, physical space on the page is very expensive, so creating charts like the preceding is the best practice.

Plotting in subplots

Let's use `numpy.linspace(...)` to generate evenly spaced values on the *x* axis, and then the `numpy.square(...)`, `numpy.sin(...)`, and `numpy.cos(...)` methods to generate corresponding values on the *y* axis.

We will use the `ax1`, `ax2`, and `ax3` axes variables we got from adding subplots to plot these functions:

```
import numpy as np

x = np.linspace(0, 1, num=20)
y1 = np.square(x)
ax1.plot(x, y1, color='black', linestyle='--')

y2 = np.sin(x)
ax2.plot(x, y2, color='black', linestyle=':')

y3 = np.cos(x)
ax3.plot(x, y3, color='black', linestyle='-.')
fig
```

Now, the following figure contains the values we just plotted:

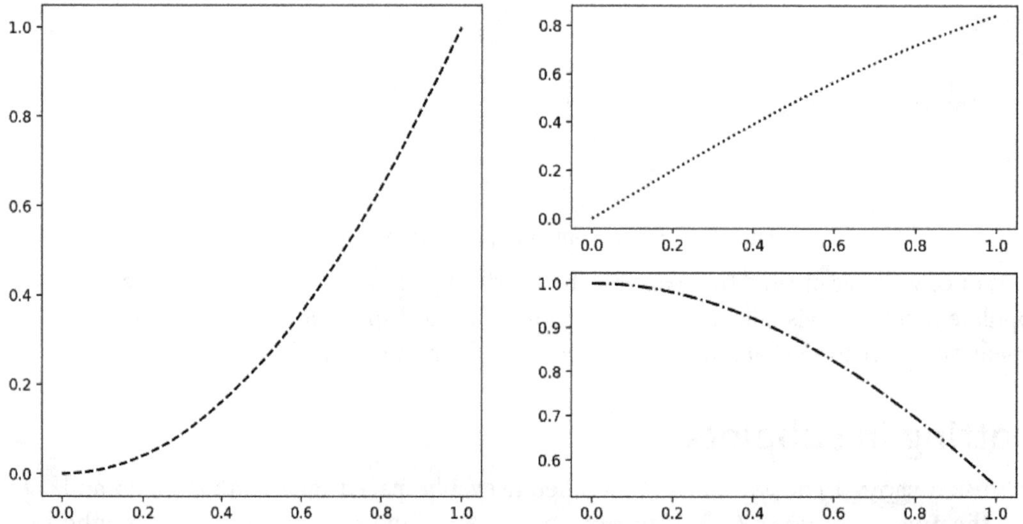

Figure 5.2 – Figure containing three subplots plotting the square, sine, and cosine functions

The `sharex=` parameter can be passed when creating subplots to specify that all the subplots should share the same *x* axis.

Let's demonstrate this functionality and plot the square, and then use the `numpy.power(...)` method to raise x to the power of 10 and plot them with the same *x* axis:

```
fig, (ax1, ax2) = plt.subplots(2, figsize=(12, 6),
                               sharex=True)
ax1.plot(x, y1, color='black', linestyle='--')
y2 = np.power(x, 10)
ax2.plot(x, y2, color='black', linestyle='-.')
```

The result is the following figure with a shared *x* axis and different functions plotted on each graph:

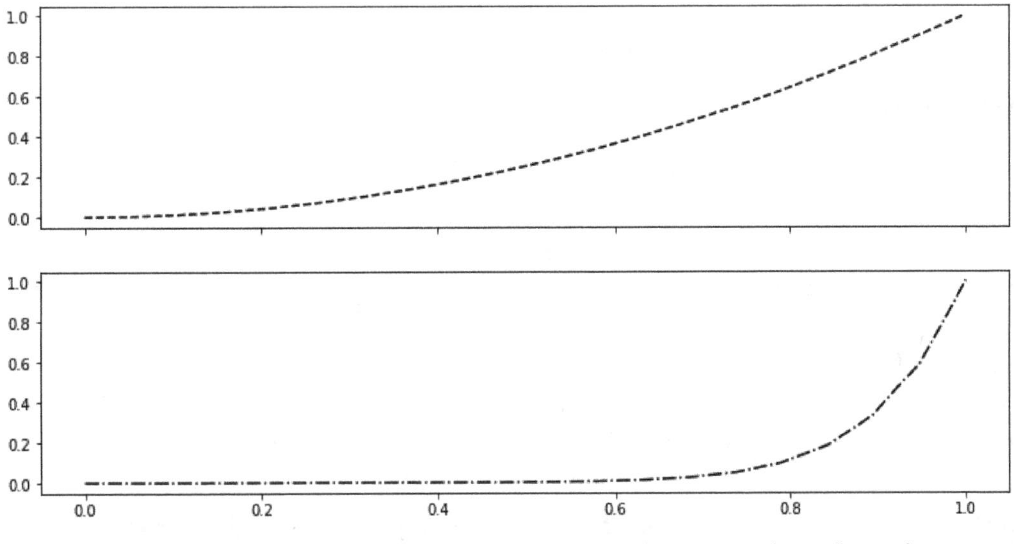

Figure 5.3 – Figure with subplots sharing an x axis, containing the square and raised to 10 functions

The charts we generated are not self-explanatory yet – it is unclear what the units on the *x* axis and the *y* axis are, and what each chart represents. To improve the charts, we need to enrich them with colors, markers, and line styles, to enrich the axes with ticks, legends, and labels and provide selected data points' annotations.

Enriching plots with colors, markers, and line styles

Colors, markers, and lines styles make charts easier to understand.

The code block that follows plots four different functions and uses the following parameters to modify the appearance:

- The `color=` parameter is used to assign colors.
- The `linewidth=` parameter is used to change the width/thickness of the lines.
- The `marker=` parameter assigns different shapes to mark the data points.
- The `markersize=` parameter changes the size of those markers.
- The `alpha=` parameter is used to modify the transparency.
- The `drawstyle=` parameter changes the default line connectivity to step connectivity between data points for one plot.

The code is as follows:

```
fig, (ax1, ax2, ax3, ax4) = plt.subplots(4,
                                          figsize=(12, 12),
                                          sharex=True)
x = np.linspace(0, 10, num=20)
y1 = np.exp(x)
y2 = x ** 3
y3 = np.sin(y2)
y4 = np.random.randn(20)

ax1.plot(x, y1, color='black', linestyle='--', linewidth=5,
         marker='x', markersize=15)
ax2.plot(x, y2, color='green', linestyle='-.', linewidth=2,
         marker='^', markersize=10, alpha=0.9)
ax3.plot(x, y3, color='red', linestyle=':', marker='*',
         markersize=15, drawstyle='steps')
ax4.plot(x, y4, color='green', linestyle='-', marker='s',
         markersize=15)
```

The output displays four functions with different attributes assigned to them:

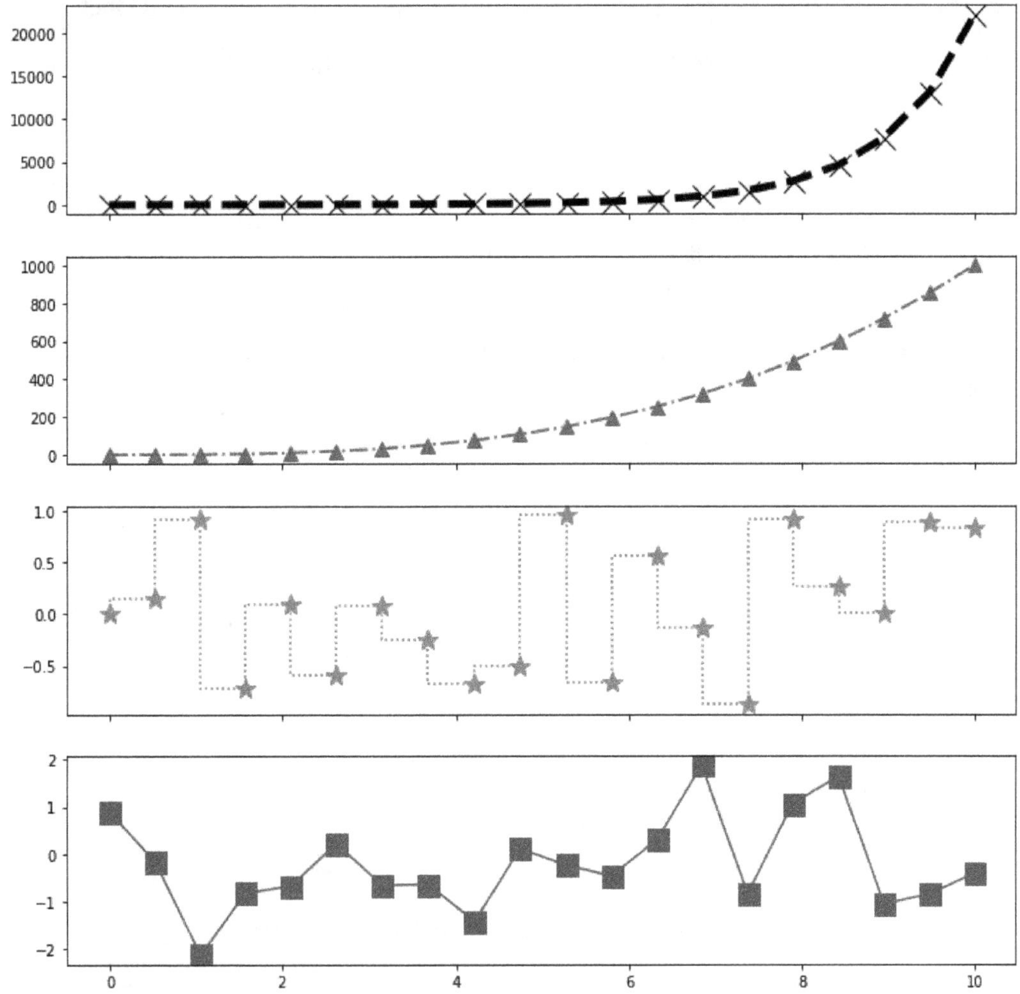

Figure 5.4 – Plot demonstrating different color, line style, marker style, transparency, and size options

Using different colors, line styles, marker styles, transparency, and size options enables us to generate rich charts with easily identifiable multiple time series. Choose the colors wisely as they may not render well on some laptop screens or on paper if printed.

Enriching axes is the next step in making outstanding charts.

Enriching axes with ticks, labels, and legends

The charts can be further improved by customizing the axes via ticks, limits, and labels.

The `matplotlib.pyplot.xlim(...)` method sets the range of values on the *x* axis.

The `matplotlib.pyplot.xticks(...)` method specifies where the ticks show up on the *x* axis:

```
plt.xlim([8, 10.5])
plt.xticks([8, 8.42, 8.94, 9.47, 10, 10.5])
plt.plot(x, y1, color='black', linestyle='--', marker='o')
```

This modifies the *x* axis to be within the specified limits and the ticks at the explicitly specified values:

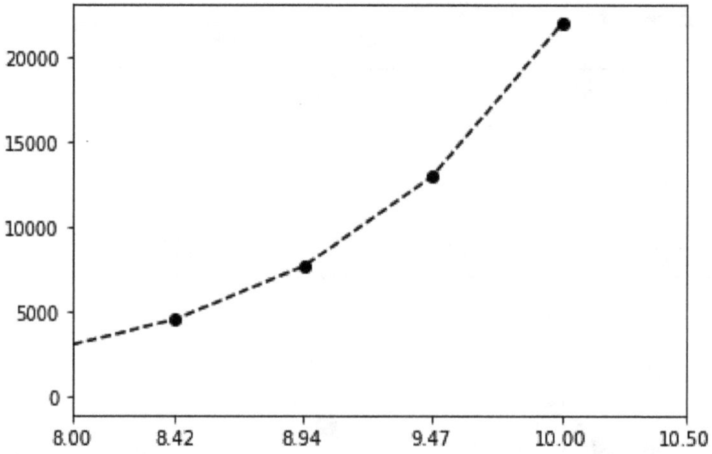

Figure 5.5 – Plot with explicit limits and ticks on the x axis

We can also change the scale of one of the axes to non-linear using the `matplotlib.Axes.set_yscale(...)` method.

The `matplotlib.Axes.set_xticklabels(...)` method changes the labels on the *x* axis:

```
fig, ax = plt.subplots(1, figsize=(12, 6))
ax.set_yscale('log')
ax.set_xticks(x)
ax.set_xticklabels(list('ABCDEFGHIJKLMNOPQRSTUV'))
ax.plot(x, y1, color='black', linestyle='--', marker='o',
        label='y=exp(x)')
```

The output of that code block shows the difference in the scale of the *y* axis, which is now logarithmic, and the *x* axis ticks have the specific tick labels:

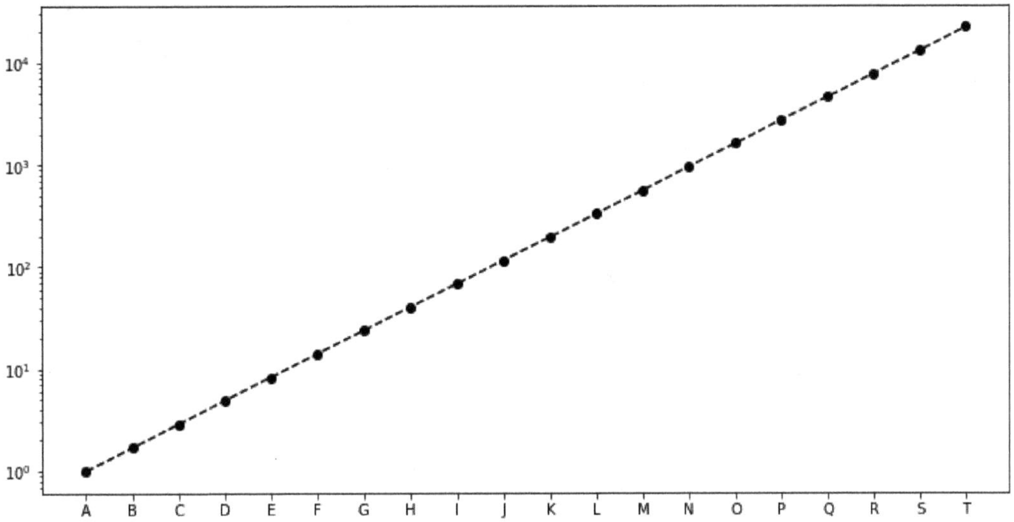

Figure 5.6 – Plot with a logarithmic y-axis scale and custom x-axis tick labels

The logarithmic scales in charts are useful if the dataset covers a large range of values and/or if we want to communicate percentage change or multiplicative factors.

The `matplotlib.Axes.set_title(...)` method adds a title to the plot and the `matplotlib.Axes.set_xlabel(...)` and `matplotlib.Axes.set_ylabel(...)` methods set labels for the *x* and *y* axes.

The `matplotlib.Axes.legend(...)` method adds a legend, which makes the plots easier to interpret. The `loc=` parameter specifies the location of the legend on the plot with `loc='best'`, meaning Matplotlib picks the best location automatically:

```
ax.set_title('xtickslabel example')
ax.set_xlabel('x labels')
ax.set_ylabel('log scale y values')
ax.legend(loc='best')
fig
```

The following plot shows the title, the *x*- and *y*-axis labels, and the legend:

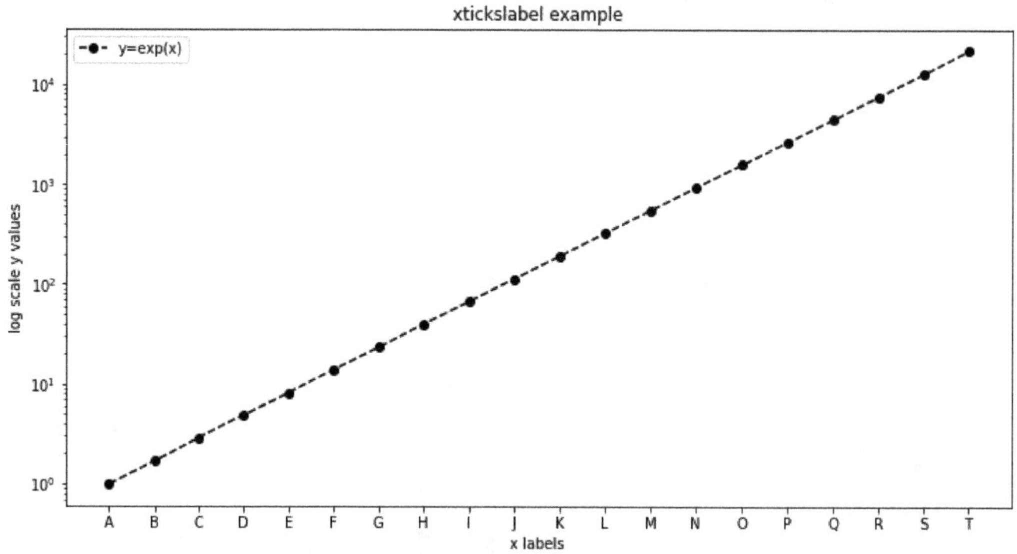

Figure 5.7 – Plot demonstrating a title, x- and y-axis labels, and a legend

Charts with a different rendering of each time series and with explained units and labels of the axes are sufficient for understanding charts. However, there are always some special data points that would benefit from being pointed out.

Enriching data points with annotations

The `matplotlib.Axes.text(...)` method adds a text box to our plots:

```
ax.text(1, 10000, 'Generated using numpy and matplotlib')
fig
```

The output is as follows:

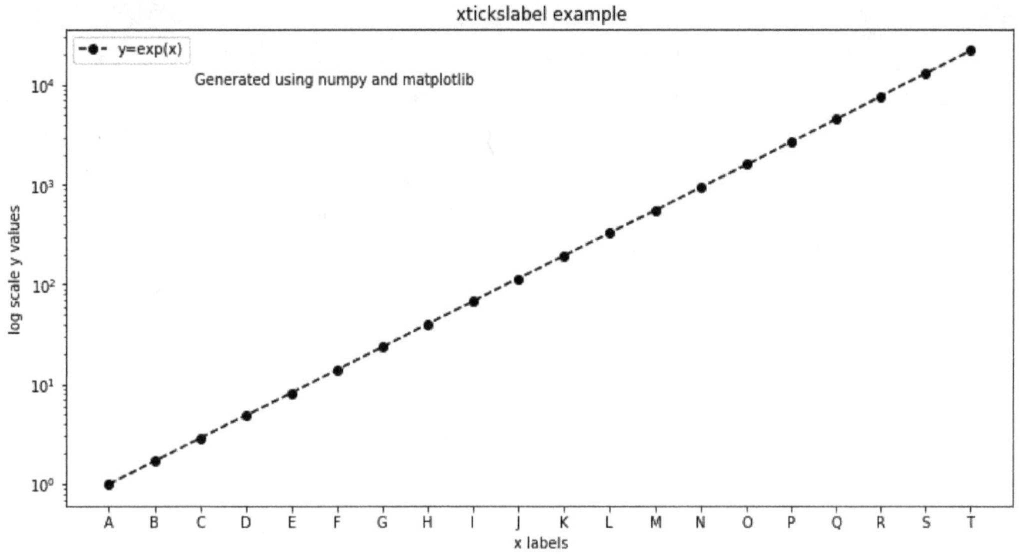

Figure 5.8 – Plot displaying Matplotlib text annotations

The `matplotlib.Axes.annotate(...)` method provides more control over the annotations.

The code block that follows uses the following parameters to control the annotation:

- The `xy=` parameter specifies the location of the data point.
- The `xytext=` parameter specifies the location of the text box.
- The `arrowprops=` parameter accepts a dictionary specifying parameters to control the arrow from the text box to the data point.
- The `facecolor=` parameter specifies the color and the `shrink=` parameter specifies the size of the arrow.
- The `horizontalalignment=` and `verticalalignment=` parameters specify the orientation of the text box relative to the data point.

The code is as follows:

```
for i in [5, 10, 15]:
    s = '(x=' + str(x[i]) + ',y=' + str(y1[i]) + ')'
    ax.annotate(s, xy=(x[i], y1[i]), xytext=(x[i]+1,
                y1[i]-5),
                arrowprops=dict(facecolor='black',
                shrink=0.05), horizontalalignment='left',
                verticalalignment='top')
fig
```

The result is as follows:

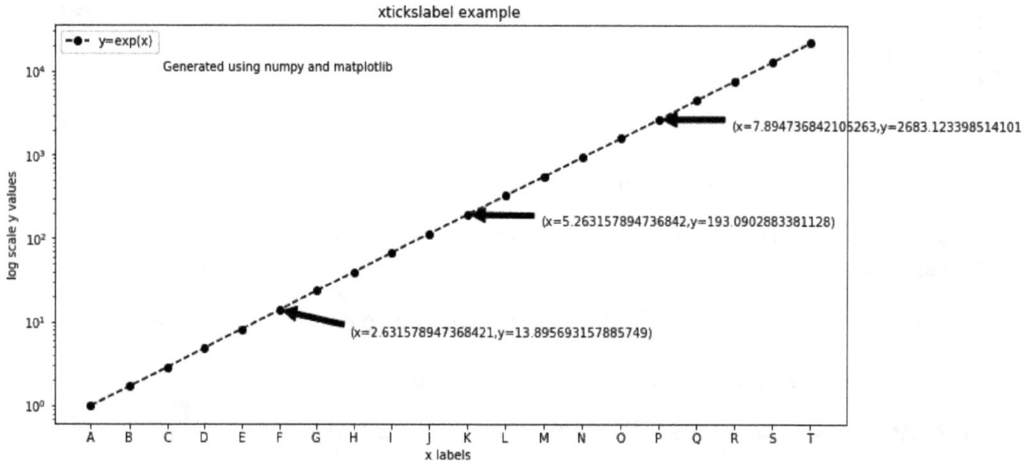

Figure 5.9 – Plot with text and arrow annotations of data points

Drawing attention to the key data points helps the reader focus on the message of the chart.

The `matplotlib.Axes.add_patch(...)` method can be used to add different shape annotations.

The code block that follows adds a `matplotlib.pyplot.Circle` object, which accepts the following:

- The `xy=` parameter to specify the location
- The `radius=` parameter to specify the circle radius
- The `color=` parameter to specify the color of the circle

The code is as follows:

```
fig, ax = plt.subplots(1, figsize=(12, 6))
ax.plot(x, x, linestyle='--', color='black', marker='*',
        markersize=15)
for val in x:
    ax.add_patch(plt.Circle(xy=(val, val), radius=0.3,
                 color='darkgray'))
```

This generates the following plot with circles around the data points:

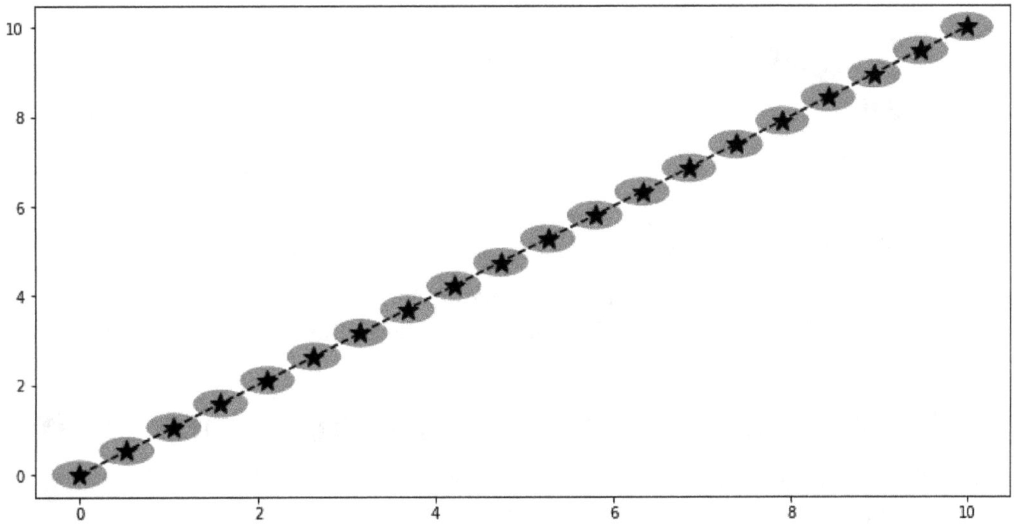

Figure 5.10 – Plot containing circle annotations around data points generated from adding a patch

Now that we have generated beautiful, professional charts, we need to learn how to share the images.

Saving plots to files

The `matplotlib.pyplot.figure` object enables us to save plots to disk in different file formats with many size and resolution specifiers, such as the `dpi=` parameter:

```
fig.savefig('fig.png', dpi=200)
```

This writes the following plot to the `fig.png` file:

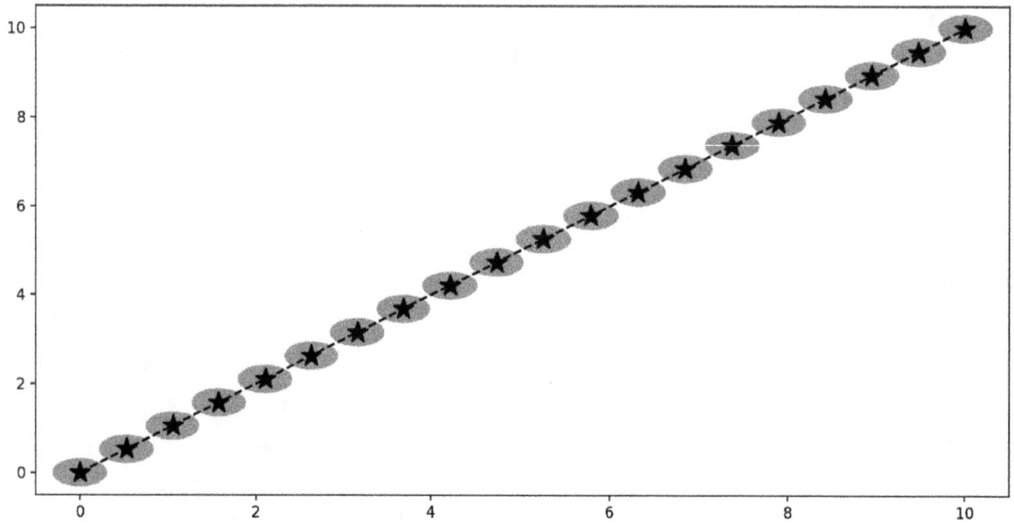

Figure 5.11 – Matplotlib plot written to a file on disk and opened with an external viewer

Exported images of trading strategies' performance are frequently used for HTML or email reports. For printing, choose the DPI of your printer as the DPI of the charts.

Charting a pandas DataFrame with Matplotlib

The `pandas` library provides plotting capabilities for Series and DataFrame objects using Matplotlib.

Let's create a `pandas` DataFrame with the `Cont` value containing continuous values that mimic prices and the `Delta1` and `Delta2` values to mimic price changes. The `Cat` value contains categorical data from five possibilities:

```
import pandas as pd

df = pd.DataFrame(index=range(1000),
                  columns=['Cont value', 'Delta1 value',
                           'Delta2 value', 'Cat value'])
df['Cont value'] = np.random.randn(1000).cumsum()
df['Delta1 value'] = np.random.randn(1000)
df['Delta2 value'] = np.random.randn(1000)
```

```
df['Cat value'] = np.random.permutation(['Very high',
                                         'High', 'Medium',
                                         'Low',
                                         'Very Low']*200)
df['Delta1 discrete'] = pd.cut(df['Delta1 value'],
                               labels=[-2, -1, 0, 1, 2],
                               bins=5).astype(np.int64)
df['Delta2 discrete'] = pd.cut(df['Delta2 value'],
                               labels=[-2, -1, 0, 1, 2],
                               bins=5).astype(np.int64)
df
```

This generates the following DataFrame:

```
    Cont value  Delta1 val  Delta2 val  Cat value  Delta1
discrete  Delta2 discrete
0   -1.429618    0.595897   -0.552871   Very high    1    0
1   -0.710593    1.626343    1.123142      Medium    1    1
...    ...         ...         ...          ...     ...  ...
998 -4.928133   -0.426593   -0.141742   Very high    0    0
999 -5.947680   -0.183414   -0.358367      Medium    0    0
1000 rows × 6 columns
```

Let's explore different ways of how this DataFrame can be visualized.

Creating line plots of a DataFrame column

We can plot `'Cont value'` in a line plot using the `pandas.DataFrame.plot(...)` method with the `kind=` parameter:

```
df.plot(y='Cont value', kind='line', color='black',
        linestyle='-', figsize=(12, 6))
```

This command produces the following chart:

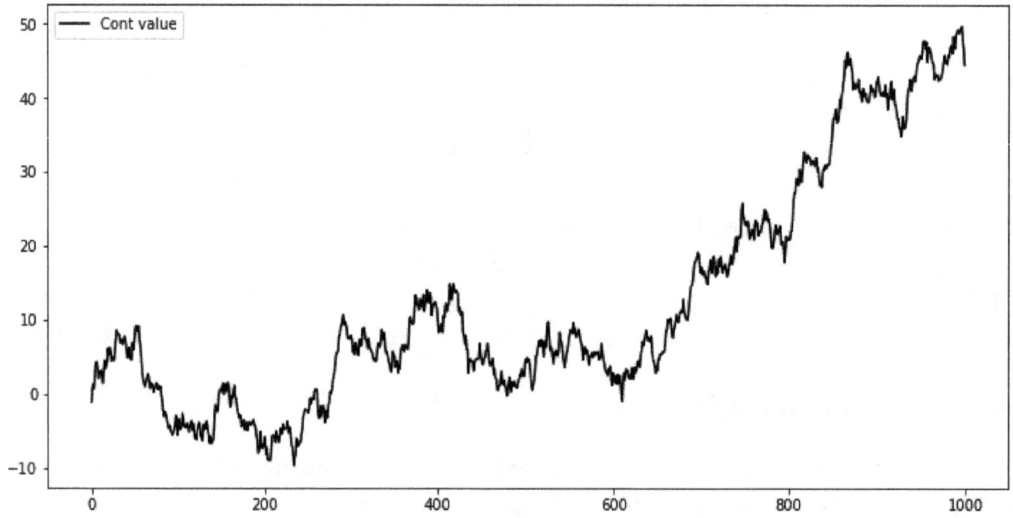

Figure 5.12 – Line plot generated using the pandas.DataFrame.plot(…) method

Line charts are typically used for displaying time series.

Creating bar plots of a DataFrame column

The `pandas.DataFrame.plot(...)` method can be used with the `kind='bar'` parameter to build a bar chart.

Let's first group the DataFrame by the `'Cat value'` value, and then plot the `Delta1 discrete` value counts in a bar chart:

```
df.groupby('Cat value')['Delta1 discrete']\
.value_counts().plot(kind='bar', color='darkgray',
                     title='Occurrence by (Cat,Delta1)',
                     figsize=(12, 6))
```

This generates the following plot showing the frequency of `(Cat value, Delta1 discrete)` value pairs:

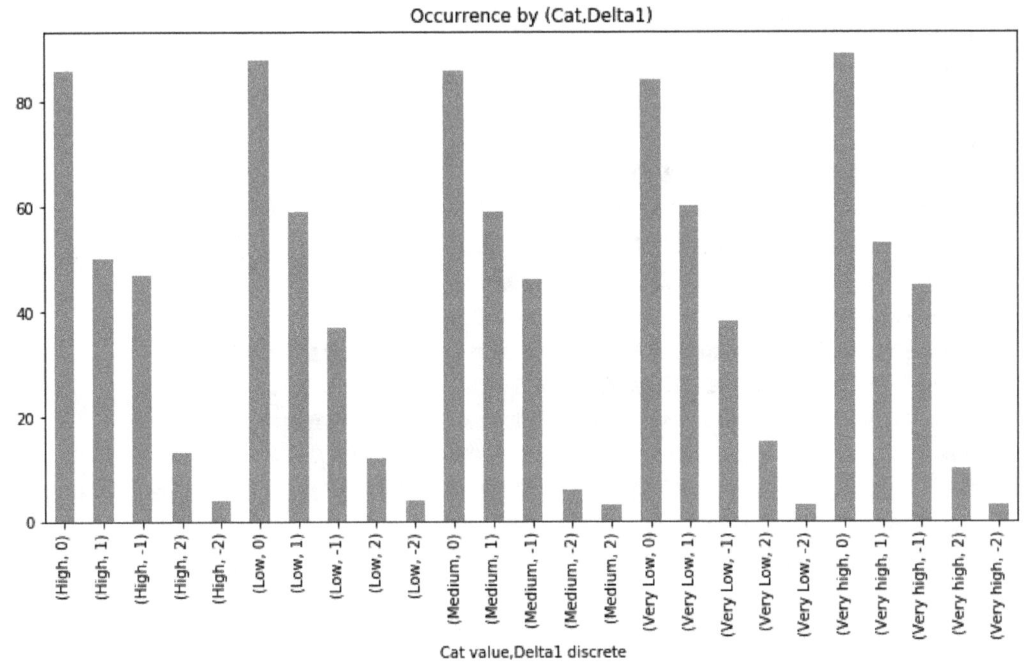

Figure 5.13 – Vertical bar plot displaying the frequency of (Cat value, Delta1 discrete) value pairs

The `kind='barh'` parameter builds a horizontal bar plot instead of a vertical one:

```
df.groupby('Delta2 discrete')['Cat value'].value_counts()\
.plot(kind='barh', color='darkgray',
      title='Occurrence by (Delta2,Cat)',
      figsize=(12, 12))
```

The output is as follows:

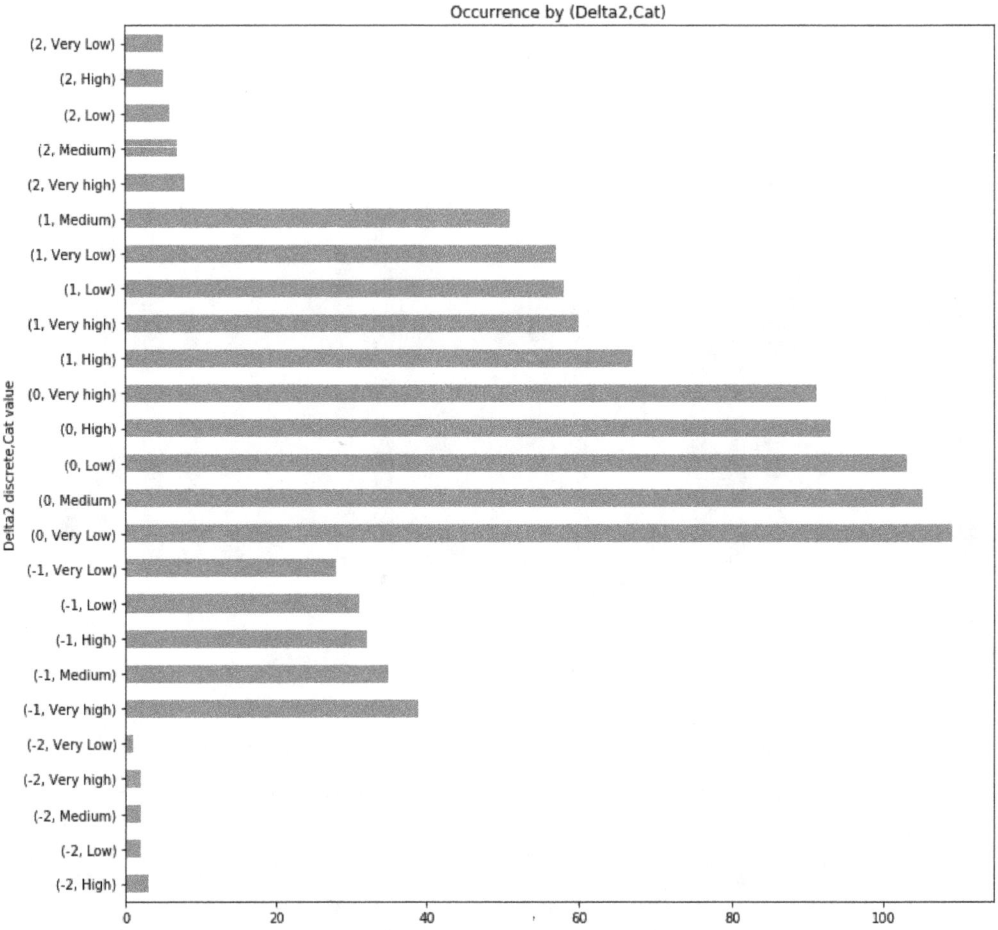

Figure 5.14 – Horizontal bar plot displaying the frequency of (Delta2 discrete, Cat value) pairs

Bar plots are most suitable for comparing the magnitude of categorical values.

Creating histogram and density plots of a DataFrame column

The `kind='hist'` parameter in the `pandas.DataFrame.plot(...)` method builds a histogram.

Let's create a histogram of the `Delta1 discrete` values:

```
df['Delta1 discrete'].plot(kind='hist', color='darkgray',
                           figsize=(12, 6), label='Delta1')
plt.legend()
```

The histogram generated is shown:

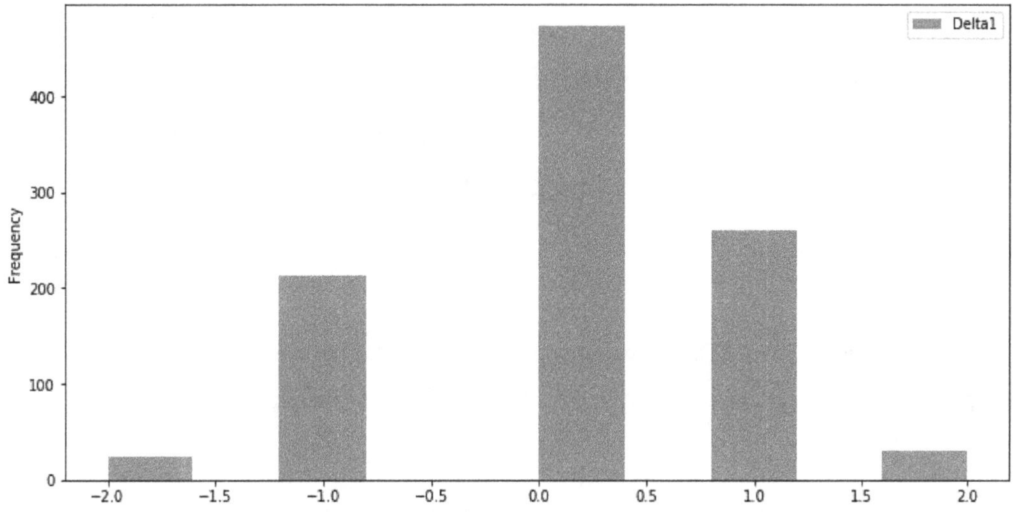

Figure 5.15 – Histogram of Delta1 discrete frequency

We can build a **Probability Density Function** (**PDF**) by specifying the `kind='kde'` parameter, which generates a PDF using the **Kernel Density Estimation** (**KDE**) of the `Delta2 discrete` value:

```
df['Delta2 discrete'].plot(kind='kde', color='black',
                           figsize=(12, 6),
                           label='Delta2 kde')
plt.legend()
```

The output is as follows:

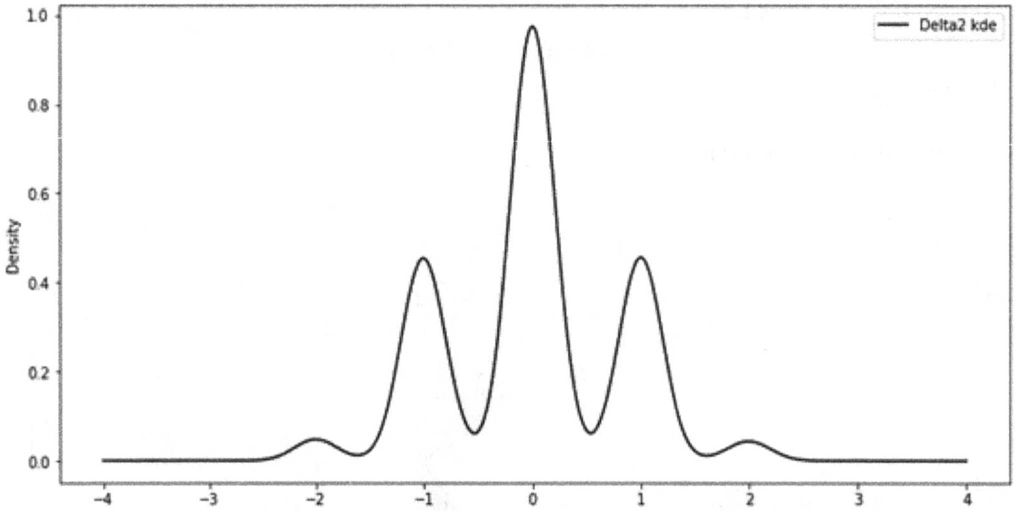

Figure 5.16 – KDE plot displaying the PDF of Delta2 discrete values

Histograms and PDFs/KDEs are used to assess the probability distribution of some random variables.

Creating scatter plots of two DataFrame columns

Scatter plots from the `pandas.DataFrame.plot(...)` method are generated using the `kind='scatter'` parameter.

The following code block plots a scatter plot between the `Delta1` and `Delta2` values:

```
df.plot(kind='scatter', x='Delta1 value', y='Delta2 value',
          alpha=0.5, color='black', figsize=(8, 8))
```

The output is as follows:

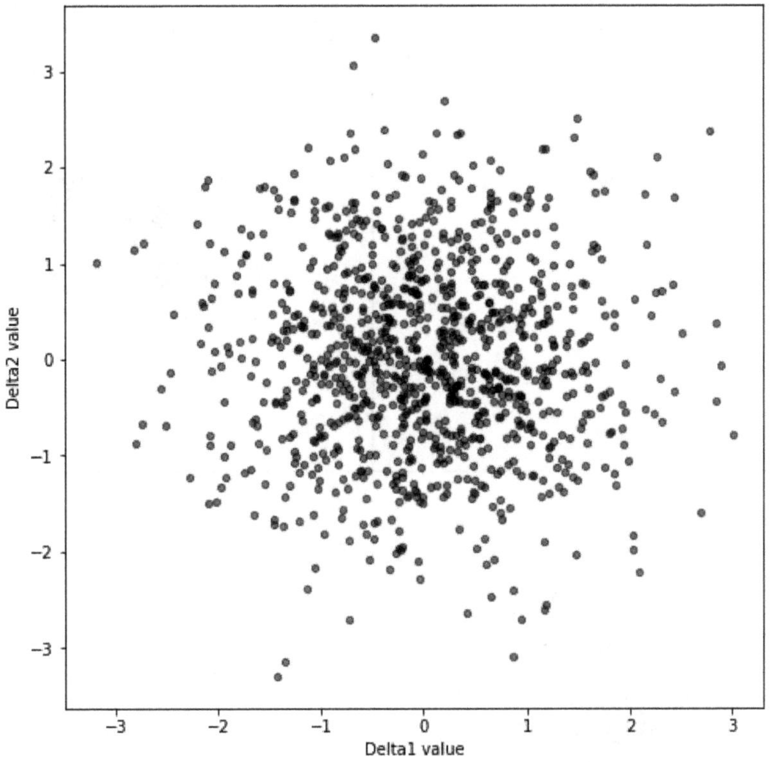

Figure 5.17 – Scatter plot of the Delta1 value and Delta2 value fields

The `pandas.plotting.scatter_matrix(...)` method builds a matrix of scatter plots on non-diagonal entries and histogram/KDE plots on the diagonal entries of the matrix between the `Delta1` and `Delta2` values:

```
pd.plotting.scatter_matrix(df[['Delta1 value',
                               'Delta2 value']],
                           diagonal='kde', color='black',
                           figsize=(8, 8))
```

The output is as follows:

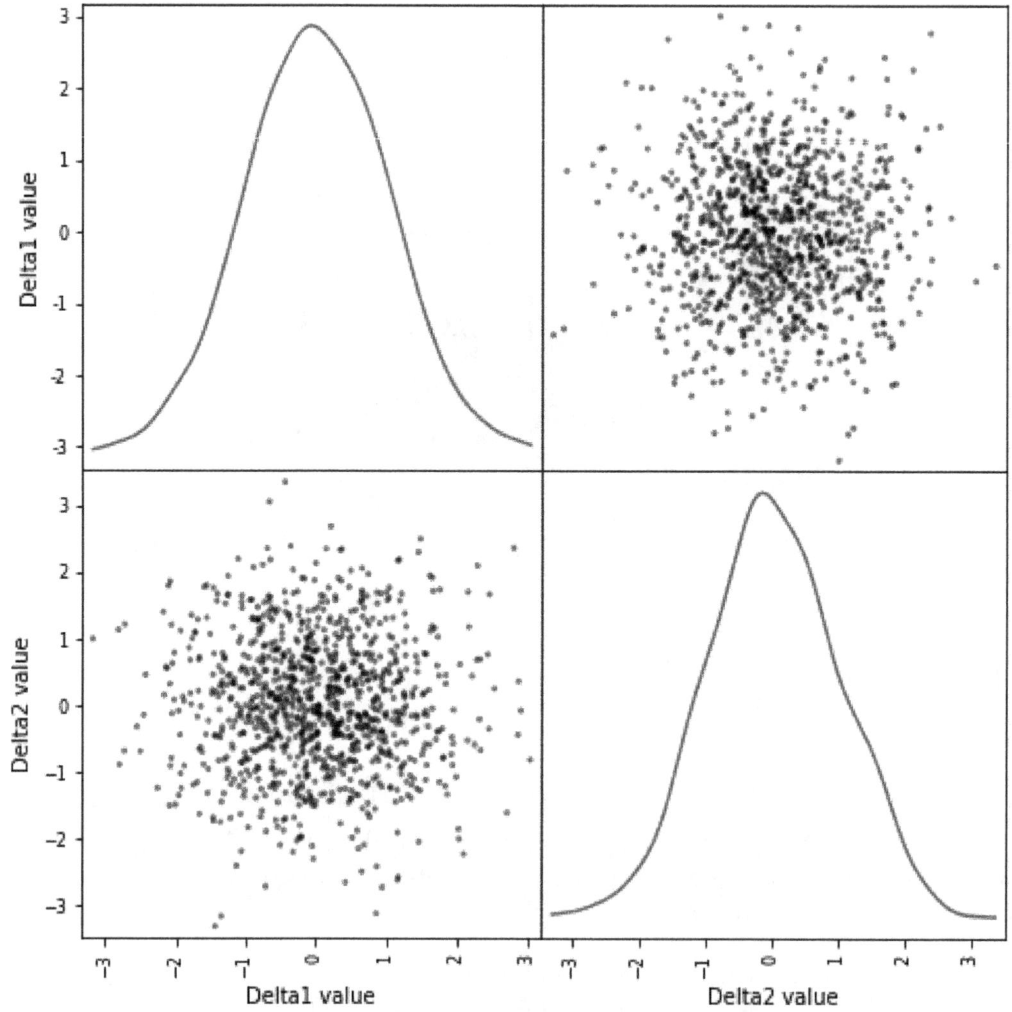

Figure 5.18 – Scatter matrix plot of the Delta1 value and Delta2 value fields

Scatter plots/scatter matrices are used to observe relationships between two variables.

Plotting time series data

The following code block creates a pandas DataFrame containing prices for two hypothetical trading instruments, A and B. The DataFrame is indexed by the DateTimeIndex objects representing daily dates from 1992 to 2012:

```
dates = pd.date_range('1992-01-01', '2012-10-22')
time_series = pd.DataFrame(index=dates, columns=['A', 'B'])
time_series['A'] = \
np.random.randint(low=-100, high=101,
                  size=len(dates)).cumsum() + 5000
time_series['B'] = \
np.random.randint(low=-75, high=76,
                  size=len(dates)).cumsum() + 5000
time_series
```

The resulting DataFrame is as follows:

```
                A       B
1992-01-01   5079    5042
1992-01-02   5088    5047
   ...        ...     ...
2012-10-21   6585    7209
2012-10-22   6634    7247
7601 rows × 2 columns
```

Let's use this time series for representative types of plots.

Plotting prices in a line plot

First, let's plot the daily prices for A and B over 20 years with line plots:

```
time_series['A'].plot(kind='line', linestyle='—',
                      color='black', figsize=(12, 6),
                      label='A')
time_series['B'].plot(kind='line', linestyle='-.',
                      color='darkgray', figsize=(12, 6),
                      label='B')
plt.legend()
```

The output is as follows:

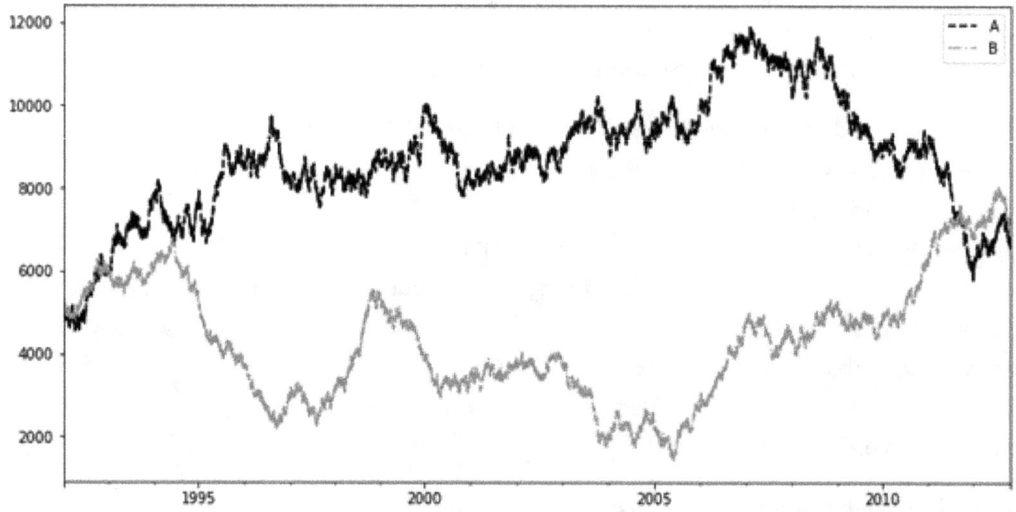

Figure 5.19 – Plot displaying prices for hypothetical instruments A and B over a period of 20 years

While most time series charts are line plots, the additional chart types provide additional insight.

Plotting price change histograms

The usual next stop in financial time series analysis is to inspect changes in price over some duration.

The following code block generates six new fields representing changes in prices over 1 day, 5 days, and 20 days, using the `pandas.DataFrame.shift(...)` and `pandas.DataFrame.fillna(...)` methods. We also drop rows with missing data due to the shift and the final DataFrame is saved in the `time_series_delta` DataFrame:

```
time_series['A_1_delta'] = \
time_series['A'].shift(-1) - time_series['A'].fillna(0)
time_series['B_1_delta'] = \
time_series['B'].shift(-1) - time_series['B'].fillna(0)

time_series['A_5_delta'] = \
time_series['A'].shift(-5) - time_series['A'].fillna(0)
time_series['B_5_delta'] = \
```

```
time_series['B'].shift(-5) - time_series['B'].fillna(0)

time_series['A_20_delta'] = \
time_series['A'].shift(-20) - time_series['A'].fillna(0)
time_series['B_20_delta'] = \
time_series['B'].shift(-20) - time_series['B'].fillna(0)

time_series_deltas = time_series[['A_1_delta', 'B_1_delta',
                                  'A_5_delta', 'B_5_delta',
                                  'A_20_delta',
                                  'B_20_delta']].dropna()
time_series_deltas
```

The DataFrame contains the following:

```
           A_1_delta    B_1_delta    A_5_delta    B_5_
delta    A_20_delta    B_20_delta
1992-01-01      9.0     5.0    -49.0    118.0    -249.0    -56.0
1992-01-02    -91.0    69.0    -84.0    123.0    -296.0    -92.0
...             ...     ...      ...      ...       ...      ...
2012-10-01     88.0    41.0    -40.0   -126.0    -148.0    -84.0
2012-10-02    -10.0   -44.0    -71.0   -172.0    -187.0    -87.0
7581 rows × 6 columns
```

We can plot the price change histogram for `A` based on what we have learned in this chapter with the following block of code:

```
time_series_delt's['A_20_de'ta'].plot(ki'd='h'st',
                                      col'r='bl'ck',
                                      alpha=0.5,
                                      lab'l='A_20_de'ta',
                                      figsize=(8,8))
time_series_delt's['A_5_de'ta'].plot(ki'd='h'st',
                                     col'r='darkg'ay',
                                     alpha=0.5,
                                     lab'l='A_5_de'ta',
                                     figsize=(8,8))
```

```
time_series_delt's['A_1_de'ta'].plot(ki'd='h'st',
                                       col'r='lightg'ay',
                                       alpha=0.5,
                                       lab'l='A_1_de'ta',
                                       figsize=(8,8))

plt.legend()
```

The output is as follows:

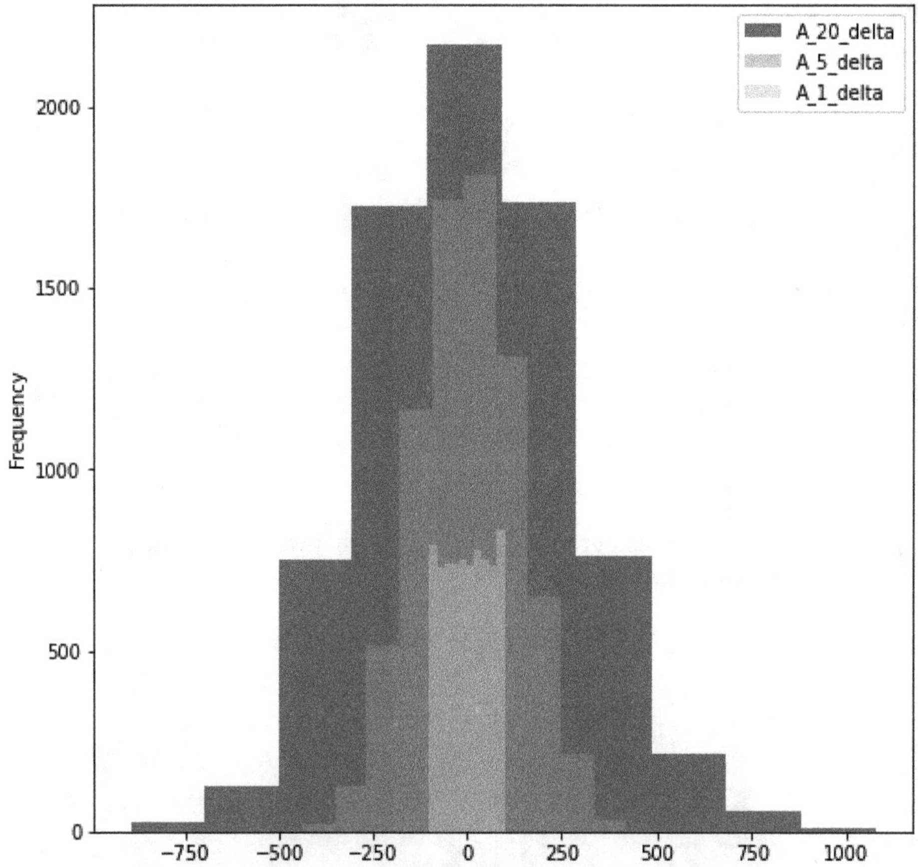

Figure 5.20 – Histogram of A_1, A_5, and A_20 deltas

Histograms are used for assessing the probability distribution of the underlying data. This particular histogram suggests that the `A_20` delta has the greatest variability, which makes sense since the underlying data exhibits a strong trend.

Creating price change density plots

We can also plot the density of price changes using the KDE PDF.

The following code block plots the density function for price changes in `B`:

```
time_series_deltas['B_20_delta'].plot(kind='kde',
                                      linestyle='-',
                                      linewidth=2,
                                      color='black',
                                      label='B_20_delta',
                                      figsize=(8,8))
time_series_deltas['B_5_delta'].plot(kind='kde',
                                     linestyle=':',
                                     linewidth=2,
                                     color='black',
                                     label='B_5_delta',
                                     figsize=(8,8))
time_series_deltas['B_1_delta'].plot(kind='kde',
                                     linestyle='--',
                                     linewidth=2,
                                     color='black',
                                     label='B_1_delta',
                                     figsize=(8,8))
plt.legend()
```

The output is as follows:

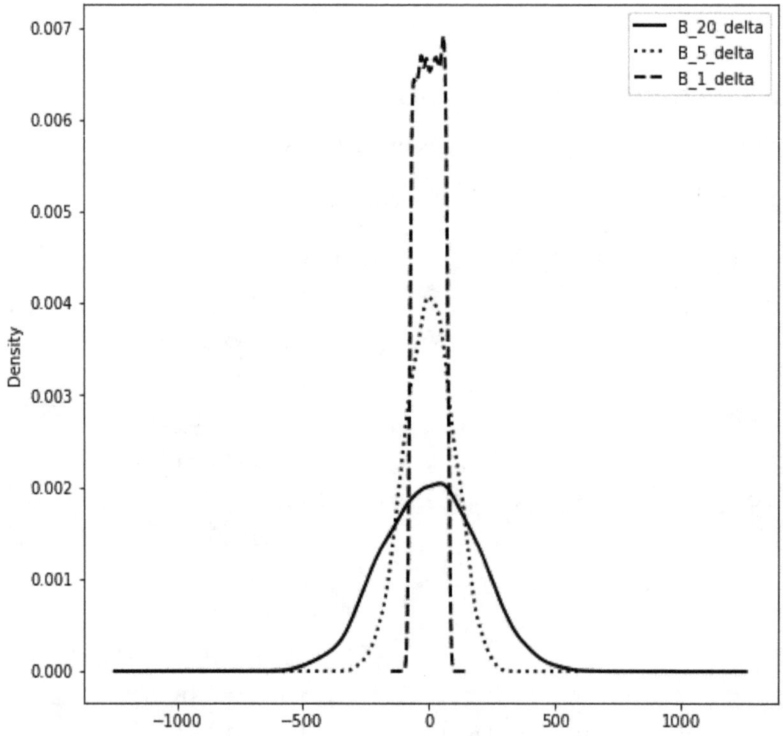

Figure 5.21 – KDE density plot for price changes in B over 1, 5, and 20 days

KDE density plots are very similar to histograms. In contrast to histograms consisting of discrete boxes, KDEs are continuous lines.

Creating box plots by interval

We can group daily prices by different intervals, such as yearly, quarterly, monthly, or weekly, and display the distribution of those prices using box plots.

The following piece of code first uses the `pandas.Grouper` object with `freq='A'` to specify annual periodicity, and then applies to the result the `pandas.DataFrame.groupby(...)` method to build a `pandas.DataFrameGroupBy` object. Finally, we call the `pandas.DataFrameGroupBy.boxplot(...)` method to generate the box plot. We specify the `rot=90` parameter to rotate the *x*-axis tick labels to make it more readable:

```
group_A = time_series[['A']].groupby(pd.Grouper(freq='A'))
group_A.boxplot(color='black', subplots=False, rot=90,
                figsize=(12,12))
```

The output is as follows:

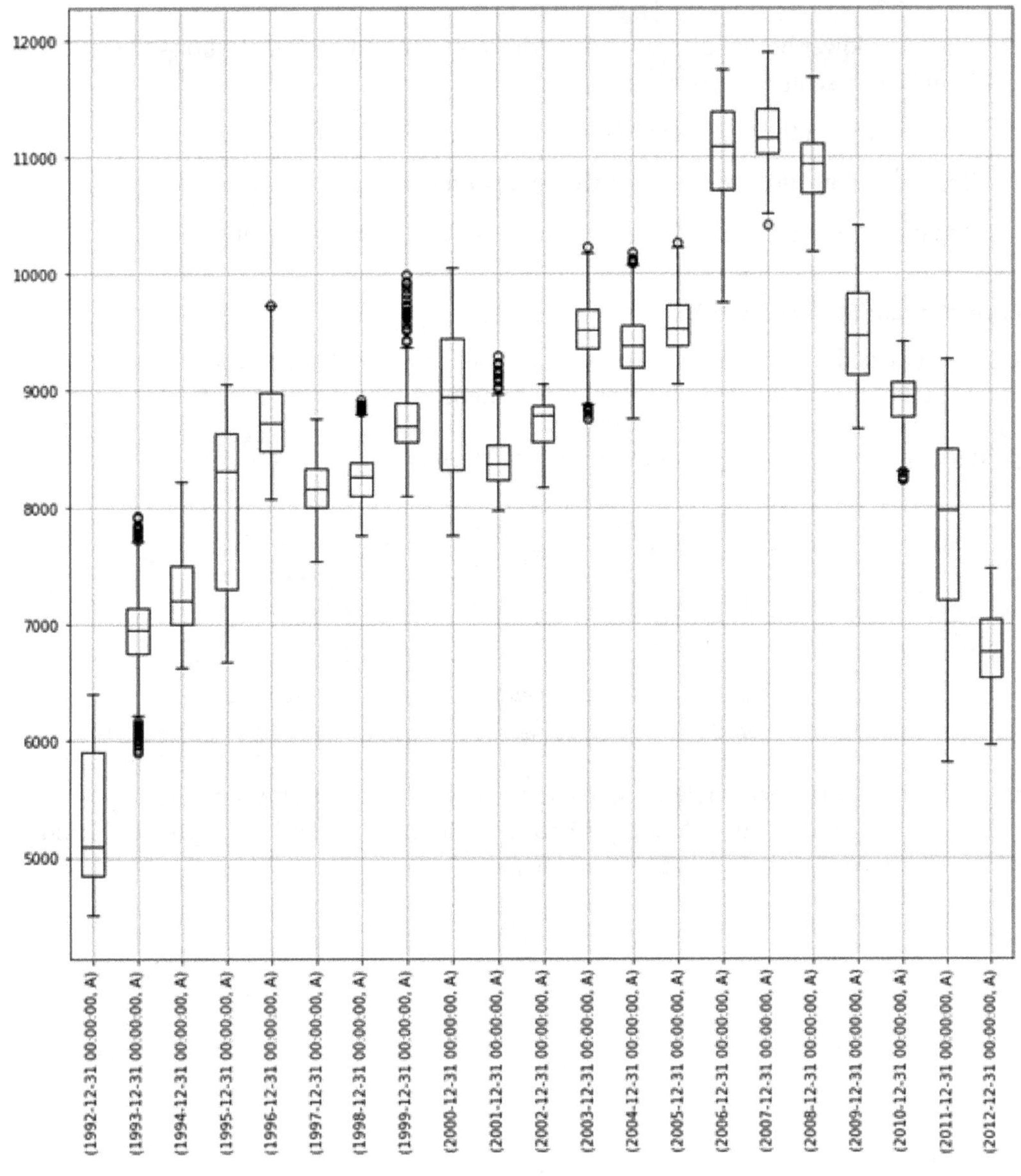

Figure 5.22 – Figure containing the box plot distribution of A's prices grouped by year

Box plots with whiskers are used for visualizing groups of numerical data through their corresponding quartiles:

- The box's lower bound corresponds to the lower quartile, while the box's upper bound represents the group's upper quartile.
- The line within the box displays the value of the median of the interval.
- The line below the box ends with the value of the lowest observation.
- The line above the box ends with the value of the highest observation.

Creating lag scatter plots

We can visualize the relationships between the different price change variables using the `pandas.plotting.scatter_matrix(…)` method:

```
pd.plotting.scatter_matrix(time_series[['A_1_delta',
                                        'A_5_delta',
                                        'A_20_delta',
                                        'B_1_delta',
                                        'B_5_delta',
                                        'B_20_delta']],
                           diagonal='kde', color='black',
                           alpha=0.25, figsize=(12, 12))
```

The result shows some linear relationships between the `(A_5_Delta and A_1_Delta)`, `(A_5_Delta and A_20_Delta)`, `(B_1_Delta and B_5_Delta)`, and `(B_5_Delta and B_20_Delta)` variable pairs:

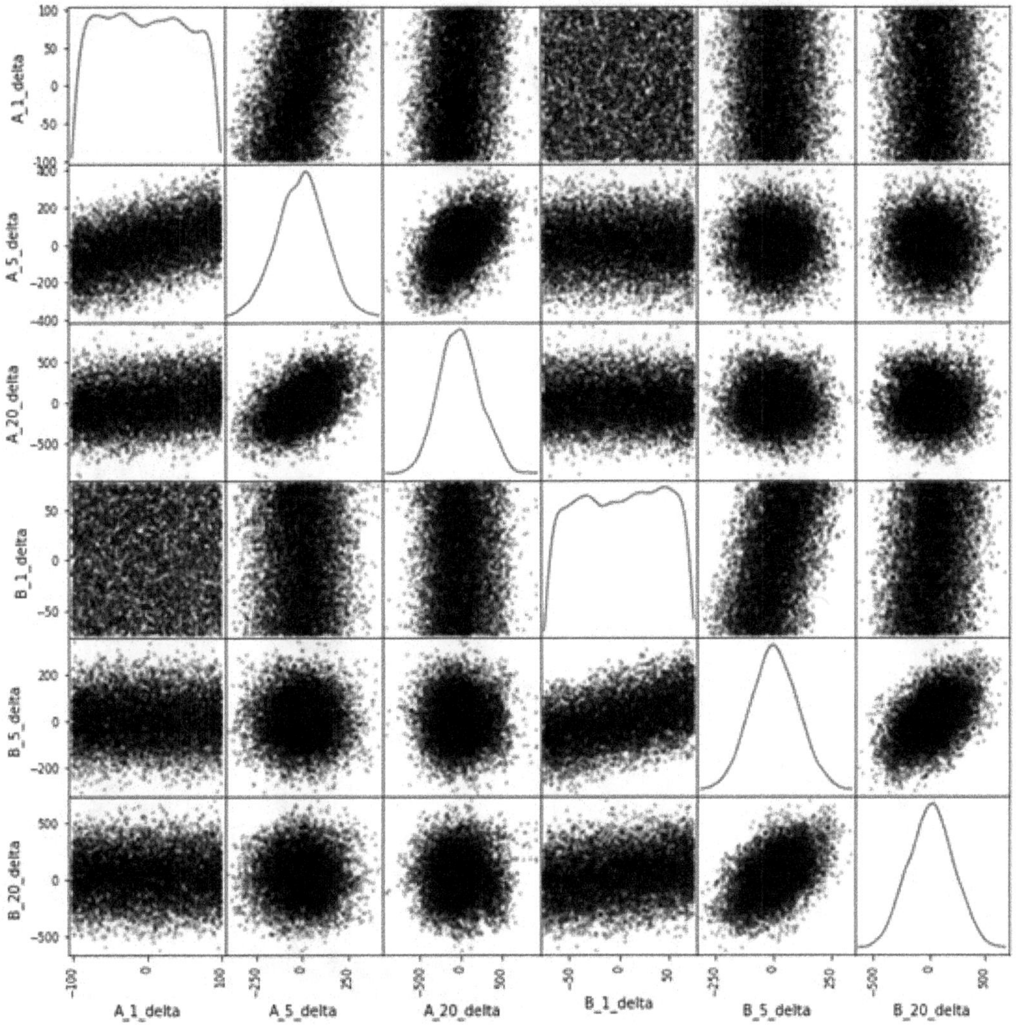

Figure 5.23 – Scatter matrix plot for A and B price delta variables

We can also use the `pandas.plotting.lag_plot(...)` method with different `lag=` values to specify different levels of lag to generate the scatter plots between prices and lagged prices for `A`:

```
fig, (ax1, ax2, ax3) = plt.subplots(3, figsize=(12, 12))
pd.plotting.lag_plot(time_series['A'], ax=ax1, lag=1,
                     c='black', alpha=0.2)
pd.plotting.lag_plot(time_series['A'], ax=ax2, lag=7,
```

```
                          c='black', alpha=0.2)
pd.plotting.lag_plot(time_series['A'], ax=ax3, lag=20,
                          c='black', alpha=0.2)
```

This generates the following three plots for lags of 1, 7, and 20 days:

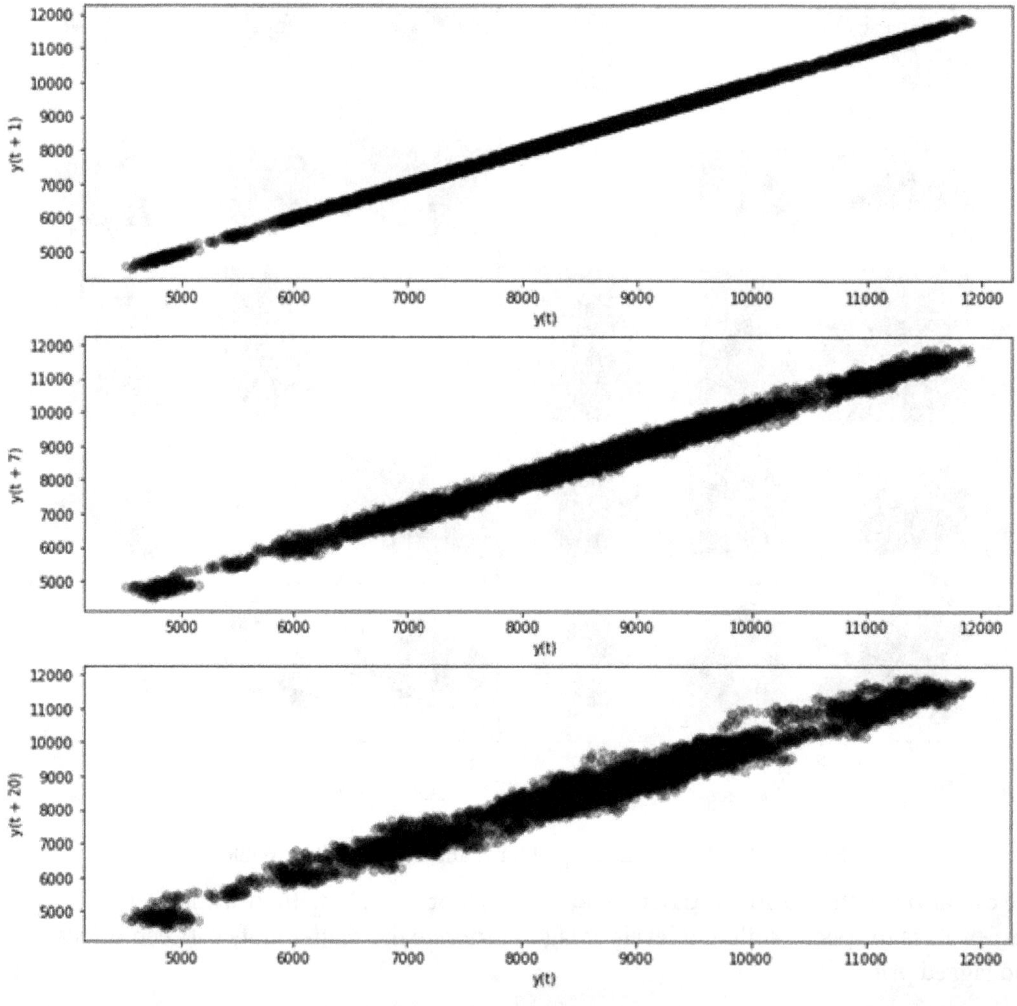

Figure 5.24 – Lag plots for A's prices with lag values of 1, 7, and 20 days, showing martingale properties

Log plots check whether a time series is random without any trend. For a random time series, its lag plots show no structure. The preceding plots show a clear linear trend; that is, we may succeed in modeling it with an auto-regressive model.

Creating autocorrelation plots

Autocorrelation plots visualize the relationships with prices at a certain point in time and the prices lagged by a certain number of periods.

We can use the `pandas.plotting.autocorrelation_plot(...)` method to plot lag values on the *x* axis and the correlation between price and price lagged by the specified value on the *y* axis:

```
fig, ax = plt.subplots(1, figsize=(12, 6))
pd.plotting.autocorrelation_plot(time_series['A'], ax=ax)
```

We can see that as lag values increase, the autocorrelation slowly deteriorates:

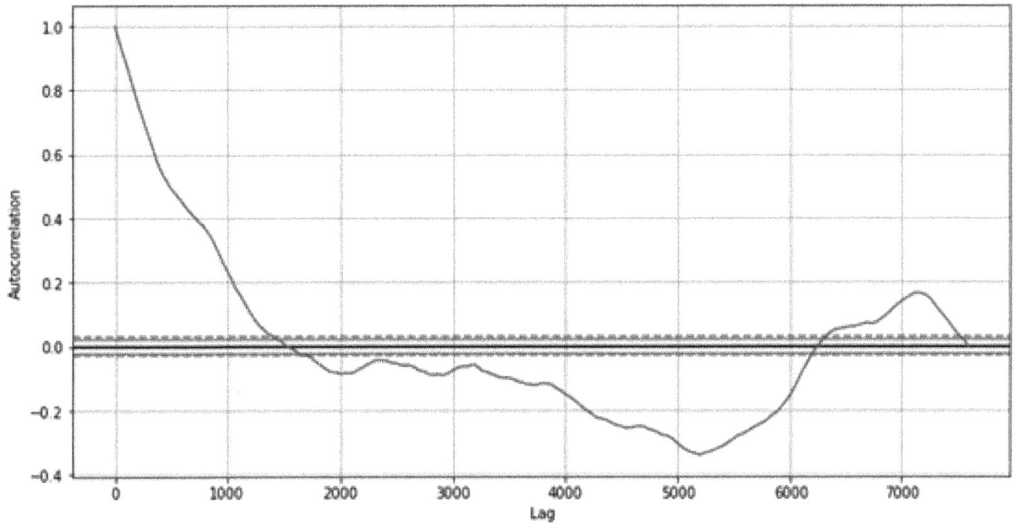

Figure 5.25 – Plot displaying the relationship between lag values versus autocorrelation between prices and prices lagged by a specified value

Autocorrelation plots summarize the randomness of a time series. For a random time series, all autocorrelations would be close to 0 for all lags. For a non-random time series, at least one of the autocorrelations would be significantly non-zero.

Summary

In this chapter, we have learned how to create visually appealing charts of `pandas` DataFrames with Matplotlib. While we can calculate many numerical statistics, charts usually offer greater insight more rapidly. You should always plot as many different charts as possible since each provides a different view of the data.

In the next chapter, we will learn how to perform statistical tests and estimate statistical models in Python.

6
Statistical Estimation, Inference, and Prediction

In this chapter, we introduce four key statistical libraries in Python—`statsmodels`, `pmdarima`, `fbprophet`, and `scikitlearn`—by outlining key examples. These libraries are used to model time series and provide their forecast values, along with confidence intervals. In addition, we demonstrate how to use a classification model to predict percentage changes of a time series.

For this, we are going to cover the following use cases:

- Introduction to statsmodels
- Using a **Seasonal Auto-Regressive Integrated Moving Average with eXogenous factors** (**SARIMAX**) time-series model with pmdarima
- Time series forecasting with Facebook's Prophet library
- Introduction to scikit-learn regression and classification

Technical requirements

The Python code used in this chapter is available in the `Chapter06 folder` in the book's code repository.

Introduction to statsmodels

statsmodels is a Python library that allows us to explore data, perform statistical tests, and estimate statistical models.

This chapter focuses on statsmodels' modeling, analysis, and forecasting of time series.

Normal distribution test with Q-Q plots

An underlying assumption of many statistical learning techniques is that the observations/fields are normally distributed.

While there are many robust statistical tests for normal distributions, an intuitive visual method is known as a **quantile-quantile plot** (**Q-Q plot**). If a sample is normally distributed, its Q-Q plot is a straight line.

In the following code block, the `statsmodels.graphics.api.qqplot(...)` method is used to check if a `numpy.random.uniform(...)` distribution is normally distributed:

```
from statsmodels.graphics.api import qqplot
import numpy as np
fig = qqplot(np.random.uniform(size=10000), line='s')
fig.set_size_inches(12, 6)
```

The resulting plot depicted in the following screenshot shows a non-linear relationship between the two distributions, which was expected since we used a uniform distribution:

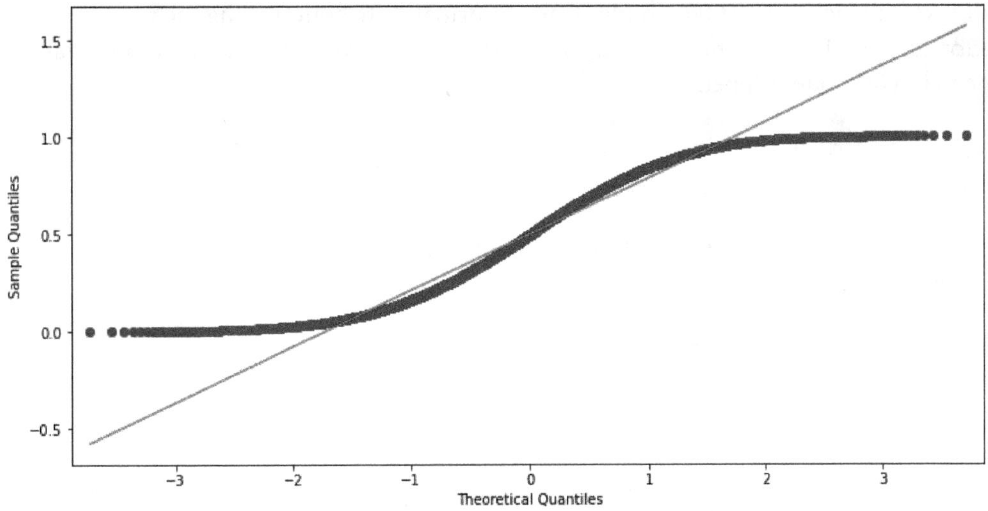

Figure 6.1 – Q-Q plot for a dataset generated from a uniform distribution

In the following code block, we repeat the test, but this time with a `numpy.random.exponential(...)` distribution as our sample distribution:

```
fig = qqplot(np.random.exponential(size=10000), line='s')
fig.set_size_inches(12, 6)
```

The resulting Q-Q plot again confirms a non-normal relationship between the two distributions, as illustrated in the following screenshot:

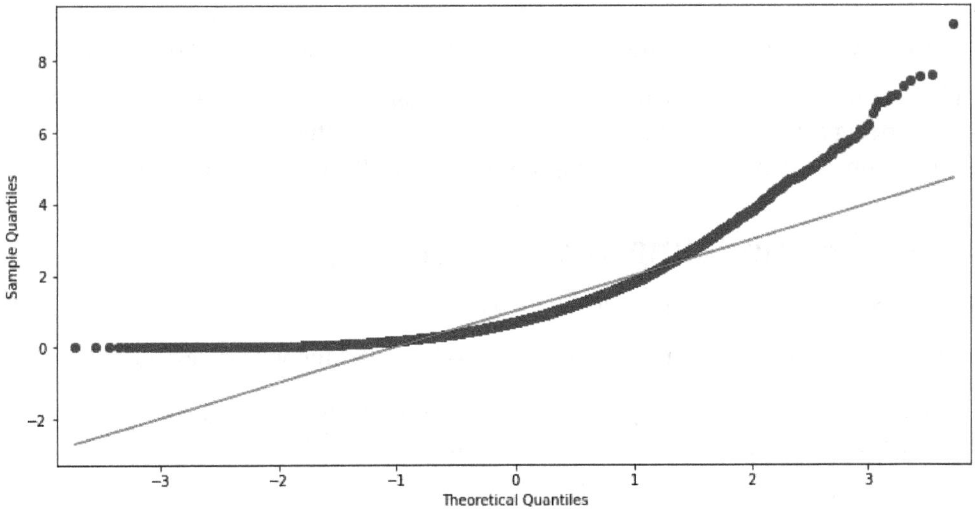

Figure 6.2 – Q-Q plot for a dataset generated from an exponential distribution

Finally, we will pick out 10,000 samples from a normal distribution using the `numpy.random.normal(...)` method and use `qqplot(...)` to observe them, as illustrated in the following code snippet:

```
fig = qqplot(np.random.normal(size=10000), line='s')
fig.set_size_inches(12, 6)
```

The result is a plot with a linear relationship as expected, as illustrated in the following screenshot:

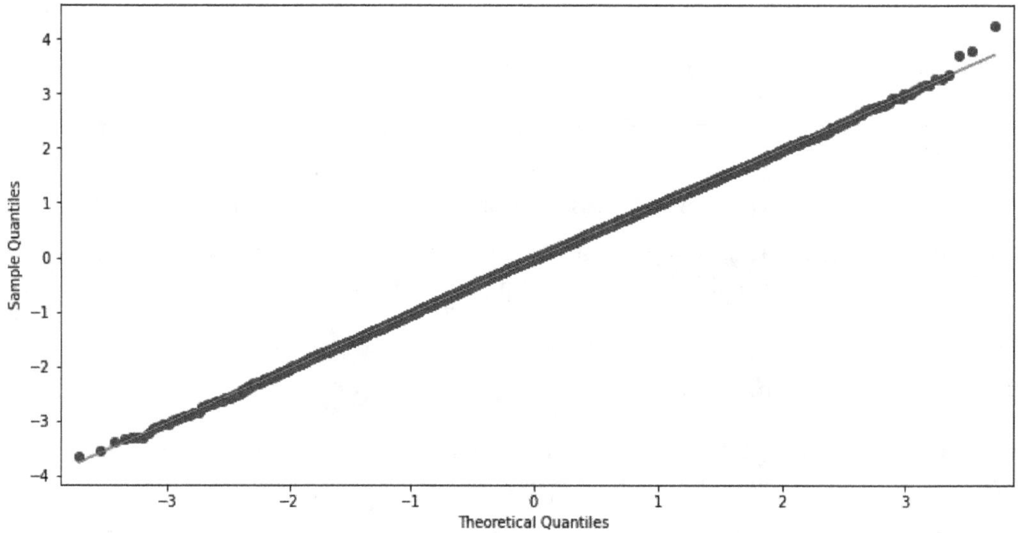

Figure 6.3 – Q-Q plot for 10,000 samples sampled from a standard normal distribution

Q-Q plots are used for comparison between two probability distributions—with one of them most often being a normal distribution—by plotting their quantiles against one another. The preceding examples demonstrate how easy it is to test visually for normal distribution.

Time series modeling with statsmodels

A time series is a sequence of numerical data points in time order.

A crucial part of working with time series data involves working with dates and times.

The `statsmodels.api.tsa.datetools` model provides some basic methods for generating and parsing dates and date ranges, such as `dates_from_range(...)`.

In the following code snippet, we generate 12 `datetime.datetime` objects using a `length=12` parameter and starting from `2010` with a yearly frequency:

```
import statsmodels.api as sm
sm.tsa.datetools.dates_from_range('2010', length=12)
```

That yields the following list of `datetime` objects:

```
[datetime.datetime(2010, 12, 31, 0, 0),
 datetime.datetime(2011, 12, 31, 0, 0),
...
 datetime.datetime(2020, 12, 31, 0, 0),
 datetime.datetime(2021, 12, 31, 0, 0)]
```

The frequency of dates in the `dates_from_range(...)` method can be specified by the start date and a special format, where the `m1` suffix means first month and monthly frequency, and `q1` means first quarter and quarterly frequency, as illustrated in the following code snippet:

```
sm.tsa.datetools.dates_from_range('2010m1', length=120)
```

That yields the following list of `datetime` objects with monthly frequency:

```
[datetime.datetime(2010, 1, 31, 0, 0),
 datetime.datetime(2010, 2, 28, 0, 0),
...
 datetime.datetime(2019, 11, 30, 0, 0),
 datetime.datetime(2019, 12, 31, 0, 0)]
```

Let's now perform an **Error, Trend, Seasonality** (**ETS**) analysis of a time series.

ETS analysis of a time series

The ETS analysis of a time series breaks down the data into three different components, as follows:

- The **trend** component captures the overall trend of the time series.
- The **seasonality** component captures cyclical/seasonal changes.
- The **error** component captures noise in the data that could not be captured with the other two components.

Let's generate 20 years of monthly dates as an index to the Pandas DataFrame dataset using the `datetools.dates_from_range(...)` method, as follows:

```
import pandas as pd
n_obs = 12 * 20
linear_trend = np.linspace(100, 200, num=n_obs)
cycle = np.sin(linear_trend) * 10
error_noise = np.random.randn(n_obs)
dataset = \
pd.DataFrame(
    linear_trend + cycle + error_noise,
    index=sm.tsa.datetools.dates_from_range('2000m1',
                                            length=n_obs),
    columns=['Price'])
dataset
```

The result is the following DataFrame with a `Price` field that is composed of ETS components:

```
                 Price
2000-01-31   96.392059
2000-02-29   99.659426
       ...         ...
2019-11-30  190.067039
2019-12-31  190.676568
240 rows x 1 columns
```

Let's visualize the time series dataset that we generated, as follows:

```
import matplotlib.pyplot as plt
dataset.plot(figsize=(12, 6), color='black')
```

The resulting time series dataset has an apparent linearly increasing trend with seasonal components mixed in, as illustrated in the following screenshot:

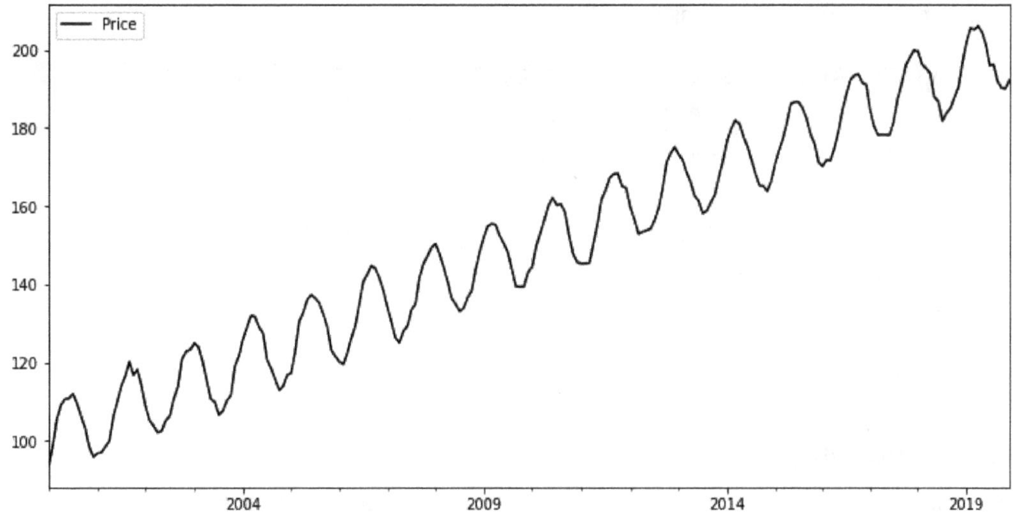

Figure 6.4 – Plot displaying synthetic prices with ETS components

In the preceding screenshot, we do see the seasonality component very clearly—the oscillation up and down from the median value. We also see the error noise since the oscillations are not perfect. Finally, we see that the values are increasing—the trend component.

The Hodrick-Prescott filter

The **Hodrick-Prescott** (**HP**) filter is used to separate the trend and cyclical components from time series data by removing short-term fluctuations from the longer-term trend. In `statsmodels`, this is implemented as `statsmodels.api.tsa.filters.hpfilter(...)`.

Let's use it with a `lamb=129600` smoothing parameter to perform the decomposition (the value `129600` is the recommended value for monthly data). We use a pair of series values returned to generate a DataFrame with `Price`, `hp_cycle`, and `hp_trend` fields to represent the price, the seasonal component, and the trend components, as illustrated in the following code snippet:

```
hp_cycle, hp_trend = \
sm.tsa.filters.hpfilter(dataset['Price'], lamb=129600)
decomp = dataset[['Price']]
decomp['HP_Cycle'] = hp_cycle
decomp['HP_Trend'] = hp_trend
decomp
```

The `decomp` DataFrame contains the following data:

	Price	HP_Cycle	HP_Trend
2000-01-31	96.392059	-4.731153	101.123212
2000-02-29	99.659426	-1.839262	101.498688
...	...	...	...
2019-11-30	190.067039	-8.350371	198.417410
2019-12-31	190.676568	-8.107701	198.784269

240 rows × 3 columns

In the next section, we will look at the `UnobservedComponents` model.

UnobservedComponents model

Another way of breaking down a time series into ETS components is to use a `statsmodels.api.tsa.UnobservedComponents` object.

The `UnobservedComponentsResults.summary(...)` method generates statistics for the model, as follows:

```
uc = sm.tsa.UnobservedComponents(dataset['Price'],
                                 level='lltrend',
                                 cycle=True,
                                 stochastic_cycle=True)
res_uc = uc.fit(method='powell', disp=True)
res_uc.summary()
```

The output contains details about the model, as illustrated in the following code block:

```
Optimization terminated successfully.
         Current function value: 2.014160
         Iterations: 6
         Function evaluations: 491
Unobserved Components Results
Dep. Variable:               Price No. Observations:     240
        Model: local linear trend  Log Likelihood  -483.399
                   + stochastic cycle             AIC   976.797
         Date:    Fri, 12 Jun 2020             BIC   994.116
         Time:            08:09:46            HQIC  983.779
       Sample:          01-31-2000
```

```
                    - 12-31-2019
Covariance Type:                opg
                       coef  std err        z   P>|z|  [0.025  0.975]
sigma2.irregular   0.4962    0.214    2.315   0.021   0.076   0.916
sigma2.level   6.954e-17   0.123   5.63e-16  1.000  -0.242  0.242
sigma2.trend   2.009e-22  4.03e-05  4.98e-18  1.000  -7.91e-
05   7.91e-05
sigma2.cycle       1.5485   0.503    3.077   0.002   0.562   2.535
frequency.cycle   0.3491    0.013   27.768   0.000   0.324   0.374
Ljung-Box (Q):              347.56    Jarque-Bera (JB):      0.42
Prob(Q):                      0.00            Prob(JB):      0.81
Heteroskedasticity (H):   0.93                   Skew:     -0.09
Prob(H) (two-sided):      0.73               Kurtosis:      2.91
```

We can access the ETS/cyclical components using the `resid`, `cycle.smoothed`, and `level.smoothed` attributes and add them to the decomp DataFrame, as follows:

```
decomp['UC_Cycle'] = res_uc.cycle.smoothed
decomp['UC_Trend'] = res_uc.level.smoothed
decomp['UC_Error'] = res_uc.resid
decomp
```

The `decomp` DataFrame has the following new columns containing the `Cycle`, `Trend`, and `Error` terms from the `UnobservedComponents` model:

```
                ...       UC_Cycle     UC_Trend     UC_Error
2000-01-31      ...      -3.358954    99.743814    96.392059
2000-02-29      ...      -0.389834   100.163434     6.173967
    ...         ...          ...          ...          ...
2019-11-30      ...      -9.725420   199.613395     1.461497
2019-12-31      ...      -9.403885   200.033015     0.306881
240 rows × 6 columns
```

Next, we will look at the `statsmodel.tsa.seasonal.seasonal_decompose(...)` method.

statsmodels.tsa.seasonal.seasonal_decompose(...) method

Another way to perform ETS decomposition is by using the `statsmodels.tsa.seasonal.seasonal_decompose(...)` method.

The following code block uses an additive model by specifying a `model='additive'` parameter and adds `SDC_Cycle`, `SDC_Trend`, and `SDC_Error` columns to the `decomp` DataFrame by accessing the `season`, `trend`, and `resid` attributes in the `DecomposeResult` object:

```
from statsmodels.tsa.seasonal import seasonal_decompose
s_dc = seasonal_decompose(dataset['Price'],
                          model='additive')
decomp['SDC_Cycle'] = s_dc.seasonal
decomp['SDC_Trend'] = s_dc.trend
decomp['SDC_Error'] = s_dc.resid
decomp[118:122]
```

The `decomp` DataFrame now has three additional fields with values, as shown in the following code block:

```
                ...  SDC_Cycle   SDC_Trend   SDC_Error
2009-11-30      ...   0.438633  146.387392   -8.620342
2009-12-31      ...   0.315642  147.240112   -6.298764
2010-01-31      ...   0.228229  148.384061   -3.538544
2010-02-28      ...   0.005062  149.912202   -0.902362
```

Next, we will plot the various results we got from the preceding sections.

Plotting of the results of HP filter, the UnobservedComponents model, and the seasonal_decompose method

Let's plot the trend components extracted from the `HP` filter, the `UnobservedComponents` model, and the `seasonal_decompose` method, as follows:

```
plt.title('Trend components')
decomp['Price'].plot(figsize=(12, 6), color='black',
                     linestyle='-', legend='Price')
decomp['HP_Trend'].plot(figsize=(12, 6), color='darkgray',
                        linestyle='--', lw=2,
                        legend='HP_Trend')
decomp['UC_Trend'].plot(figsize=(12, 6), color='black',
                        linestyle=':', lw=2,
                        legend='UC_Trend')
```

```
decomp['SDC_Trend'].plot(figsize=(12, 6), color='black',
                         linestyle='-.', lw=2,
                         legend='SDC_Trend')
```

That gives us the following plot, with the trend components plotted next to the original price. All three models did a good job in identifying the overall increasing trend, with the `seasonal_decompose(...)` method capturing some non-linear/cyclical trend components, in addition to the overall linearly increasing trend:

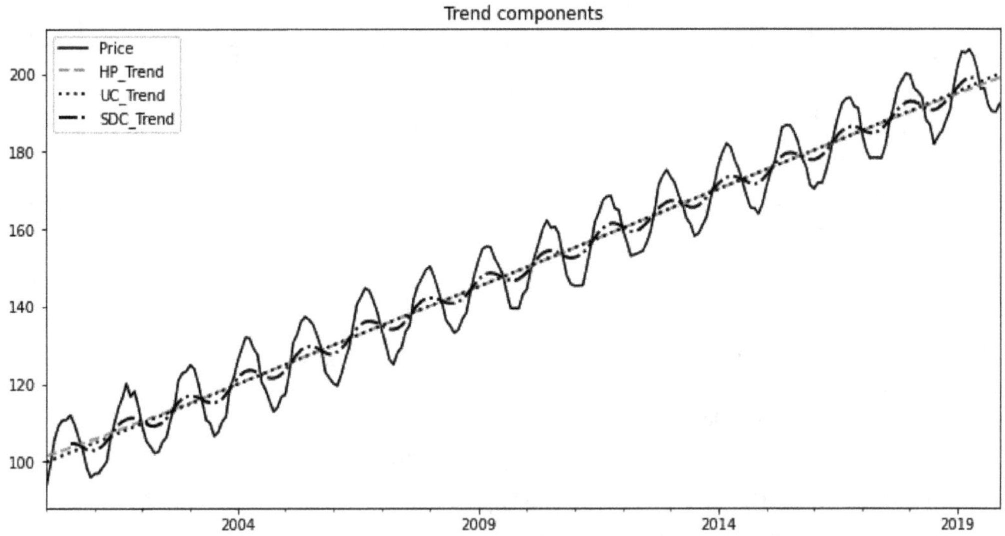

Figure 6.5 – Plot showing trend components extracted from different ETS decomposition methods

The following code block plots the cycle/seasonal components obtained from the three models:

```
plt.title('Cycle/Seasonal components')
decomp['HP_Cycle'].plot(figsize=(12, 6), color='darkgray',
                        linestyle='--', lw=2,
                        legend='HP_Cycle')
decomp['UC_Cycle'].plot(figsize=(12, 6), color='black',
                        linestyle=':', lw=2,
                        legend='UC_Cycle')
decomp['SDC_Cycle'].plot(figsize=(12, 6), color='black',
                         linestyle='-.', lw=2,
                         legend='SDC_Cycle')
```

The following result shows that the `seasonal_decompose(...)` method generates seasonal components with very small fluctuations, and that is because some part of the seasonal components was built into the trend plot we saw before:

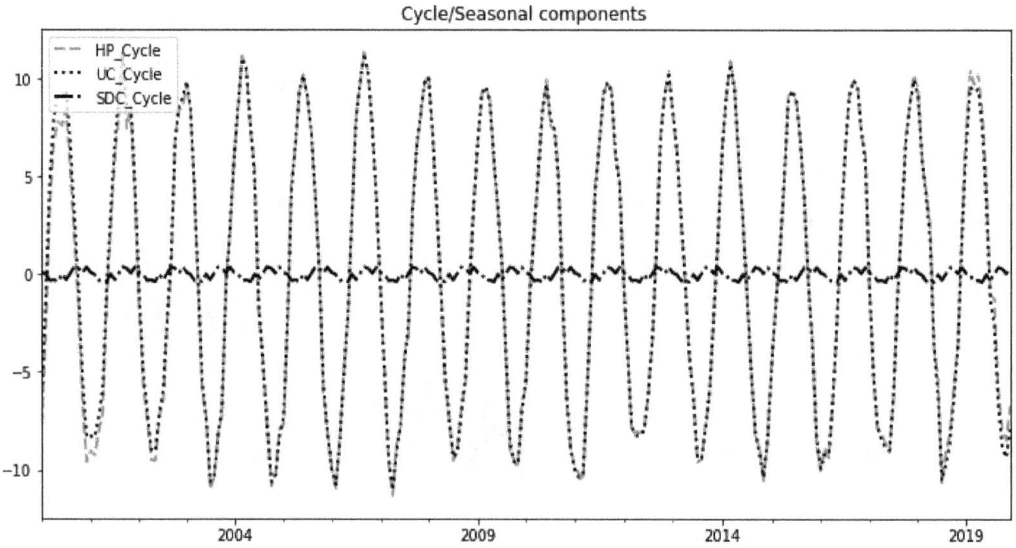

Figure 6.6 – Plot showing cyclical/seasonal components extracted by different ETS decomposition methods

Finally, we will visualize the error terms in the `UnobservedComponents` and `seasonal_decompose` methods, as follows:

```
plt.title('Error components')
plt.ylim((-20, 20))
decomp['UC_Error'].plot(figsize=(12, 6), color='black',
                        linestyle=':', lw=2,
                        legend='UC_Error')
decomp['SDC_Error'].plot(figsize=(12, 6), color='black',
                         linestyle='-.', lw=2,
                         legend='SDC_Error')
```

The output is shown in the following screenshot:

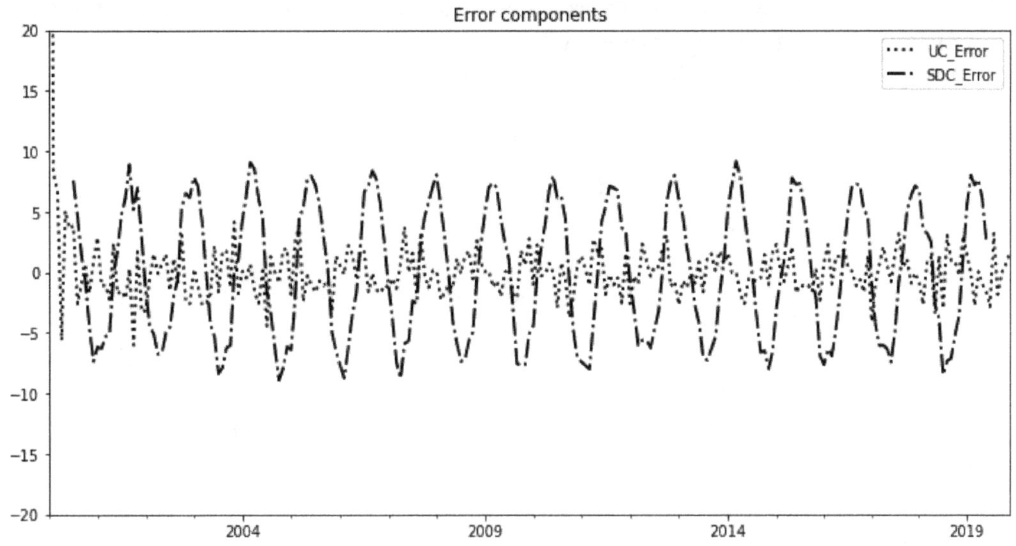

Figure 6.7 – Plot displaying error terms from different ETS decomposition models

The plot shown in the preceding screenshot demonstrates that the error terms oscillate around `0` and that they have no clear trend.

Augmented Dickey-Fuller test for stationarity of a time series

Stationary time series are time series whose statistical properties such as mean, variance, and autocorrelation are constant over time. Many statistical forecasting models assume that time series datasets can be transformed into stationary datasets by some mathematical operations, such as differencing.

An **Augmented Dickey-Fuller** (**ADF**) test is used to check if a dataset is stationary or not—it computes the likelihood that a dataset is not stationary, and when that probability (*p-value*) is very low, we can conclude that the dataset is stationary. We will look at the detailed steps in the following sections.

Step 1 – ADF test on the prices

Let's check for stationarity, as well as converting our dataset into a stationary dataset by using a differencing method. We start with the `statsmodels.tsa.stattools.adfuller(...)` method, as illustrated in the following code snippet:

```
from statsmodels.tsa.stattools import adfuller
result = adfuller(dataset['Price'])
print('Test Stat: {}\np value: {}\nLags: {}\nNum \
      observations: {}'.format(result[0], result[1],
                               result[2], result[3]))
```

That outputs the following values when applied to the `Price` field. The `Test` statistic is a positive value and the p-value is 98%, meaning there is strong evidence that the `Price` field is not stationary. We knew this was expected, since the `Price` field has strong trend and seasonality components in it:

```
Test Stat: 0.47882793726850786
p value: 0.9842151821849324
Lags: 14
Num observations: 225
```

Step 2 – First differencing on prices

Next, we apply a **first differencing** transformation; this finds the first difference from one observation to the next one. If we difference the differenced dataset again, that yields a **second difference**, and so on.

We store the first-differenced `pandas.Series` dataset in the `price_diff` variable, as shown in the following code block:

```
price_diff = \
(dataset['Price'].shift(-1) - dataset['Price']).fillna(0)
price_diff
```

That dataset contains the following values:

```
2000-01-31    4.951062
2000-02-29    5.686832
                ...
2019-11-30    3.350694
2019-12-31    0.000000
Name: Price, Length: 240, dtype: float64
```

Step 3 – ADF test on the differenced prices

Now, we rerun the ADF test on this transformed dataset to check for stationarity, as follows:

```
result = adfuller(price_diff)
print('Test Stat: {}\np value: {}\nLags: {}\nNum \
      observations: {}'.format(result[0], result[1],
                               result[2], result[3]))
```

The test statistic now has a large negative value (values under -4 have a very high likelihood of being stationary). The probability of not being stationary now reduces to an extremely low value, indicating that the transformed dataset is stationary, as illustrated in the following code snippet:

```
Test Stat: -7.295184662866956
p value: 1.3839111942229784e-10
Lags: 15
Num observations: 224
```

Autocorrelation and partial autocorrelation of a time series

Autocorrelation or serial correlation is the correlation of an observation—a delayed copy of itself—as a function of delay. It measures if the currently observed value has any relationship to the value in the future/past.

In our dataset with a clear linear trend and some seasonal components, the autocorrelation slowly decreases as the number of lags increases, but for smaller lag values the dataset has high autocorrelation values due to the large overall linear trend. The `statsmodels.graphics.tsaplots.plot_acf(...)` method plots the autocorrelation of the `Price` field with lag values ranging from `0` to `100`, as illustrated in the following code snippet:

```
from statsmodels.graphics.tsaplots import plot_acf, plot_pacf
fig = plot_acf(dataset['Price'], lags=100)
fig.set_size_inches(12, 6)
```

The result indicates that autocorrelation remains relatively strong up to lag values of around 36, where it dips below 0.5. This is illustrated in the following screenshot:

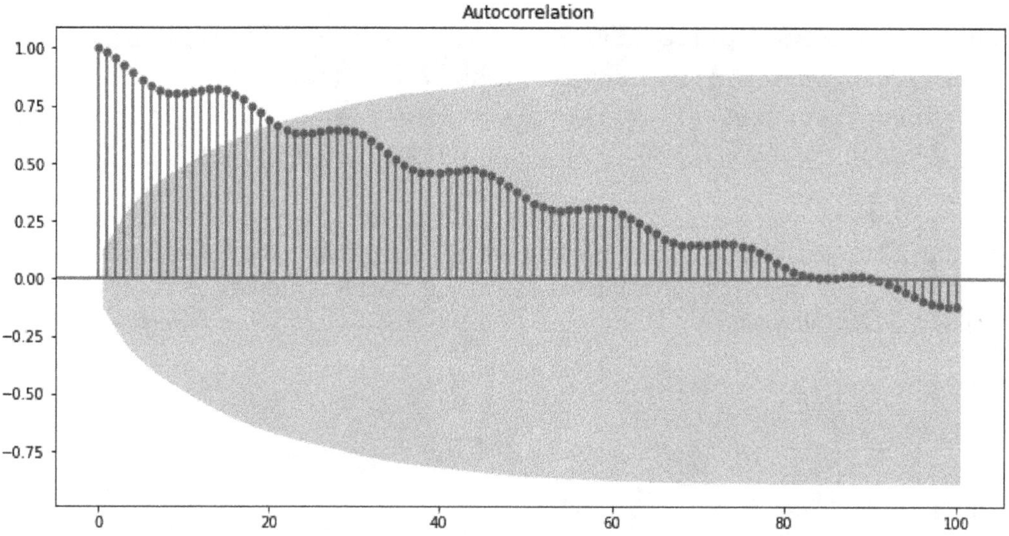

Figure 6.8 – Autocorrelation plot showing autocorrelation against different lag values

The `statsmodels.graphics.tsaplots.plot_pacf(...)` method lets us plot the partial autocorrelation values against different lag values. The difference between autocorrelation and partial autocorrelation is that with partial autocorrelation, only the correlation between that observation and the previous observation that lag periods is used, and correlation effects from lower lag-value terms are removed. This method is shown in the following code snippet:

```
fig = plot_pacf(dataset['Price'], lags=100)
fig.set_size_inches(12, 6)
```

The output can be seen in the following screenshot:

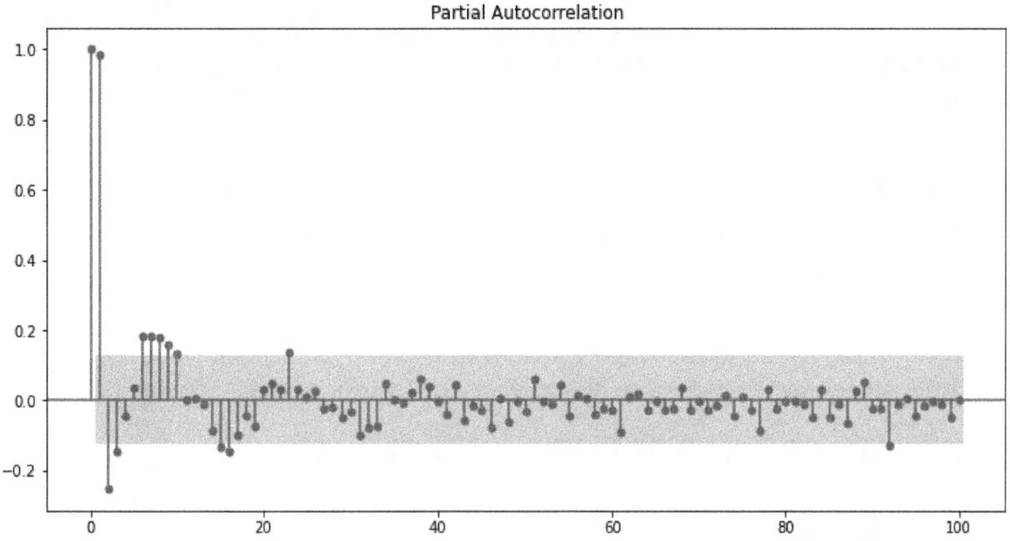

Figure 6.9 – Partial autocorrelation plot showing partial autocorrelations against lag values

The plot shown in the preceding screenshot drops in autocorrelation sharply after the first two lag terms and then seasonally varies from positive to negative values every 10 lag terms.

ARIMA time series model

The **Auto-Regressive Integrated Moving Average** (**ARIMA**) model is one of the most well-known time series modeling and forecasting models available. It is used to predict time series data for time series with correlated data points.

The ARIMA model is composed of three components, outlined as follows:

- **Auto-regression** (**AR**): This model uses the autocorrelation relationship we explored in the previous section. It accepts a `p` parameter, specifying the number of lags to use. For our case based on the autocorrelation plots, we will specify `p=36` when modeling the `Price` series with ARIMA.
- **Integrated** (**I**): This is the differencing transformation for the model to use to convert the time series into a stationary dataset. It accepts a `d` parameter, specifying the order of differencing to perform, which in our case will be `d=1`. As we saw in the *Augmented Dickey-Fuller test for stationarity of a time series* section, the first-order differencing led to a stationary dataset.

- **Moving Average (MA)**: This is the component that applies a MA model to lagged observations. This accepts a single parameter, q, which is the size of the MA window. In our case, we will set this parameter based on the partial autocorrelation plots and use a value of `q=2` because of the sharp drop-off in partial autocorrelation past the lag value of `1`.

In statsmodels, the `statsmodels.tsa.arima.model.ARIMA` model builds a time series as an ARIMA model. Using an `order=(36, 1, 2)` parameter, we specify `p=36`, `d=1`, and `q=2`. Then, we call the `ARIMA.fit(...)` method to fit the model to our `Price` series, and call the `ARIMA.summary(...)` method to output information about the fitted ARIMA model.

Some other packages—for example, `pmdarima`—offer `auto_arima` methods that find the ARIMA models by themselves, as illustrated in the following code snippet:

```
from statsmodels.tsa.arima.model import ARIMA
arima = ARIMA(dataset['Price'], order=(36,1,2))
res_ar = arima.fit()
res_ar.summary()
```

The following output describes fitting parameters:

```
SARIMAX Results
Dep. Variable:              Price  No. Observations:          240
        Model:    ARIMA(36, 1, 2)    Log Likelihood      -360.195
         Date:  Sat, 13 Jun 2020                AIC       798.391
         Time:          09:18:46                BIC       933.973
       Sample:        01-31-2000               HQIC       853.027
                    - 12-31-2019
Covariance Type:              opg
           coef   std err       z   P>|z|    [0.025     0.975]
ar.L1   -0.8184     0.821  -0.997   0.319    -2.428      0.791
ar.L2   -0.6716     0.495  -1.358   0.175    -1.641      0.298
...
ar.L35   0.3125     0.206   1.514   0.130    -0.092      0.717
ar.L36   0.1370     0.161   0.851   0.395    -0.178      0.452
ma.L1   -0.0244     0.819  -0.030   0.976    -1.630      1.581
ma.L2    0.1694     0.454   0.373   0.709    -0.721      1.060
sigma2   1.0911     0.144   7.586   0.000     0.809      1.373
```

```
          Ljung-Box (Q):   13.99  Jarque-Bera (JB):   1.31
                Prob(Q):   1.00           Prob(JB):   0.52
   Heteroskedasticity (H):   1.15               Skew:   0.09
      Prob(H) (two-sided):   0.54           Kurtosis:   2.69
```

Using the `statsmodels.tsa.arima.ARIMAResults.predict(...)` method, we can use the fitted model to predict values over the specified start and end datetime indices (in this case, the entire dataset). We will save the predicted prices in the `PredPrice` field for comparison later. The code can be seen in the following snippet:

```
dataset['PredPrice'] = res_ar.predict(dataset.index[0],
                                      dataset.index[-1])
dataset
```

The result adds the new column with the predicted prices, as follows:

```
                   Price          PredPrice
2000-01-31     95.317833           0.000000
2000-02-29    100.268895          95.317901
       ...           ...                ...
2019-11-30    188.524009         188.944216
2019-12-31    191.874704         190.614641
240 rows × 2 columns
```

Now, we will plot the original `Price` and the `PredPrice` fields in the following code block to visually compare the two:

```
plt.ylim(70, 250)
dataset['Price'].plot(figsize=(12, 6), color='darkgray',
                      linestyle='-', lw=4, legend='Price')
dataset['PredPrice'].plot(figsize=(12, 6), color='black',
                          linestyle='-.',
                          legend='PredPrice')
```

The predicted prices are quite accurate, and that is because the specified parameters (`p`, `d`, `q`) were precise. The result can be seen in the following screenshot:

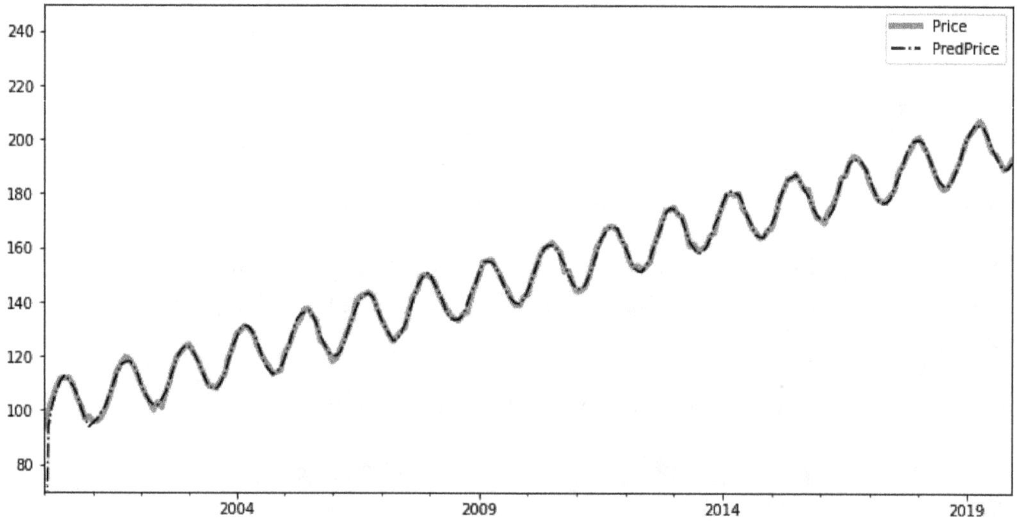

Figure 6.10 – Plot comparing the original price and the price predicted by an ARIMA (36, 1, 2) model

Let's use this fitted model to forecast values for dates out in the future. First, we build an `extended_dataset` DataFrame with another 4 years' worth of datetime indices and no data (which will be filled in with `NaN` values) using the `datetools.dates_from_range(...)` method and the `pandas.DataFrame.append(...)` method, as follows:

```
extended_dataset = pd.DataFrame(index=sm.tsa.datetools.dates_
from_range('2020m1', length=48))
extended_dataset = dataset.append(extended_dataset)
extended_dataset
                   Price          PredPrice
2000-01-31     95.317833           0.000000
2000-02-29     100.268895        95.317901
       ...           ...                ...
2023-11-30           NaN                NaN
2023-12-31           NaN                NaN
288 rows x 2 columns
```

Then, we can call the `ARIMAResults.predict(...)` method again to generate predicted prices for the entire time series and thus forecast onto the new dates we added, as follows:

```
extended_dataset['PredPrice'] = \
res_ar.predict(extended_dataset.index[0],
               extended_dataset.index[-1])
extended_dataset
                 Price         PredPrice
2000-01-31     95.317833        0.000000
2000-02-29    100.268895       95.317901
   ...           ...              ...
2023-11-30          NaN       215.441777
2023-12-31          NaN       220.337355
288 rows × 2 columns
```

The following code block plots the last 100 observations from the `extended_dataset` DataFrame:

```
extended_dataset['Price'].iloc[-100:].plot(figsize=(12, 6),
                                           color='darkgray',
                                           linestyle='-',
                                           lw=4,
                                           legend='Price')
extended_dataset['PredPrice'].iloc[-100:].plot(figsize=(12, 6),
                                           color='black',
                                           linestyle='-.',
                                           legend='PredPrice')
```

And that yields a plot with the forecasted `PredPrice` values, as illustrated in the following screenshot:

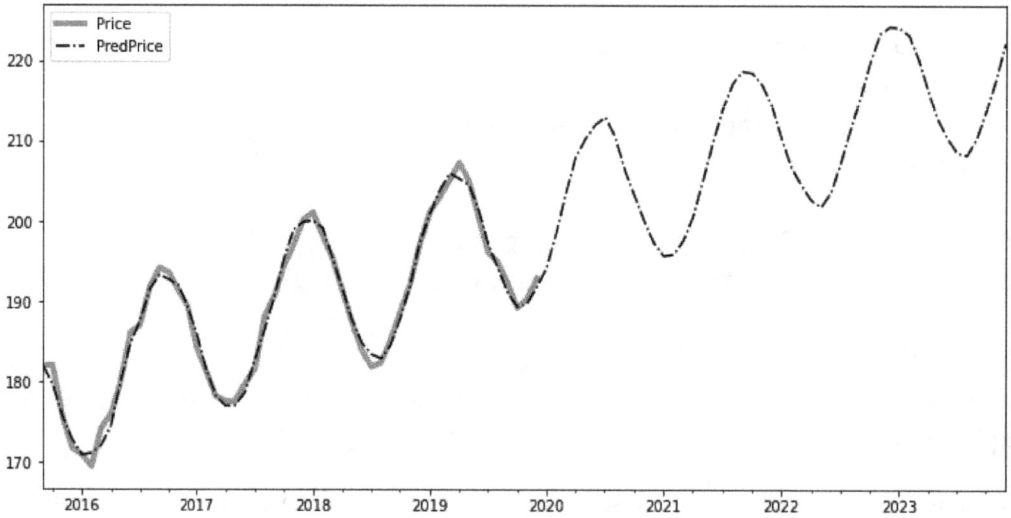

Figure 6.11 – Historical and predicted prices forecasted by the ARIMA model

In the plot shown in the preceding screenshot, the predicted prices visibly follow the trend of past prices.

Using a SARIMAX time series model with pmdarima

SARIMA is an extension of the ARIMA model for univariate time series with a seasonal component.

SARIMAX is, then, the name of the model, which also supports **exogenous** variables.

These are the three ARIMA parameters:

- `p` = trend auto-regressive order
- `d` = trend difference order
- `q` = trend MA order

In addition to the preceding parameters, SARIMA introduces four more, as follows:

- `P` = seasonal auto-regressive order
- `D` = seasonal difference order
- `Q` = seasonal MA order
- `m` = the length of a single seasonal period in the number of time steps

To find these parameters manually can be time-consuming, and it may be advantageous to use an auto-ARIMA model.

In Python, auto-ARIMA modeling is provided by the `pmdarima` library. Its documentation is available at `http://alkaline-ml.com/pmdarima/index.html`.

The installation is straightforward, as can be seen here:

```
pip install pmdarima
```

The auto-ARIMA model attempts to automatically discover the SARIMAX parameters by conducting various statistical tests, as illustrated here:

Parameter	Statistical Tests
d = trend difference order	Kwiatkowski-Phillips-Schmidt-Shin (KPSS) Augmented Dickey-Fuller (ADF) Phillips-Perron (PP)
D = seasonal difference order	Canova-Hansen (CH)

Figure 6.12 – Table of the various statistical tests

Once we find the optimal `d` value, the auto-ARIMA model searches for the best fitting model within the ranges defined by `start_p`, `max_p`, `start_q`, and `max_q`. If the `seasonal` parameter is enabled, once we determine the optimal `D` value we use a similar procedure to find `P` and `Q`.

The best model is determined by minimizing the value of the information criterion (**Akaike information criterion** (AIC), **Corrected AIC**, **Bayesian information criterion** (BIC), **Hannan-Quinn information criterion** (HQC), or **out-of-bag** (OOB)—for validation scoring—respectively).

If no suitable model is found, auto-ARIMA returns a `ValueError` output.

Let's use auto-ARIMA with the previous dataset. The time series has a clear seasonality component with a periodicity of 12.

Notice in the following code block that we generate 95% confidence intervals for the predicted values, which is very useful for trading rules—for example, sell if the price is above the upper confidence interval value:

```
import pmdarima as pm
model = pm.auto_arima(dataset['Price'], seasonal=True,
                      stepwise=True, m=12)
print(model.summary())

extended_dataset = \
pd.DataFrame(
    index=sm.tsa.datetools.dates_from_range('2020m1',
    length=48))

extended_dataset['PredPrice'], conf_int = \
model.predict(48, return_conf_int=True, alpha=0.05)

plt.plot(dataset['Price'], c='blue')
plt.plot(extended_dataset['PredPrice'], c='green')
plt.show()
print(extended_dataset)
print(conf_int)
```

The output is shown here:

```
                               SARIMAX Results
==============================================================================
Dep. Variable:                      y   No. Observations:                  240
Model:               SARIMAX(4, 1, 2)   Log Likelihood                -392.059
Date:                Thu, 18 Mar 2021   AIC                            800.119
Time:                        11:15:38   BIC                            827.930
Sample:                             0   HQIC                           811.326
                                - 240
Covariance Type:                  opg
==============================================================================
                 coef    std err          z      P>|z|      [0.025      0.975]
------------------------------------------------------------------------------
intercept      0.1222      0.013      9.356      0.000       0.097       0.148
ar.L1          1.2502      0.096     13.059      0.000       1.063       1.438
ar.L2         -0.0985      0.135     -0.732      0.464      -0.362       0.165
ar.L3         -0.3111      0.126     -2.479      0.013      -0.557      -0.065
ar.L4         -0.1326      0.089     -1.487      0.137      -0.307       0.042
ma.L1         -1.8235      0.061    -30.098      0.000      -1.942      -1.705
ma.L2          0.8357      0.060     13.874      0.000       0.718       0.954
sigma2         1.6801      0.203      8.263      0.000       1.282       2.079
===================================================================================
Ljung-Box (Q):                       55.54   Jarque-Bera (JB):                 1.44
Prob(Q):                              0.05   Prob(JB):                         0.49
Heteroskedasticity (H):               0.77   Skew:                             0.06
Prob(H) (two-sided):                  0.25   Kurtosis:                         2.64
===================================================================================

Warnings:
[1] Covariance matrix calculated using the outer product of gradients (complex-step).
```

Figure 6.13 – SARIMAX result statistics from auto-ARIMA

The plot is shown in the following screenshot:

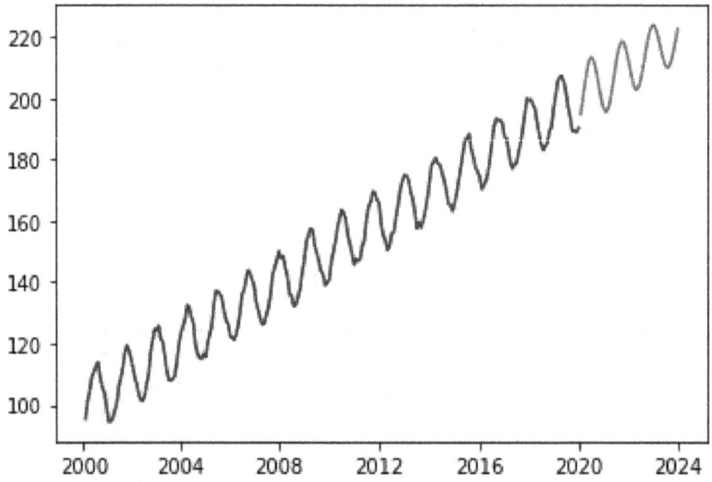

Figure 6.14 – Historical and predicted price forecasted by the auto-ARIMA model

The output also includes the predicted prices, as follows:

```
            PredPrice
2020-01-31  194.939195
       ...         ...
2023-12-31  222.660698

[48 rows x 1 columns]
```

In addition, the output provides the confidence intervals for each predicted price, as follows:

```
[[192.39868933 197.4797007 ]
 [196.80033117 202.32443987]
 [201.6275806  207.60042584]
...
 [212.45091331 225.44676173]
 [216.11548707 229.20590827]]
```

We will now see time series forecasting with Facebook's Prophet library.

Time series forecasting with Facebook's Prophet library

Facebook Prophet is a Python library used for forecasting univariate time series with strong support for seasonality and holiday effects. It is especially suitable for time series with frequent changes of trends and is robust enough to handle outliers.

More specifically, the `Prophet` model is an additive regression model with the following attributes:

- Piecewise linear or logistic growth trend
- Yearly seasonal component modeled with a Fourier series
- Weekly seasonal component modeled with dummy variables
- A user-provided list of holidays

Installation of `Prophet` is more complicated, since it requires a compiler. The easiest way to install it is by using Anaconda, as follows:

```
conda install -c conda-forge fbprophet
```

The accompanying Git repository contains the `conda` environment set up with `Prophet`.

The `Prophet` library requires the input DataFrame to include two columns—`ds` for date, and `y` for the value.

Let's fit the `Prophet` model onto the previous dataset. Notice in the following code snippet that we explicitly tell `Prophet` we wish to receive monthly predictions (`freq='M'`):

```
from fbprophet import Prophet

prophet_dataset = \
dataset.rename(columns={'Price' : 'y'}).rename_axis('ds')\
.drop('PredPrice', 1).reset_index()

print(prophet_dataset)
model = Prophet()
model.fit(prophet_dataset)
df_forecast = model.make_future_dataframe(periods=48,
                                          freq='M')
df_forecast = model.predict(df_forecast)
```

```
print(df_forecast[['ds', 'yhat', 'yhat_lower',
                   'yhat_upper']].tail())
model.plot(df_forecast, xlabel='Date', ylabel='Value')
model.plot_components(df_forecast)
```

The predicted values are very similar to the SARIMAX model, as can be seen here:

```
             ds           y
0    2000-01-31   95.434035
..          ...         ...
239 2019-12-31  190.440912

[240 rows x 2 columns]
             ds       trend  trend_lower  ...  yearly_lower  \
0    2000-01-31  100.442384   100.442384  ...      0.158596
..          ...         ...          ...  ...           ...
287 2023-12-31  219.455470   219.455392  ...     -0.041164

     yearly_upper        yhat
0        0.158596  100.600980
..            ...         ...
287     -0.041164  219.414306

[288 rows x 16 columns]
```

Figure 6.15 – The Prophet library's output includes prediction values, along with the model components' values

The predicted values are stored in the `yhat` column with the `yhat_lower` and `yhat_upper` confidence intervals.

`Prophet` does produce charts of Prophet components, which is useful for understanding the model's prediction powers. A trend component chart can be seen here:

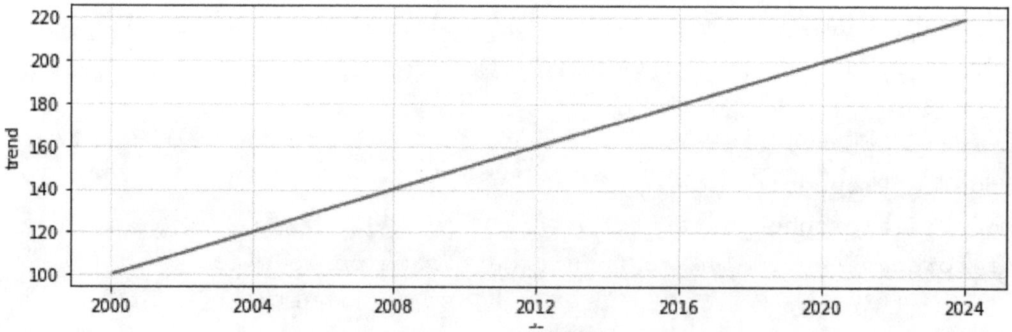

Figure 6.16 – The trend component chart of the Prophet model

The following screenshot shows the yearly seasonality output:

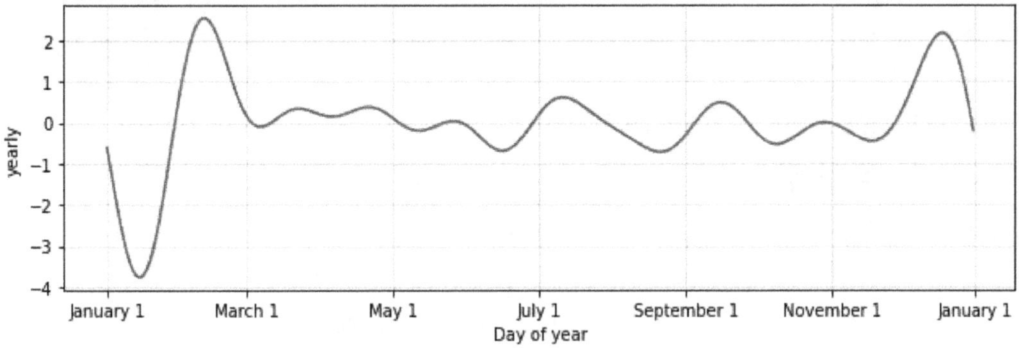

Figure 6.17 – The yearly seasonality component chart of the Prophet model

Here is the output of the forecast chart:

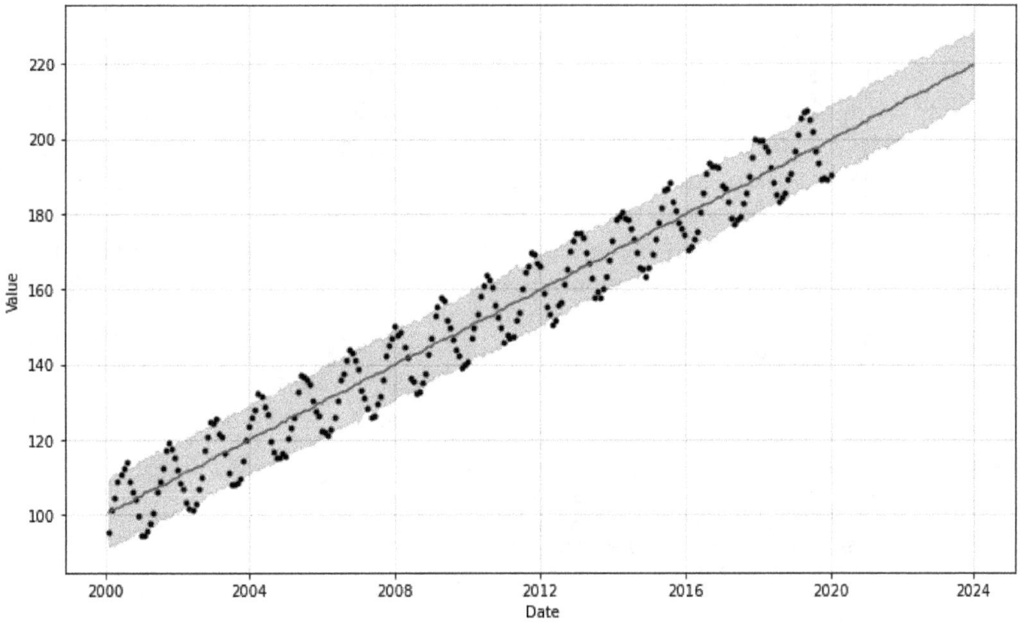

Figure 6.18 – The forecast chart of the Prophet model along with the confidence intervals

Each time series model is slightly different and is best suited for different classes of time series. In general, however, the `Prophet` model is very robust and easiest to use in most scenarios.

Introduction to scikit-learn regression and classification

scikit-learn is a Python *supervised* and *unsupervised* machine learning library built on top of the `numpy` and `scipy` libraries.

Let's demonstrate how to forecast price changes on a dataset with `RidgeCV` regression and classification using scikit-learn.

Generating the dataset

Let's start by generating the dataset for the following examples—a Pandas DataFrame containing daily data for 20 years with `BookPressure`, `TradePressure`, `RelativeValue`, and `Microstructure` fields to represent some synthetic trading signals built on this dataset (also known as **features** or **predictors**). The `PriceChange` field represents the daily change in prices that we are trying to predict (also known as **response** or **target variable**). For simplicity, we make the `PriceChange` field a linear function of our predictors with random weights and some random noise. The `Price` field represents the actual price of the instrument generated using the `pandas.Series.cumsum(...)` method. The code can be seen in the following snippet:

```
import numpy as np
import pandas as pd

df = pd.DataFrame(index=pd.date_range('2000', '2020'))
df['BookPressure'] = np.random.randn(len(df)) * 2
df['TradePressure'] = np.random.randn(len(df)) * 100
df['RelativeValue'] = np.random.randn(len(df)) * 50
df['Microstructure'] = np.random.randn(len(df)) * 10

true_coefficients = np.random.randint(low=-100, high=101,
                                      size=4) / 10
```

```
df['PriceChange'] = ((df['BookPressure'] * true_
coefficients[0])
+ (df['TradePressure'] * true_coefficients[1])
+ (df['RelativeValue'] * true_coefficients[2])
+ (df['Microstructure'] * true_coefficients[3])
+ (np.random.randn(len(df)) * 200))

df['Price'] = df['PriceChange'].cumsum(0) + 100000
```

Let's quickly inspect the true weights assigned to our four features, as follows:

```
true_coefficients
array([10. ,  6.2, -0.9,  5. ])
```

Let's also inspect the DataFrame containing all the data, as follows:

```
Df
            BookPressure  TradePressure  RelativeValue
Microstructure  PriceChange  Price
2000-01-01  4.545869  -2.335894  5.953205  -15.025576
-263.749500  99736.250500
2000-01-02  -0.302344  -186.764283  9.150213  13.795346
-758.298833  98977.951667
...    ...    ...    ...    ...    ...    ...
2019-12-31  -1.890265  -113.704752  60.258456  12.229772
-295.295108  182827.332185
2020-01-01  1.657811  -77.354049  -39.090108  -3.294086
-204.576735  182622.755450
7306 rows × 6 columns
```

Let's visually inspect the `Price` field, as follows:

```
df['Price'].plot(figsize=(12, 6), color='black',
                 legend='Price')
```

The plot shows the following realistic-looking price evolution over 20 years:

Figure 6.19 – Price plot for the synthetically generated dataset

Let's display a scatter matrix of all columns but the `Price` column, as follows:

```
pd.plotting.scatter_matrix(df.drop('Price', axis=1),
                           color='black', alpha=0.2,
                           grid=True, diagonal='kde',
                           figsize=(10, 10))
```

The output is shown here:

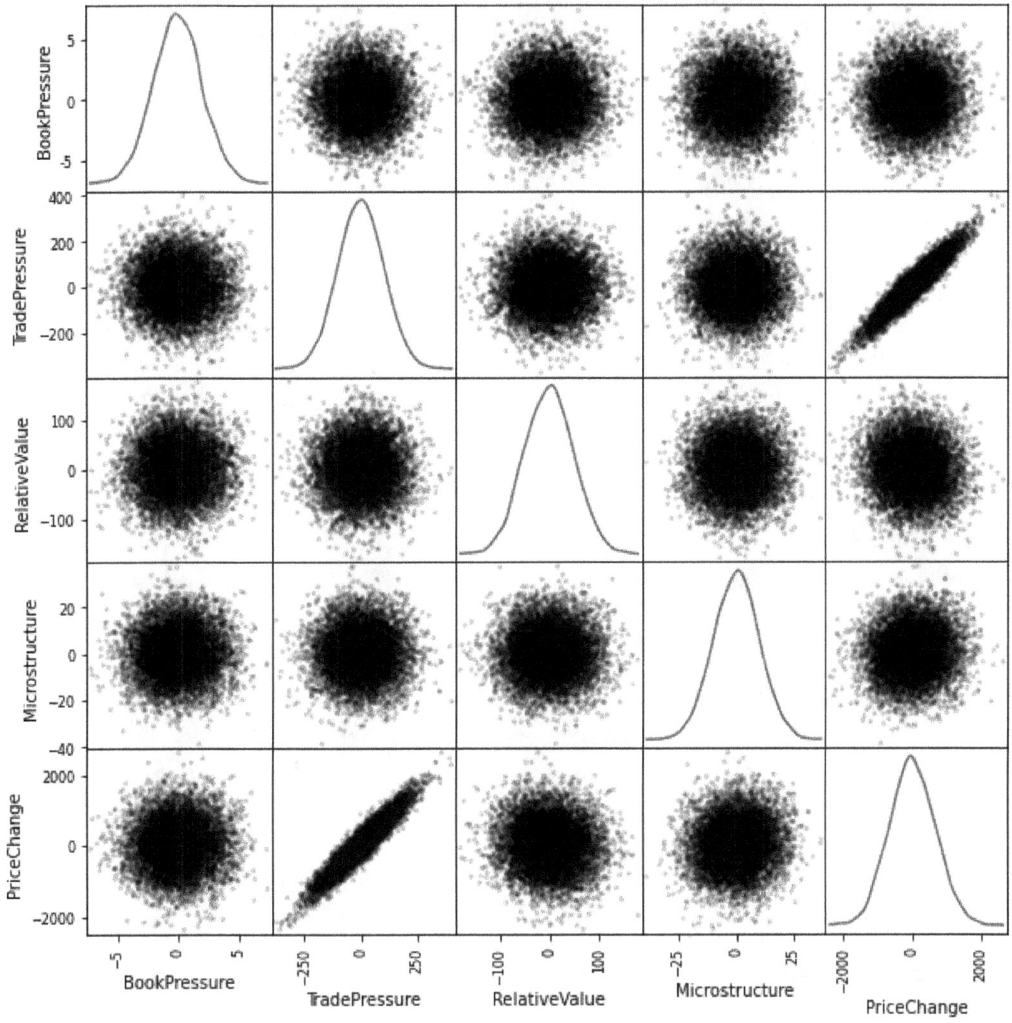

Figure 6.20 – Scatter matrix for the synthetically generated dataset

The scatter matrix shows that there is a strong relationship between `PriceChange` and `TradePressure`.

Running RidgeCV regression on the dataset

Let's use a scikit-learn regression method to fit a linear regression model to our dataset. We will use the four features to try to fit to and predict the `PriceChange` field.

First, we collect the features and target into a DataFrame and a Series, as follows:

```
features = df[['BookPressure', 'TradePressure',
               'RelativeValue', 'Microstructure']]
target = df['PriceChange']
```

We will use `sklearn.linear_model.RidgeCV`, a linear regression model with L2 regularization (an L2 norm penalty factor to avoid overfitting) that uses cross-validation to learn the optimal coefficients. We will use the `sklearn.linear_model.RidgeCV.fit(...)` method to fit the target values using the features. The code is shown in the following snippet:

```
from sklearn.linear_model import RidgeCV
ridge = RidgeCV()
ridge.fit(features, target)
```

The result is a `RidgeCV` object, as can be seen here:

```
RidgeCV(alphas=array([ 0.1,  1. , 10. ]), cv=None,
                     fit_intercept=True, gcv_mode=None,
                     normalize=False, scoring=None,
                     store_cv_values=False)
```

We can access the weights/coefficients learned by the `Ridge` model using the `RidgeCV.coef_` attribute and compare it with the actual coefficients, as follows:

```
true_coefficients, ridge.coef_
```

It seems the coefficients learned by the model are very close to the true weights, with some errors on each one of them, as can be seen in the following code snippet:

```
(array([10. ,  6.2, -0.9,  5. ]),
 array([11.21856334, 6.20641632, -0.93444009, 4.94581522]))
```

The `RidgeCV.score(...)` method returns the R2 score, representing the accuracy of a fitted model, as follows:

```
ridge.score(features, target)
```

That returns the following R2 score with a maximum value of 1, so this model fits the data quite well:

```
0.9076861352499385
```

The `RidgeCV.predict(...)` method outputs the predicted price change values, which we combine with the `pandas.Series.cumsum(...)` method to generate the predicted price series, and then save it in the `PredPrice` field, as follows:

```
df['PredPrice'] = \
ridge.predict(features).cumsum(0) + 100000; df
```

That adds a new column to our DataFrame, as shown here:

```
                ...          Price        PredPrice
2000-01-01  ...   99736.250500    99961.011495
2000-01-02  ...   98977.951667    98862.549185
   ...      ...       ...              ...
2019-12-31  ...  182827.332185   183059.625653
2020-01-01  ...  182622.755450   182622.755450
7306 rows x 7 columns
```

In the following code block, the true `Price` field is plotted alongside the predicted `PredPrice` field:

```
df['Price'].plot(figsize=(12, 6), color='gray',
                 linestyle='--', legend='Price')
df['PredPrice'].plot(figsize=(12, 6), color='black',
                     linestyle='-.', legend='PredPrice')
```

The plot generated, as shown in the following screenshot, reveals that `PredPrice` mostly tracks `Price`, with some prediction errors during some time periods:

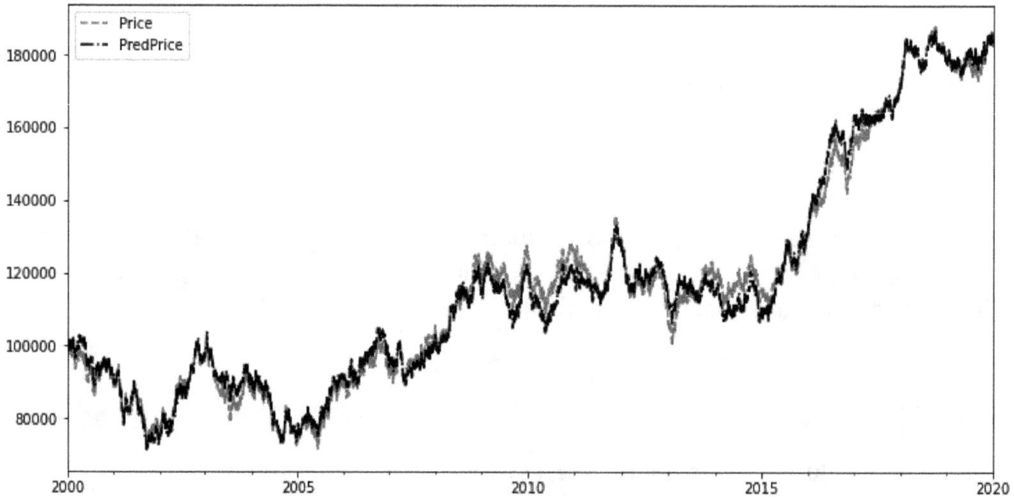

Figure 6.21 – Plot comparing the original price and the predicted price from a Ridge regression model

We can zoom in to the first quarter of 2010 to inspect the prediction errors, as follows:

```
df['Price'].loc['2010-01-01':'2010-03-31']\
.plot(figsize=(12, 6), color='darkgray', linestyle='-',
      legend='Price')
df['PredPrice'].loc['2010-01-01':'2010-03-31']\
.plot(figsize=(12, 6), color='black', linestyle='-.',
      legend='PredPrice')
```

This yields the following plot, displaying the differences between `Price` and `PredPrice` for that period:

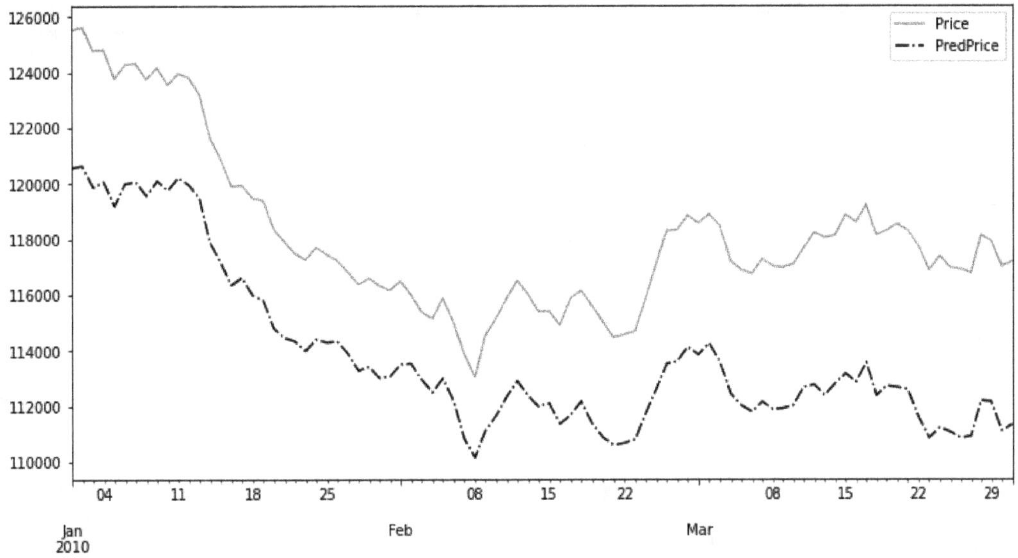

Figure 6.22 – Plot comparing the original and predicted price from a Ridge regression model for 2010 Q1

We can compute the prediction errors and plot them using a density plot, as shown in the following code snippet:

```
df['Errors'] = df['Price'] - df['PredPrice']
df['Errors'].plot(figsize=(12, 6), kind='kde',
                  color='black', legend='Errors')
```

This generates the plot shown in the following screenshot, displaying the distribution of errors:

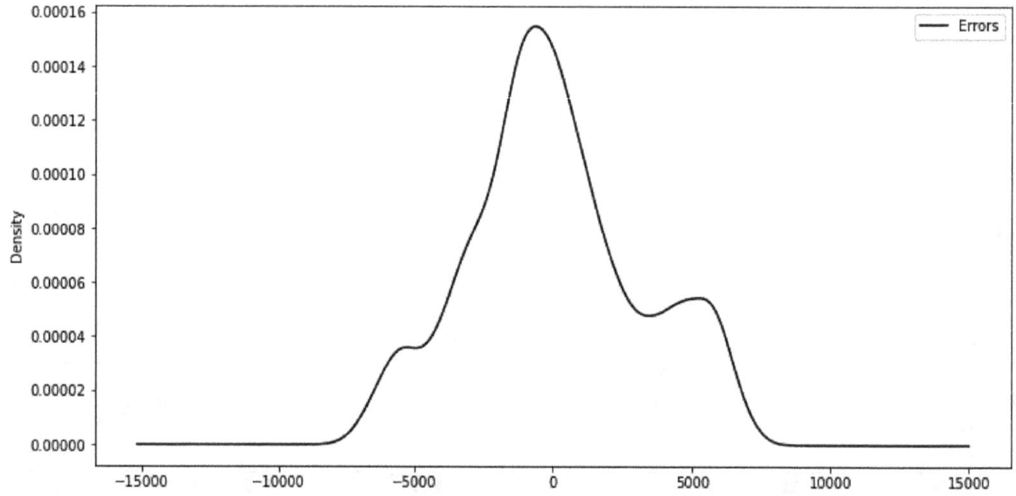

Figure 6.23 – Plot displaying the distribution of prediction errors for the Ridge regression model

The error plot displayed in the preceding screenshot shows that there is no strong bias in the errors.

Running a classification method on the dataset

Let's demonstrate scikit-learn's classification methods.

First, we need to create discrete categorical target labels for the classification model to predict. We assign `-2`, `-1`, `0`, `1`, and `2` numeric labels to these conditions respectively and save the discrete target labels in the `target_discrete pandas.Series` object, as follows:

```
target_discrete = pd.cut(target, bins=5,
                         labels = \
                         [-2, -1, 0, 1, 2]).astype(int);
target_discrete
```

The result is shown here:

```
2000-01-01     0
2000-01-02    -1
             ...
2019-12-28    -1
```

```
2019-12-29    0
2019-12-30    0
2019-12-31    0
2020-01-01    0
Freq: D, Name: PriceChange, Length: 7306, dtype: int64
```

We can visualize the distribution of the five labels by using the following code:

```
target_discrete.plot(figsize=(12, 6), kind='hist',
                     color='black')
```

The result is a plot of frequency of occurrence of the five labels, as shown in the following screenshot:

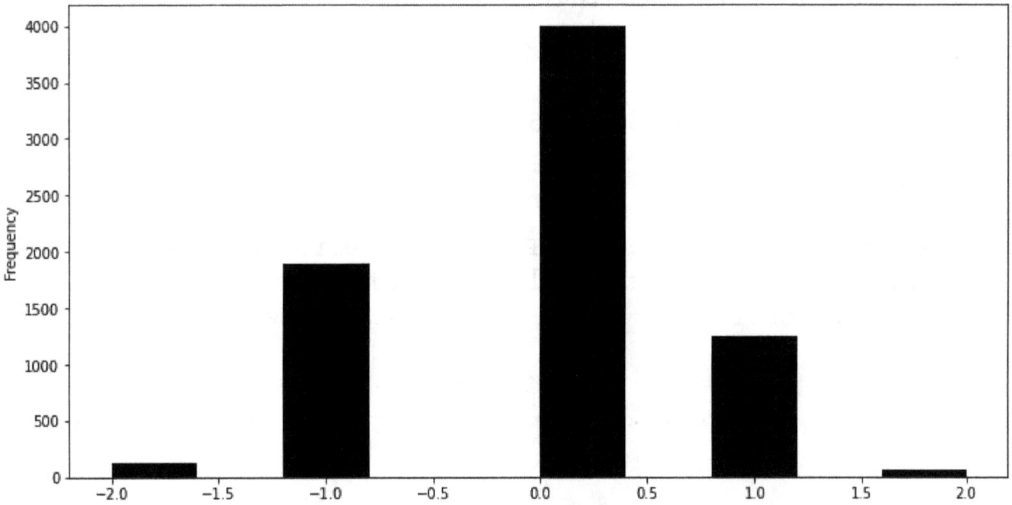

Figure 6.24 – Frequency distribution of our discrete target-price change-label values [-2, -1, 0, 1, 2]

For the classification, we use an ensemble of decision tree classifiers provided by `sklearn.ensemble.RandomForestClassifier`. Random forest is a classifier that uses the bagging ensemble method and builds a forest of decision trees by training each tree on datasets generated by random sampling with replacements from the original dataset. Using a `max_depth=5` parameter, we limit the height of each tree to reduce overfitting and then call the `RandomForestClassifier.fit(...)` method to fit the model, as follows:

```
from sklearn.ensemble import RandomForestClassifier
rf = RandomForestClassifier(max_depth=5)
rf.fit(features, target_discrete)
```

This builds the following `RandomForestClassifier` fitted model:

```
RandomForestClassifier(
        bootstrap=True, ccp_alpha=0.0, class_weight=None,
        criterion='gini', max_depth=5, max_features='auto',
        max_leaf_nodes=None, max_samples=None,
        min_impurity_decrease=0.0, min_impurity_split=None,
        min_samples_leaf=1, min_samples_split=2,
        min_weight_fraction_leaf=0.0, n_estimators=100,
        n_jobs=None, oob_score=False, random_state=None,
        verbose=0, warm_start=False)
```

The `RandomForestClassifier.score(...)` method returns the mean accuracy of the predictions compared to the `True` labels, as follows:

```
rf.score(features, target_discrete)
```

As we can see here, the accuracy score is 83.5%, which is excellent:

```
0.835340815767862
```

We add the `DiscretePriceChange` and `PredDiscretePriceChange` fields to the DataFrame to hold the true labels and the predicted labels using the `RandomForestClassifier.predict(...)` method, as follows:

```
df['DiscretePriceChange'] = target_discrete
df['PredDiscretePriceChange'] = rf.predict(features)
df
```

The result is the following DataFrame with the two additional fields:

```
            ... DiscretePriceChange PredDiscretePriceChange
2000-01-01  ...                   0                       0
2000-01-02  ...                  -1                      -1
       ...  ...                 ...                     ...
2019-12-31  ...                   0                      -1
2020-01-01  ...                   0                      -1
7306 rows x 10 columns
```

In the following code block, we plot two fields for the first quarter of 2010:

```
df['DiscretePriceChange'].loc['2010-01-01':'2010-03-31'].
plot(figsize=(12, 6), color='darkgray', linestyle='-',
legend='DiscretePriceChange')
df['PredDiscretePriceChange'].loc['2010-01-01':'2010-03-
31'].plot(figsize=(12, 6), color='black', linestyle='-.',
legend='PredDiscretePriceChange')
```

That yields a plot, as shown in the following screenshot, with some dislocations between the `True` and predicted labels:

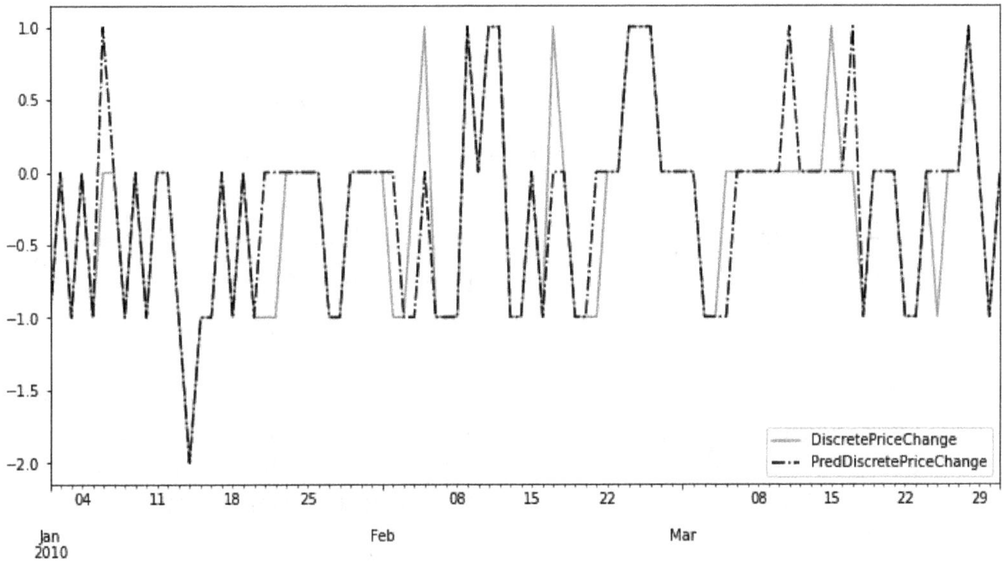

Figure 6.25 – Comparison of original and predicted discrete price-change labels from the RandomForest classification model for 2010 Q1

We can compute and plot the distribution of the `ClassificationErrors` DataFrame with the following code:

```
df['ClassificationErrors'] = \
df['DiscretePriceChange'] - df['PredDiscretePriceChange']
df['ClassificationErrors'].plot(figsize=(12, 6),
                             kind='kde', color='black',
                             legend='ClassificationErrors')
```

This yields the following error distribution:

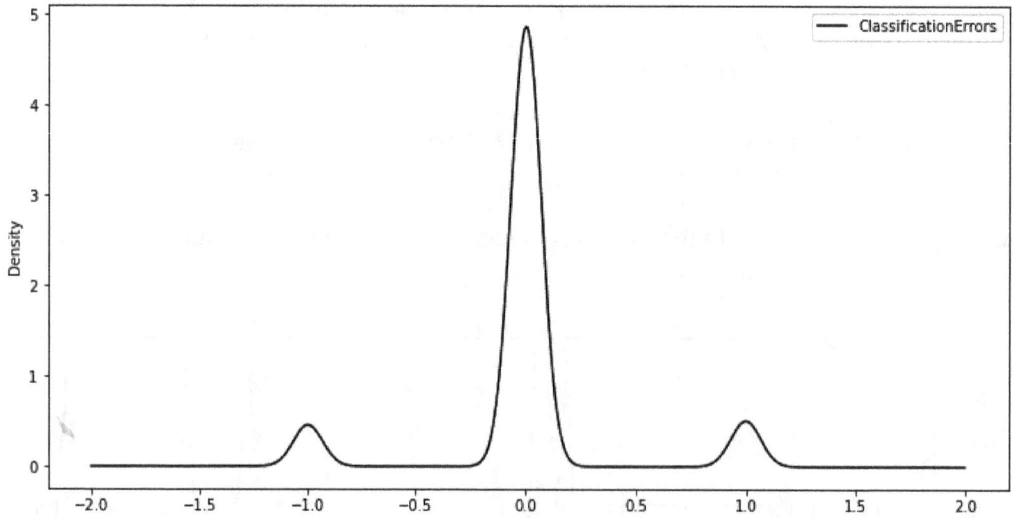

Figure 6.26 – Plot of distribution of classification errors from the RandomForest classifier model

The classification errors are again without bias and are negligible.

Summary

All advanced trading algorithms use statistical models, whether for a direct trading rule or just for deciding when to enter/leave trading. In this chapter, we have covered the four key statistical libraries for Python—`statsmodels`, `pmdarima`, `fbprophet`, and `scikitlearn`.

In the next chapter, we discuss how to import key financial and economic data into Python.

Section 3: Algorithmic Trading in Python

This section teaches you how to retrieve market data in Python, how to run basic algorithmic trading backtesting, and describes in detail the key algorithmic trading algorithms.

This section comprises the following chapters:

- *Chapter 7, Financial Market Data Access in Python*
- *Chapter 8, Introduction to Zipline and PyFolio*
- *Chapter 9, Fundamental Algorithmic Trading Strategies*

7
Financial Market Data Access in Python

This chapter outlines several key market data sources, ranging from free to paid data sources. A more complete list of available resources can be obtained from `https://github.com/wilsonfreitas/awesome-quant#data-sources`.

The quality of algorithmic trading models' signals fundamentally depends on the quality of market data being analyzed. Has the market data been cleaned of erroneous records and is there a quality assurance process in place to rectify any errors as they occur? If there is a problem with the market data feed, how quickly can the data be corrected?

The following free data sources described are suitable for learning purposes, but not fit for purpose as regards professional trading – there may be a very low limit on the number of API calls per day, the APIs may be slow, and there is no support and no rectification of the data should it not be correct. In addition, when using any of these data providers, be aware of their terms of use.

In this chapter, we are going to cover the following key topics:

- Exploring the yahoofinancials Python library
- Exploring the pandas_datareader Python library

- Exploring the Quandl data source
- Exploring the IEX Cloud data source
- Exploring the MarketStack data source

Technical requirements

The Python code used in this chapter is available in the `Chapter07/marketdata.ipynb` notebook in the book's code repository.

Exploring the yahoofinancials Python library

The yahoofinancials Python library provides free access to the market data available from Yahoo Finance, whose provider is ICE Data Services. The library repository is available at `https://github.com/JECSand/yahoofinancials`.

It provides access to historical and, for most assets, also real-time pricing data for the following:

- Currencies
- Indexes
- Stocks
- Commodities
- ETFs
- Mutual funds
- US Treasuries
- Cryptocurrencies

To find the right ticker, use the lookup at `https://finance.yahoo.com/`.

There is a very strict limit on the number of calls per hour per IP address (about 1,000-2,000 requests per hour per IP address) and once you reach it, your IP address gets blocked for an extensive period of time. In addition, the functionality provided constantly changes.

Installation of the library is standard:

```
pip install yahoofinancials
```

Access to the data is very straightforward, as follows:

```
from yahoofinancials import YahooFinancials
```

The library supports both single-ticker retrieval and multiple-tickers retrieval.

Single-ticker retrieval

The steps regarding single-ticker retrieval are as follows:

1. First, we define the AAPL ticker object:

```
aapl = yf.Ticker("AAPL")
```

2. Then, there is the issue of historical data retrieval. Let's print all historical daily price data for the year of 2020:

```
hist = aapl.get_historical_price_data('2020-01-01',
                                      '2020-12-31',
                                      'daily')
print(hist)
```

The output starts with the following:

```
{'AAPL': {'eventsData': {'dividends': {'2020-02-07':
{'amount': 0.1925, 'date': 1581085800, 'formatted_
date': '2020-02-07'}, '2020-05-08': {'amount': 0.205,
'date': 1588944600, 'formatted_date': '2020-05-08'},
'2020-08-07': {'amount': 0.205, 'date': 1596807000,
'formatted_date': '2020-08-07'}, '2020-11-06':
{'amount': 0.205, 'date': 1604673000, 'formatted_
date': '2020-11-06'}}, 'splits': {'2020-08-31':
{'date': 1598880600, 'numerator': 4, 'denominator': 1,
'splitRatio': '4:1', 'formatted_date': '2020-08-31'}}},
'firstTradeDate': {'formatted_date': '1980-12-12',
'date': 345479400}, 'currency': 'USD', 'instrumentType':
'EQUITY', 'timeZone': {'gmtOffset': -18000}, 'prices':
[{'date': 1577975400, 'high': 75.1500015258789, 'low':
73.79750061035156, 'open': 74.05999755859375, 'close':
75.0875015258789, 'volume': 135480400, 'adjclose':
74.4446029663086, 'formatted_date': '2020-01-02'},
{'date': 1578061800, 'high': 75.1449966430664,
'low': 74.125, 'open': 74.2874984741211, 'close':
74.35749816894531, 'volume': 146322800, 'adjclose':
73.72084045410156, 'formatted_date': '2020-01-03'},
{'date': 1578321000, 'high': 74.98999786376953,
'low': 73.1875, 'open': 73.44750213623047, 'close':
74.94999694824219, 'volume': 118387200, 'adjclose':
74.30826568603516, 'formatted_date': '2020-01-06'},
{'date': 1578407400, 'high': 75.2249984741211, 'low':
74.37000274658203, 'open': 74.95999908447266, 'close':
74.59750366210938, 'volume': 108872000, 'adjclose':
```

```
73.95879364013672, 'formatted_date': '2020-01-07'},
{'date': 1578493800, 'high': 76.11000061035156, 'low':
74.29000091552734, 'open': 74.29000091552734, 'close':
75.79750061035156, 'volume': 132079200, 'adjclose':
75.14852142333984, 'formatted_date': '2020-01-08'},
{'date': 1578580200, 'high': 77.60749816894531,
'low': 76.55000305175781, 'open': 76.80999755859375,
'close': 77.40750122070312, 'volume': 170108400,
'adjclose': 76.7447280883789, 'formatted_date': '2020-
01-09'}, {'date': 1578666600, 'high': 78.1675033569336,
'low': 77.0625, 'open': 77.6500015258789, 'close':
77.5824966430664, 'volume': 140644800, 'adjclose':
76.91822052001953, 'formatted_date': '2020-01-10'},
{'date': 1578925800, 'high': 79.26750183105469, 'low':
77.7874984741211, 'open': 77.91000366210938, 'close':
79.23999786376953, 'volume': 121532000, 'adjclose':
78.56153106689453, 'formatted_date': '2020-01-13'},
{'date': 1579012200, 'high': 79.39250183105469,
'low': 78.0425033569336, 'open': 79.17500305175781,
'close': 78.16999816894531, 'volume': 161954400,
'adjclose': 77.50070190429688, 'formatted_date': '2020-
01-14'}, {'date': 1579098600, 'high': 78.875, 'low':
77.38749694824219, 'open': 77.9625015258789, 'close':
77.83499908447266, 'volume': 121923600, 'adjclose':
77.16856384277344, 'formatted_date': '2020-01-15'},
{'date': 1579185000, 'high': 78.92500305175781, 'low':
78.02249908447266, 'open': 78.39749908447266, 'close':
78.80999755859375, 'volume': 108829200, 'adjclose':
78.13522338867188, 'formatted_date': '2020-01-16'},
{'date': 1579271400, 'high': 79.68499755859375,
'low': 78.75, 'open': 79.06749725341797, 'close':
79.68250274658203, 'volume': 137816400, 'adjclose':
79.000244140625, 'formatted_date': '2020-01-17'},
{'date': 1579617000, 'high': 79.75499725341797,
'low': 79.0, 'open': 79.29750061035156, 'close':
79.14250183105469, 'volume': 110843200, 'adjclose':
78.4648818969726б, 'formatted_date': '2020-01-21'},
{'date': 1579703400, 'high': 79.99749755859375, 'low':
79.32749938964844, 'open': 79.6449966430664, 'close':
79.42500305175781, 'volume': 101832400, 'adjclose':
78.74495697021484, 'formatted_date': '2020-01-22'}, ...
```


Note

You can change the frequency from `'daily'` to `'weekly'` or `'monthly'`.

3. Now, let's inspect the weekly data results:

```
hist = aapl.get_historical_price_data('2020-01-01',
                                      '2020-12-31',
                                      'weekly')
print(hist)
```

The output is as follows:


```
{'AAPL': {'eventsData': {'dividends': {'2020-02-05':
{'amount': 0.1925, 'date': 1581085800, 'formatted_
date': '2020-02-07'}, '2020-05-06': {'amount': 0.205,
'date': 1588944600, 'formatted_date': '2020-05-08'},
'2020-08-05': {'amount': 0.205, 'date': 1596807000,
'formatted_date': '2020-08-07'}, '2020-11-04': {'amount':
0.205, 'date': 1604673000, 'formatted_date': '2020-11-
06'}}, 'splits': {'2020-08-26': {'date': 1598880600,
'numerator': 4, 'denominator': 1, 'splitRatio': '4:1',
'formatted_date': '2020-08-31'}}}, 'firstTradeDate':
{'formatted_date': '1980-12-12', 'date': 345479400},
'currency': 'USD', 'instrumentType': 'EQUITY',
'timeZone': {'gmtOffset': -18000}, 'prices': [{'date':
1577854800, 'high': 75.2249984741211, 'low': 73.1875,
'open': 74.05999755859375, 'close': 74.59750366210938,
'volume': 509062400, 'adjclose': 73.95879364013672,
'formatted_date': '2020-01-01'}, {'date': 1578459600,
'high': 79.39250183105469, 'low': 74.29000091552734,
'open': 74.29000091552734, 'close': 78.16999816894531,
'volume': 726318800, 'adjclose': 77.50070190429688,
'formatted_date': '2020-01-08'}, {'date': 1579064400,
'high': 79.75499725341797, 'low': 77.38749694824219,
'open': 77.9625015258789, 'close': 79.14250183105469,
'volume': 479412400, 'adjclose': 78.46488189697266,
'formatted_date': '2020-01-15'}, {'date': 1579669200,
'high': 80.8324966430664, 'low': 76.22000122070312,
'open': 79.6449966430664, 'close': 79.42250061035156,
'volume': 677016000, 'adjclose': 78.74247741699219,
'formatted_date': '2020-01-22'}, {'date': 1580274000,
'high': 81.9625015258789, 'low': 75.55500030517578,
'open': 81.11250305175781, 'close': 79.7125015258789,
'volume': 853162800, 'adjclose': 79.02999877929688,
'formatted_date': '2020-01-29'}, {'date': 1580878800,
'high': 81.30500030517578, 'low': 78.4625015258789,
'open': 80.87999725341797, 'close': 79.90249633789062,
'volume': 545608400, 'adjclose': 79.21836853027344,
```

```
'formatted_date': '2020-02-05'}, {'date': 1581483600,
'high': 81.80500030517578, 'low': 78.65249633789062,
'open': 80.36750030517578, 'close': 79.75, 'volume':
441122800, 'adjclose': 79.25482177734375, 'formatted_
date': '2020-02-12'}, {'date': 1582088400, 'high':
81.1624984741211, 'low': 71.53250122070312, 'open':
80.0, 'close': 72.0199966430664, 'volume': 776972800,
'adjclose': 71.57282257080078, 'formatted_date': '2020-
02-19'}, {'date': 1582693200, 'high': 76.0, 'low':
64.09249877929688, 'open': 71.63249969482422, 'close':
72.33000183105469, 'volume': 1606418000, 'adjclose':
71.88089752197266, 'formatted_date': '2020-02-
26'}, {'date': 1583298000, 'high': 75.8499984741211,
'low': 65.75, 'open': 74.11000061035156, 'close':
71.33499908447266, 'volume': 1204962800, 'adjclose':
70.89207458496094, 'formatted_date': '2020-03-04'},
{'date': 1583899200, 'high': 70.3050003051757 ...
```


4. Then, we check the monthly data results:

```
hist = aapl.get_historical_price_data('2020-01-01',
                                      '2020-12-31',
                                      'monthly')
print(hist)
```

The output is as follows:


```
{'AAPL': {'eventsData': {'dividends': {'2020-05-01':
{'amount': 0.205, 'date': 1588944600, 'formatted_
date': '2020-05-08'}, '2020-08-01': {'amount': 0.205,
'date': 1596807000, 'formatted_date': '2020-08-07'},
'2020-02-01': {'amount': 0.1925, 'date': 1581085800,
'formatted_date': '2020-02-07'}, '2020-11-01': {'amount':
0.205, 'date': 1604673000, 'formatted_date': '2020-11-
06'}}, 'splits': {'2020-08-01': {'date': 1598880600,
'numerator': 4, 'denominator': 1, 'splitRatio': '4:1',
'formatted_date': '2020-08-31'}}}, 'firstTradeDate':
{'formatted_date': '1980-12-12', 'date': 345479400},
'currency': 'USD', 'instrumentType': 'EQUITY',
'timeZone': {'gmtOffset': -18000}, 'prices': [{'date':
1577854800, 'high': 81.9625015258789, 'low': 73.1875,
'open': 74.05999755859375, 'close': 77.37750244140625,
'volume': 2934370400, 'adjclose': 76.7149887084961,
'formatted_date': '2020-01-01'}, {'date': 1580533200,
'high': 81.80500030517578, 'low': 64.09249877929688,
```

```
'open': 76.07499694824219, 'close': 68.33999633789062,
'volume': 3019851200, 'adjclose': 67.75486755371094,
'formatted_date': '2020-02-01'}, {'date': 1583038800,
'high': 76.0, 'low': 53.15250015258789, 'open':
70.56999969482422, 'close': 63 ...
```

5. The nested JSON can easily be converted to a pandas' DataFrame:

```
import pandas as pd

hist_df = \
pd.DataFrame(hist['AAPL']['prices']).drop('date',
axis=1).set_index('formatted_date')
print(hist_df)
```

The output is as follows:

```
                  adjclose       close        high         low        open  \
formatted_date
2020-01-01       76.714989   77.377502   81.962502   73.187500   74.059998
2020-02-01       67.754868   68.339996   81.805000   64.092499   76.074997
2020-03-01       63.177769   63.572498   76.000000   53.152500   70.570000
2020-04-01       72.993935   73.449997   73.632500   59.224998   61.625000
2020-05-01       78.991470   79.485001   81.059998   71.462502   71.562500
2020-06-01       90.879066   91.199997   93.095001   79.302498   79.437500
2020-07-01      105.886086  106.260002  106.415001   89.144997   91.279999
2020-08-01      128.585907  129.039993  131.000000  107.892502  108.199997
2020-09-01      115.610542  115.809998  137.979996  103.099998  132.759995
2020-10-01      108.672516  108.860001  125.389999  107.720001  117.639999
2020-11-01      118.844963  119.050003  121.989998  107.320000  109.110001
2020-12-01      132.690002  132.690002  138.789993  120.010002  121.010002

                    volume
formatted_date
2020-01-01      2934370400
2020-02-01      3019851200
2020-03-01      6280072400
2020-04-01      3266123200
2020-05-01      2806405200
2020-06-01      3243375600
2020-07-01      3020496000
2020-08-01      4070623100
2020-09-01      3885767100
2020-10-01      2895016800
2020-11-01      2123077300
2020-12-01      2322830600
```

Figure 7.1 – Nested JSON converted to a pandas' DataFrame

Notice the two columns – `adjclose` and `close`. The adjusted close is the close price adjusted for dividends, stock splits, and other corporate events.

Real-time data retrieval

To get real-time stock price data, use the `get_stock_price_data()` function:

```
print(aapl.get_stock_price_data())
```

The output is as follows:


```
{'AAPL': {'quoteSourceName': 'Nasdaq Real Time Price',
'regularMarketOpen': 137.35, 'averageDailyVolume3Month':
107768827, 'exchange': 'NMS', 'regularMarketTime':
'2021-02-06 03:00:02 UTC+0000', 'volume24Hr': None,
'regularMarketDayHigh': 137.41, 'shortName': 'Apple Inc.',
'averageDailyVolume10Day': 115373562, 'longName': 'Apple
Inc.', 'regularMarketChange': -0.42500305, 'currencySymbol':
'$', 'regularMarketPreviousClose': 137.185, 'postMarketTime':
'2021-02-06 06:59:58 UTC+0000', 'preMarketPrice':
None, 'exchangeDataDelayedBy': 0, 'toCurrency': None,
'postMarketChange': -0.0800018, 'postMarketPrice': 136.68,
'exchangeName': 'NasdaqGS', 'preMarketChange': None,
'circulatingSupply': None, 'regularMarketDayLow': 135.86,
'priceHint': 2, 'currency': 'USD', 'regularMarketPrice':
136.76, 'regularMarketVolume': 72317009, 'lastMarket': None,
'regularMarketSource': 'FREE_REALTIME', 'openInterest': None,
'marketState': 'CLOSED', 'underlyingSymbol': None, 'marketCap':
2295940513792, 'quoteType': 'EQUITY', 'volumeAllCurrencies':
None, 'postMarketSource': 'FREE_REALTIME', 'strikePrice':
None, 'symbol': 'AAPL', 'postMarketChangePercent':
-0.00058498, 'preMarketSource': 'FREE_REALTIME', 'maxAge':
1, 'fromCurrency': None, 'regularMarketChangePercent':
-0.0030980287}}
```


Real-time data for free data sources is usually delayed by 10 to 30 minutes.

As regards the retrieval of financial statements, let's get financial statements for Apple's stock – the income statement, cash flow, and balance sheet:

```
statements = aapl.get_financial_stmts('quarterly',
                                      ['income', 'cash',
                                       'balance'])
print(statements)
```

The output is as follows:

```
{'incomeStatementHistoryQuarterly': {'AAPL': [{'2020-
12-26': {'researchDevelopment': 5163000000,
'effectOfAccountingCharges': None, 'incomeBeforeTax':
33579000000, 'minorityInterest': None, 'netIncome':
28755000000, 'sellingGeneralAdministrative': 5631000000,
'grossProfit': 44328000000, 'ebit': 33534000000,
'operatingIncome': 33534000000, 'otherOperatingExpenses':
None, 'interestExpense': -638000000, 'extraordinaryItems':
None, 'nonRecurring': None, 'otherItems': None,
'incomeTaxExpense': 4824000000, 'totalRevenue': 111439000000,
'totalOperatingExpenses': 77905000000, 'costOfRevenue':
67111000000, 'totalOtherIncomeExpenseNet': 45000000,
'discontinuedOperations': None, 'netIncomeFromContinuingOps':
28755000000, 'netIncomeApplicableToCommonShares':
28755000000}}, {'2020-09-26': {'researchDevelopment':
4978000000, 'effectOfAccountingCharges': None,
'incomeBeforeTax': 14901000000, 'minorityInterest': None,
'netIncome': 12673000000, 'sellingGeneralAdministrative':
4936000000, 'grossProfit': ...
```

There are multiple uses of financial statement data in relation to algorithmic trading. First, it can be used to determine the totality of stocks to trade in. Second, the creation of algorithmic trading signals from non-price data adds additional value.

Summary data retrieval

Summary data is accessible via the `get_summary_data` method:

```
print(aapl.get_summary_data())
```

The output is as follows:

```
{'AAPL': {'previousClose': 137.185, 'regularMarketOpen':
137.35, 'twoHundredDayAverage': 119.50164,
'trailingAnnualDividendYield': 0.0058825673, 'payoutRatio':
0.2177, 'volume24Hr': None, 'regularMarketDayHigh': 137.41,
'navPrice': None, 'averageDailyVolume10Day': 115373562,
'totalAssets': None, 'regularMarketPreviousClose': 137.185,
'fiftyDayAverage': 132.86455, 'trailingAnnualDividendRate':
0.807, 'open': 137.35, 'toCurrency': None,
'averageVolume10days': 115373562, 'expireDate': '-',
'yield': None, 'algorithm': None, 'dividendRate':
0.82, 'exDividendDate': '2021-02-05', 'beta':
1.267876, 'circulatingSupply': None, 'startDate': '-',
'regularMarketDayLow': 135.86, 'priceHint': 2, 'currency':
'USD', 'trailingPE': 37.092484, 'regularMarketVolume':
72317009, 'lastMarket': None, 'maxSupply': None,
'openInterest': None, 'marketCap': 2295940513792,
'volumeAllCurrencies': None, 'strikePrice': None,
'averageVolume': 107768827, 'priceToSalesTrailing12Months':
7.805737, 'dayLow': 135.86, 'ask': 136.7, 'ytdReturn': None,
'askSize': 1100, 'volume': 72317009, 'fiftyTwoWeekHigh':
145.09, 'forwardPE': 29.410751, 'maxAge': 1, 'fromCurrency':
None, 'fiveYearAvgDividendYield': 1.44, 'fiftyTwoWeekLow':
53.1525, 'bid': 136.42, 'tradeable': False, 'dividendYield':
0.0061000003, 'bidSize': 2900, 'dayHigh': 137.41}}
```

Summary data retrieved using this function is a summary of the financial statements function and the real-time data function.

Multiple-tickers retrieval

Multiple-tickers retrieval, also known as **a bulk retrieval**, is far more efficient and faster than single-ticker retrieval since most of the time associated with each download request is spent on establishing and closing the network connection.

Historical data retrieval

Let's retrieve the historical prices for these FX pairs: `EURCHF`, `USDEUR`, and `GBPUSD`:

```
currencies = YahooFinancials(['EURCHF=X', 'USDEUR=X',
                              'GBPUSD=x'])
print(currencies.get_historical_price_data('2020-01-01',
                                           '2020-12-31',
                                           'weekly'))
```

The output is as follows:


```
{'EURCHF=X': {'eventsData': {}, 'firstTradeDate': {'formatted_
date': '2003-01-23', 'date': 1043280000}, 'currency': 'CHF',
'instrumentType': 'CURRENCY', 'timeZone': {'gmtOffset': 0},
'prices': [{'date': 1577836800, 'high': 1.0877000093460083,
'low': 1.0818699598312378, 'open': 1.0872000455856323, 'close':
1.084280014038086, 'volume': 0, 'adjclose': 1.084280014038086,
'formatted_date': '2020-01-01'}, {'date': 1578441600,
'high': 1.083299994468689, 'low': 1.0758999586105347, 'open':
1.080530047416687, 'close': 1.0809999704360962, 'volume':
0, 'adjclose': 1.0809999704360962, 'formatted_date': '2020-
01-08'}, {'date': 1579046400, 'high': 1.0774999856948853,
'low': 1.0729299783706665, 'open': 1.076300024986267,
'close': 1.0744800567626953, 'volume': 0, 'adjclose':
1.0744800567626953, 'formatted_date': '2020-01-15'},
{'date': 1579651200, 'high': 1.0786099433898926, 'low':
1.0664700269699097, 'open': 1.0739500522613525, 'close':
1.068600058555603, 'volume': 0, 'adjclose': 1.068600058555603,
'formatted_date': '2020-01-22'}, {'date': 1580256000, 'high':
1.0736199617385864, 'low': 1.0663000345230103, 'open':
1.0723999738693237, 'close': 1.0683200359344482, 'volume': 0,
'adjclose': 1.068320035 ...
```


We see that the historical data does not contain any data from the financial statements.

The full list of methods supported by the library at the time of writing this book is as follows:

- `get_200day_moving_avg()`
- `get_50day_moving_avg()`
- `get_annual_avg_div_rate()`
- `get_annual_avg_div_yield()`
- `get_beta()`

- `get_book_value()`
- `get_cost_of_revenue()`
- `get_currency()`
- `get_current_change()`
- `get_current_percent_change()`
- `get_current_price()`
- `get_current_volume()`
- `get_daily_dividend_data(start_date, end_date)`
- `get_daily_high()`
- `get_daily_low()`
- `get_dividend_rate()`
- `get_dividend_yield()`
- `get_earnings_per_share()`
- `get_ebit()`
- `get_exdividend_date()`
- `get_financial_stmts(frequency, statement_type, reformat=True)`
- `get_five_yr_avg_div_yield()`
- `get_gross_profit()`
- `get_historical_price_data(start_date, end_date, time_interval)`
- `get_income_before_tax()`
- `get_income_tax_expense()`
- `get_interest_expense()`
- `get_key_statistics_data()`
- `get_market_cap()`
- `get_net_income()`
- `get_net_income_from_continuing_ops()`
- `get_num_shares_outstanding(price_type='current')`
- `get_open_price()`
- `get_operating_income()`

- `get_payout_ratio()`
- `get_pe_ratio()`
- `get_prev_close_price()`
- `get_price_to_sales()`
- `get_research_and_development()`
- `get_stock_earnings_data(reformat=True)`
- `get_stock_exchange()`
- `get_stock_price_data(reformat=True)`
- `get_stock_quote_type_data()`
- `get_summary_data(reformat=True)`
- `get_ten_day_avg_daily_volume()`
- `get_three_month_avg_daily_volume()`
- `get_total_operating_expense()`
- `get_total_revenue()`
- `get_yearly_high()`
- `get_yearly_low()`

We will explore the `pandas_datareader` library in the next section.

Exploring the pandas_datareader Python library

`pandas_datareader` is one of the most advanced libraries for financial data and offers access to multiple data sources.

Some of the data sources supported are as follows:

- Yahoo Finance
- The Federal Reserve Bank of St Louis' FRED
- IEX
- Quandl
- Kenneth French's data library
- World Bank

- OECD
- Eurostat
- Econdb
- Nasdaq Trader symbol definitions

Refer to `https://pandas-datareader.readthedocs.io/en/latest/remote_data.html` for a full list.

Installation is simple:

```
pip install pandas-datareader
```

Let's now set up the basic data retrieval parameters:

```
from pandas_datareader import data
start_date = '2010-01-01'
end_date = '2020-12-31'
```

The general access method for downloading the data is `data.DataReader(ticker, data_source, start_date, end_date)`.

Access to Yahoo Finance

Let's download the last 10 years' worth of Apple stock prices:

```
aapl = data.DataReader('AAPL', 'yahoo', start_date,
                       end_date)
aapl
      High      Low       Open      Close      Volume Adj Close
Date
2010-01-
04 7.660714 7.585000 7.622500 7.643214 493729600.0 6.593426
2010-01-
05 7.699643 7.616071 7.664286 7.656428 601904800.0 6.604825
2010-01-
06 7.686786 7.526786 7.656428 7.534643 552160000.0 6.499768
2010-01-
07 7.571429 7.466072 7.562500 7.520714 477131200.0 6.487752
2010-01-
08 7.571429 7.466429 7.510714 7.570714 447610800.0 6.530883
```

```
...  ...  ...  ...  ...  ...  ...
2020-12
-21 128.309998 123.449997 125.019997 128.229996 121251600.0
128.229996
2020-12-22 134.410004 129.649994 131.610001 131.880005
168904800.0 131.880005
2020-12-23 132.429993 130.779999 132.160004 130.960007
88223700.0 130.960007
2020-12-24 133.460007 131.100006 131.320007 131.970001
54930100.0 131.970001
2020-12-28 137.339996 133.509995 133.990005 136.690002
124182900.0 136.690002
```

The output is virtually identical to the output from the `yahoofinancials` library in the preceding section.

Access to EconDB

The list of available tickers is available at `https://www.econdb.com/main-indicators`.

Let's download the time series of monthly oil production in the US for the last 10 years:

```
oilprodus = data.DataReader('ticker=OILPRODUS', 'econdb',
                            start_date, end_date)
oilprodus
 Reference Area          United States of America
 Energy product                         Crude oil
 Flow breakdown                        Production
Unit of measure  Thousand Barrels per day (kb/d)
TIME_PERIOD
2010-01-01  5390
2010-02-01  5548
2010-03-01  5506
2010-04-01  5383
2010-05-01  5391
     ...     ...
2020-04-01  11990
2020-05-01  10001
```

```
2020-06-01  10436
2020-07-01  10984
2020-08-01  10406
```

Each data source has different output columns.

Access to the Federal Reserve Bank of St Louis' FRED

The list of available data, along with tickers, can be inspected at `https://fred.stlouisfed.org/`.

Let's download the last 10 years of real gross domestic product of the USA:

```
import pandas as pd
pd.set_option('display.max_rows', 2)

gdp = data.DataReader('GDP', 'fred', start_date, end_date)
gdp
```

We restricted the output to just two rows:

```
                  GDP
      DATE
2010-01-01  14721.350
       ...        ...
2020-07-01  21170.252
43 rows × 1 columns
```

Now, let's study 5 years of the 20-year constant maturity yields on U.S. government bonds:

```
gs10 = data.get_data_fred('GS20')
gs10
             GS20
      DATE
2016-01-01  2.49
       ...   ...
2020-11-01  1.40
59 rows × 1 columns
```

The Federal Reserve Bank of St Louis' FRED data is one of the cleanest data sources available, offering complimentary support.

Caching queries

One of the key advantages of the library is its implementation of caching the results of queries, thereby saving bandwidth, speeding up code execution, and preventing the banning of IPs due to the overuse of APIs.

By way of an example, let's download the entire history of Apple stock:

```
import datetime
import requests_cache
session = \
requests_cache.CachedSession(cache_name='cache',
                             backend='sqlite',
                             expire_after = \
                             datetime.timedelta(days=7))

aapl_full_history = \
data.DataReader("AAPL",'yahoo',datetime.datetime(1980,1,1),
                datetime.datetime(2020, 12, 31),
                session=session)
aapl_full_history
       High       Low     Open     Close       Volume Adj Close
Date
1980-12-
12 0.128906 0.128348 0.128348 0.128348 469033600.0 0.101087
...  ...  ...  ...  ...  ...  ...
2020-12-28 137.339996 133.509995 133.990005 136.690002
124182900.0 136.690002
```

Let's now access just one data point:

```
aapl_full_history.loc['2013-01-07']
High          18.903572
                 ...
Adj Close     16.284145
Name: 2013-01-07 00:00:00, Length: 6, dtype: float64
```

Caching can be enabled for all previous examples, too.

Exploring the Quandl data source

Quandl is one of the largest repositories of economic/financial data on the internet. Its data sources can be accessed free of charge. It also offers premium data sources, for which there is a charge.

Installation is straightforward:

```
pip install quandl
```

To access the data, you have to provide an access key (apply for one at `https://quandl.com`):

```
import quandl
quandl.ApiConfig.api_key = 'XXXXXXX'
```

To find a ticker and data source, use `https://www.quandl.com/search`.

Let's now download the `Monthly average consumer prices in metropolitan France - Apples (1 Kg); EUR` data:

```
papple = quandl.get('ODA/PAPPLE_USD')
papple
               Value
Date
1998-01-31  1.735999
    ...          ...
2020-11-30  3.350000
275 rows × 1 columns
```

Let's now download Apple's fundamental data:

```
aapl_fundamental_data = quandl.get_table('ZACKS/FC',
                                          ticker='AAPL')
  m_ticker  ticker  comp_name  comp_name_2  exchange  currency_
code  per_end_date  per_type  per_code  per_fisc_
year  ...  stock_based_compsn_qd  cash_flow_oper_activity_
qd  net_change_prop_plant_equip_qd  comm_stock_div_paid_
qd  pref_stock_div_paid_qd  tot_comm_pref_stock_div_qd  wavg_
shares_out  wavg_shares_out_diluted  eps_basic_net  eps_
diluted_net
None
```

```
0 AAPL AAPL APPLE INC Apple Inc. NSDQ USD
2018-09-30 A None 2018 ... NaN NaN NaN NaN
None NaN 19821.51 20000.44 3.000 2.980
... ... ... ... ... ... ... ... ... ... ... ...
... ... ... ... ... ... ... ... ... ...
4 AAPL AAPL APPLE INC Apple Inc. NSDQ USD 2018-12-31
Q None 2019 ... 1559.0 26690.0 -3355.0 -3568.0 None
-3568.0 18943.28 19093.01 1.055 1.045
5 rows × 249 columns
```

The difference between Yahoo and Quandl data is that the Quandl data is more reliable and more complete.

Exploring the IEX Cloud data source

IEX Cloud is one of the commercial offerings. It offers a plan for individuals at USD 9 per month. It also offers a free plan, with a limit of 50,000 API calls per month.

The installation of the Python library is standard:

```
pip install iexfinance
```

The full library's documentation is available at `https://addisonlynch.github.io/iexfinance/stable/index.html`.

The following code is designed to retrieve all symbols:

```
from iexfinance.refdata import get_symbols
get_symbols(output_format='pandas', token="XXXXXX")
symbol exchange exchangeSuffix exchangeName name date
type iexId region currency isEnabled figi cik lei
0 A NYS UN NEW YORK STOCK EXCHANGE, INC. Agilent
Technologies Inc. 2020-12-29 cs IEX_46574843354B2D52 US
USD True BBG000C2V3D6 0001090872 QUIX8Y7A2WP0XRMW7G29
... ... ... ... ... ... ... ... ... ... ... ...
... ... ...
9360 ZYXI NAS NASDAQ CAPITAL MARKET Zynex Inc 2020-12-29
cs IEX_4E464C4C4A462D52 US USD True BBG000BJBXZ2
0000846475 None
9361 rows × 14 columns
```

The following code is designed to obtain Apple's balance sheet (not available for free accounts):

```
from iexfinance.stocks import Stock
aapl = Stock("aapl", token="XXXXXX")
aapl.get_balance_sheet()
```

The following code is designed to get the current price (not available for free accounts):

```
aapl.get_price()
```

The following code is designed to get the sector performance report (not available for free accounts):

```
from iexfinance.stocks import get_sector_performance
get_sector_performance(output_format='pandas',
                       token =token)
```

The following code is designed to get historical market data for Apple:

```
from iexfinance.stocks import get_historical_data

get_historical_data("AAPL", start="20190101",
                    end="20200101",
                    output_format='pandas', token=token)
close  high  low  open  symbol  volume  id  key  subkey
updated  ...  uLow  uVolume  fOpen  fClose  fHigh  fLow
fVolume  label  change  changePercent
2019-01-02  39.48  39.7125  38.5575  38.7225  AAPL
148158948  HISTORICAL_PRICES  AAPL    1606830572000
...  154.23  37039737  37.8227  38.5626  38.7897  37.6615
148158948  Jan 2, 19  0.045  0.0011
...  ...  ...  ...  ...  ...  ...  ...  ...  ...  ...
...  ...  ...  ...  ...  ...  ...  ...  ...  ...  ...
2019-12-31  73.4125  73.42  72.38  72.4825  AAPL  100990500
HISTORICAL_PRICES  AAPL    1606830572000  ...  289.52
25247625  71.8619  72.7839  72.7914  71.7603  100990500
Dec 31, 19  0.5325  0.0073
252 rows x 25 columns
```

We can see that each data source offers a slightly different set of output columns.

Exploring the MarketStack data source

MarketStack offers an extensive database of real-time, intra-day, and historical market data across major global stock exchanges. It offers free access for up to 1,000 monthly API requests.

While there is no official MarketStack Python library, the REST JSON API provides comfortable access to all its data in Python.

Let's download the adjusted close data for Apple:

```
import requests

params = {
  'access_key': 'XXXXX'
}

api_result = \
requests.get('http://api.marketstack.com/v1/tickers/aapl/eod',
params)

api_response = api_result.json()
print(f"Symbol = {api_response['data']['symbol']}")
for eod in api_response['data']['eod']:
    print(f"{eod['date']}: {eod['adj_close']}")
Symbol = AAPL
2020-12-28T00:00:00+0000: 136.69
2020-12-24T00:00:00+0000: 131.97
2020-12-23T00:00:00+0000: 130.96
2020-12-22T00:00:00+0000: 131.88
2020-12-21T00:00:00+0000: 128.23
2020-12-18T00:00:00+0000: 126.655
2020-12-17T00:00:00+0000: 128.7
2020-12-16T00:00:00+0000: 127.81
2020-12-15T00:00:00+0000: 127.88
2020-12-14T00:00:00+0000: 121.78
2020-12-11T00:00:00+0000: 122.41
2020-12-10T00:00:00+0000: 123.24
2020-12-09T00:00:00+0000: 121.78
```

```
2020-12-08T00:00:00+0000: 124.38
2020-12-07T00:00:00+0000: 123.75
2020-12-04T00:00:00+0000: 122.25
```

Let's now download all tickers on the Nasdaq stock exchange:

```
api_result = \
requests.get('http://api.marketstack.com/v1/exchanges/XNAS/
tickers', params)

api_response = api_result.json()

print(f"Exchange Name = {api_response['data']['name']}")
for ticker in api_response['data']['tickers']:
    print(f"{ticker['name']}: {ticker['symbol']}")
Exchange Name = NASDAQ Stock Exchange
Microsoft Corp: MSFT
Apple Inc: AAPL
Amazoncom Inc: AMZN
Alphabet Inc Class C: GOOG
Alphabet Inc Class A: GOOGL
Facebook Inc: FB
Vodafone Group Public Limited Company: VOD
Intel Corp: INTC
Comcast Corp: CMCSA
PepsiCo Inc: PEP
Adobe Systems Inc: ADBE
Cisco Systems Inc: CSCO
NVIDIA Corp: NVDA
Netflix Inc: NFLX
```

The ticket universe retrieval function is one of the most valuable functions of MarketStack. One of the first steps for all backtesting is determining the universe (that is, the complete list) of the stocks to trade. Then, you restrict yourself to a subset of that list, for example, by trading only stocks with certain trends, or certain volumes.

Summary

In this chapter, we have outlined different ways to obtain financial and economic data in Python. In practice, you usually use multiple data sources at the same time. We explored the `yahoofinancials` Python library and saw single- and multiple-tickers retrievals. We then explored the `pandas_datareader` Python library to access Yahoo Finance, EconDB, and Fed's Fred data and cache queries. We then explored the Quandl, IEX Cloud and MarketStack data sources.

In the next chapter, we introduce the backtesting library, Zipline, as well as the trading portfolio performance and risk analysis library, PyFolio.

8
Introduction to Zipline and PyFolio

In this chapter, you will learn about the Python libraries known as Zipline and PyFolio, which abstract away the complexities of the backtesting and performance/risk analysis aspects of algorithmic trading strategies. They allow you to completely focus on the trading logic.

For this, we are going to cover the following main topics:

- Introduction to Zipline and PyFolio
- Installing Zipline and PyFolio
- Importing market data into a Zipline/PyFolio backtesting system
- Structuring Zipline/PyFolio backtesting modules
- Reviewing the key Zipline API reference
- Running Zipline backtesting from the command line
- Introduction to the key risk management figures provided by PyFolio

Technical requirements

The Python code used in this chapter is available in the `Chapter08/risk_management.ipynb` notebook in the book's code repository.

Introduction to Zipline and PyFolio

Backtesting is a computational method of assessing how well a trading strategy would have done if it had been applied to historical data. Ideally, this historical data should come from a period of time where there were similar market conditions, such as it having similar volatility to the present and the future.

Backtesting should include all relevant factors, such as slippage and trading costs.

Zipline is one of the most advanced open source Python libraries for algorithmic trading backtesting engines. Its source code can be found at `https://github.com/quantopian/zipline`. Zipline is a backtesting library ideal for daily trading (you can also backtest weekly, monthly, and so on). It is less suitable for backtesting high-frequency trading strategies.

PyFolio is an open source Python performance and risk analysis library consisting of financial portfolios that's closely integrated with Zipline. You can find its documentation at `https://github.com/quantopian/pyfolio`.

Using these two libraries to backtest your trading strategy saves you an enormous amount of time.

The objective of this chapter is to describe the key functionality of these libraries and to build your intuition. You are encouraged to debug the code in PyCharm or any other Python IDE and study the contents of each result's variables to make full use of the provided information. Once you become familiar with the contents of each resultant object, briefly study the source code of the libraries to see their full functionality.

Installing Zipline and PyFolio

We recommend setting up the development environment as described in *Appendix A*. Nevertheless, the detailed instructions are given in the following sections.

Installing Zipline

For performance reasons, Zipline is closely dependent on a particular version of Python and its related libraries. Therefore, the best way to install it is to create a `conda` virtual environment and install Zipline there. We recommend using Anaconda Python for this.

Let's create a virtual environment called `zipline_env` with Python 3.6 and install the `zipline` package:

```
conda create -n zipline_env python=3.6
conda activate zipline_env
conda install -c conda-forge zipline
```

We will now install PyFolio.

Installing PyFolio

You can install the `pyfolio` package via `pip`:

```
pip install pyfolio
```

As we can see, installing PyFolio is also an easy task.

Importing market data into a Zipline/PyFolio backtesting system

Backtesting depends on us having an extensive market data database.

Zipline introduces two market data-specific terms – bundle and ingest:

- A **bundle** is an interface for incrementally importing market data into Zipline's proprietary database from a custom source.
- An **ingest** is the actual process of incrementally importing the custom source market data into Zipline's proprietary database; the data ingest is not automatically updated. Each time you need fresh data, you must re-ingest the bundle.

By default, Zipline supports these bundles:

- Historical Quandl bundle (complimentary daily data for US equities up to 2018)
- `.csv` files bundle

We will now learn how to import these two bundles in more detail.

Importing data from the historical Quandl bundle

First, in the activated `zipline_env` environment, set the `QUANDL_API_KEY` environment variable to your free (or paid) Quandl API key. Then, ingest the `quandl` data.

For Windows, use the following code:

```
SET QUANDL_API_KEY=XXXXXXXX
zipline ingest -b quandl
```

For Mac/Linux, use the following code:

```
export QUANDL_API_KEY=XXXXXXXX
zipline ingest -b quandl
```

> **Note**
> Quandl stopped updating the complimentary bundle in 2018 but is still more than useful for the first few algorithmic trading steps.

It's best to set `QUANDL_API_KEY` in Windows' System Properties (press the Windows icon and type `Environment Variables`):

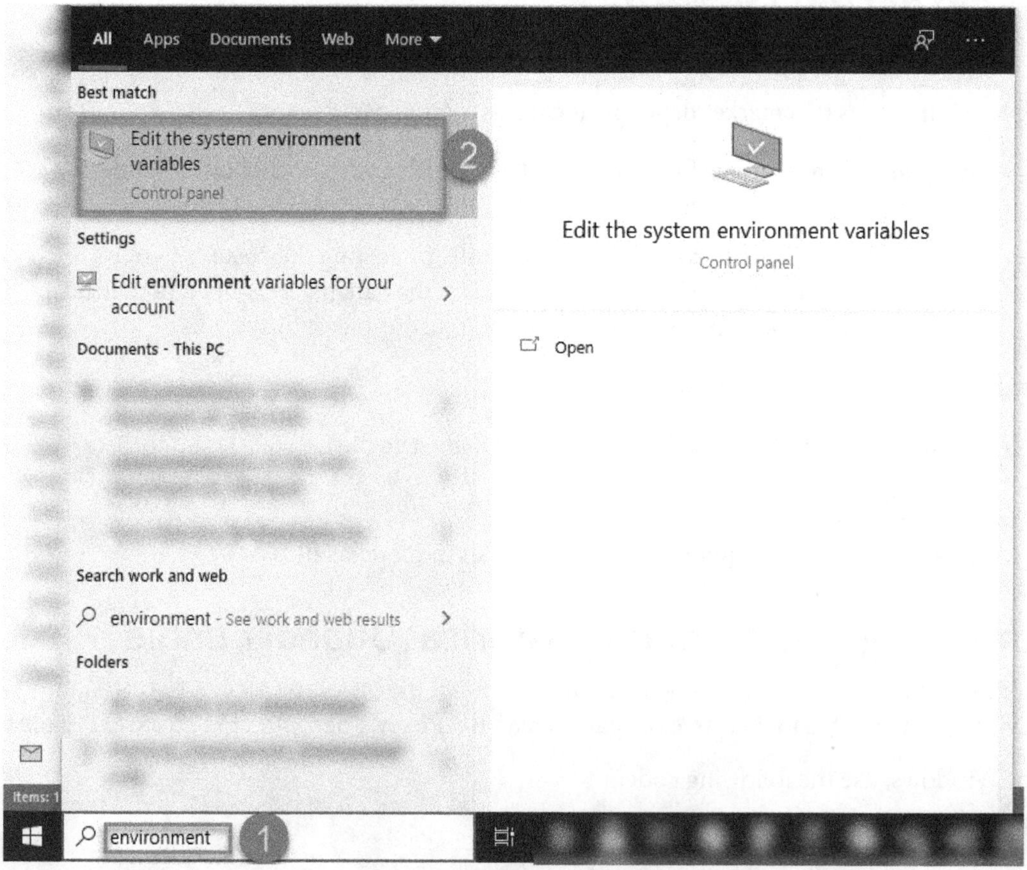

Figure 8.1 – Locating the Edit the system environment variables dialog on Windows

Then, choose **Edit the system environment variables.**

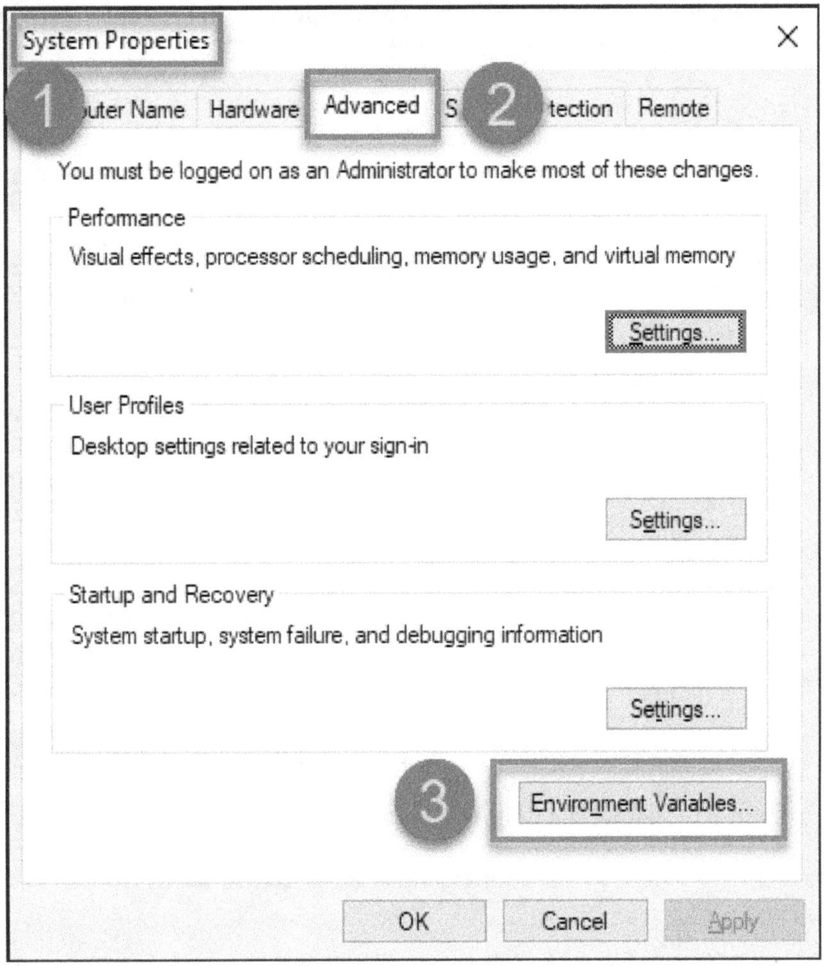

Figure 8.2 – The location of the Environment Variables… dialog in System Properties on Windows

Then, specify the variable in the **Environment Variables...** dialog.

On Mac/Linux, add the following command to `~/.bash_profile` for user-based operations or `~/.bashrc` for non-login interactive shells:

```
export QUANDL_API_KEY=xxxx
```

Now, let's learn how to import data from the CSV files bundle.

Importing data from the CSV files bundle

The default CSV bundle requires the CSV file to be in **open, high, low, close, volume** (**OHLCV**) format with dates, dividends, and splits:

```
date,open,high,low,close,volume,dividend,split
```

This book's GitHub repository contains one sample input CSV file. Its top few lines are as follows:

```
date,open,high,low,close,volume,dividend,split
2015-05-
15,18251.9707,18272.7207,18215.07031,18272.56055,108220000,0,0
2015-05-
18,18267.25,18325.53906,18244.25977,18298.88086,79080000,0,0
2015-05-
19,18300.48047,18351.35938,18261.34961,18312.39063,87200000,0,0
2015-05-
20,18315.06055,18350.13086,18272.56055,18285.40039,80190000,0,0
2015-05-
21,18285.86914,18314.89063,18249.90039,18285.74023,84270000,0,0
2015-05-
22,18286.86914,18286.86914,18217.14063,18232.01953,78890000,0,0
2015-05-
26,18229.75,18229.75,17990.01953,18041.53906,109440000,0,0
```

To use the custom CSV files bundle, follow these steps:

1. Create a directory for CSV files, for example, `C:\MarketData`, with a subdirectory called `Daily`.
2. Copy the CSV files to the created directory (for example, `C:\MarketData\Daily`).
3. Edit the `.py` file extension in the `C:\Users\<username>\.zipline\extension.py` directory on Windows or `~/.zipline/extension.py` on Mac/Linux, as shown:

```
import pandas as pd

from zipline.data.bundles import register
from zipline.data.bundles.csvdir import csvdir_equities

register(
    'packt-csvdir-bundle',
```

```
        csvdir_equities(
            ['daily'],
            'c:/MarketData/',
        ),
        calendar_name='NYSE',
        start_session=pd.Timestamp('2015-5-15', tz='utc'),
        end_session=pd.Timestamp('2020-05-14', tz='utc')
    )
```

Notice that we associate the market data with a trading calendar. In this case, we're using `NYSE`, which corresponds to the US equities.

4. Ingest the bundle, as follows:

```
zipline ingest -b packt-csvdir-bundle
```

The output is as follows:

Figure 8.3 – Output of the zipline ingest for packt-csvdir-bundle

This has created one asset with the `A` ticker.

Importing data from custom bundles

The historical Quandl bundle is most suitable for learning how to design and backtest an algorithmic strategy. The CSV files bundle is most suitable for importing prices of assets with no public prices. However, for other purposes, you should purchase a market data subscription.

Importing data from Quandl's EOD US Stock Prices data

Quandl offers a subscription service for the End of Day US Stock Prices database (`https://www.quandl.com/data/EOD-End-of-Day-US-Stock-Prices`) at 49 USD per month, with discounts for quarterly or annual payments.

The advantages of this service, compared to others, are as follows:

- Quandl is deeply integrated into Zipline and you can download the history of all the stocks using one command.
- There is no hard limit in terms of the number of API calls you can make per month, unlike other providers.

Installing the custom bundle is straightforward:

1. Find the location of the `bundles` directory using the following command:

```
python -c "import zipline.data.bundles as bdl;
print(bdl.__path__)"
```

   This results in the following output on my computer:

```
['d:\\Anaconda3\\envs\\zipline_env\\lib\\site-packages\\
zipline\\data\\bundles']
```

2. Copy the `quandl_eod.py` file from this book's GitHub repository into that directory. The file is a slight modification of the code from Zipline's GitHub.
3. In the same directory, modify the `__init__.py` file (add this line there):

```
from . import quandl_eod  # noqa
```

An example of the full `__init__.py` file is as follows:

```
# These imports are necessary to force module-scope register
calls to happen.
from . import quandl  # noqa
from . import csvdir  # noqa
from . import quandl_eod  # noqa

from .core import (
    UnknownBundle,
    bundles,
    clean,
    from_bundle_ingest_dirname,
    ingest,
    ingestions_for_bundle,
    load,
    register,
    to_bundle_ingest_dirname,
    unregister,
)


__all__ = [
```

```
    'UnknownBundle',
    'bundles',
    'clean',
    'from_bundle_ingest_dirname',
    'ingest',
    'ingestions_for_bundle',
    'load',
    'register',
    'to_bundle_ingest_dirname',
    'unregister',
]
```

Once you have set this up, ensure you have set the `QUANDL_API_KEY` environment variable to your API key and run the `ingest` command:

```
zipline ingest -b quandl_eod
```

The output is as follows:

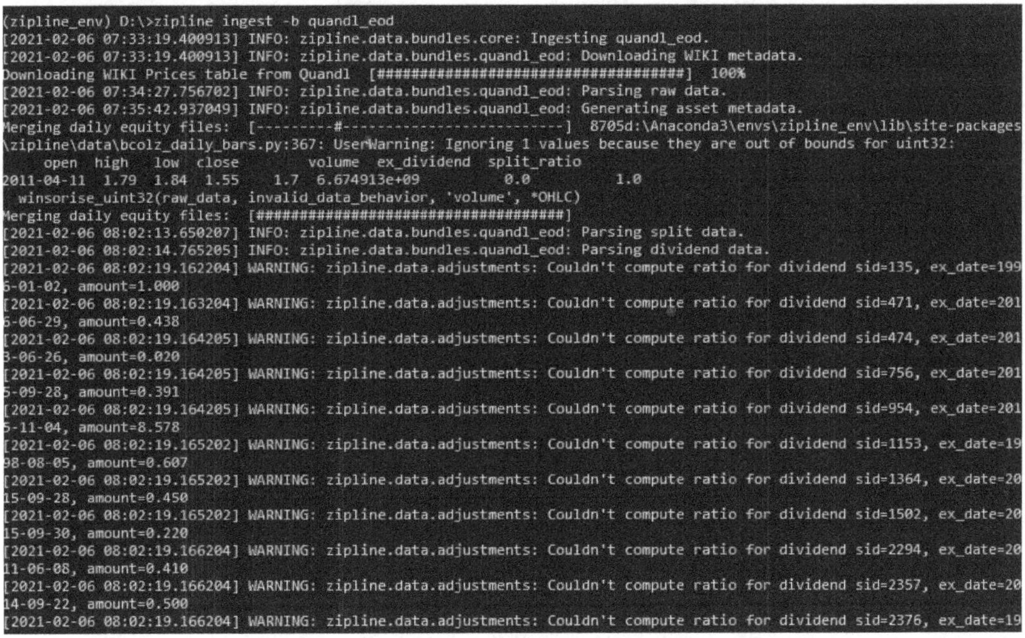

Figure 8.4 – Output of ingesting the quandl_eod bundle

The actual source code of `quandl_eod.py` is self-explanatory. The `quandl_eod_bundle` function, which is annotated with `@bundles.register("quandl_eod")`, defines the download process:

```
@bundles.register("quandl_eod")
def quandl_eod_bundle(environ,
                      asset_db_writer,
                      minute_bar_writer,
                      daily_bar_writer,
                      adjustment_writer,
                      calendar,
                      start_session,
                      end_session,
                      cache,
                      show_progress,
                      output_dir):
    """
    quandl_bundle builds a daily dataset using Quandl's WIKI
Prices dataset.

    For more information on Quandl's API and how to obtain an
API key,
    please visit https://docs.quandl.com/docs#section-
authentication
    """
    api_key = environ.get("QUANDL_API_KEY")
    if api_key is None:
        raise ValueError(
            "Please set your QUANDL_API_KEY environment
variable and retry."
        )

    raw_data = fetch_data_table(
        api_key, show_progress,
        environ.get("QUANDL_DOWNLOAD_ATTEMPTS", 5)
    )
    asset_metadata = \
    gen_asset_metadata(raw_data[["symbol", "date"]],
```

```
                          show_progress)
    asset_db_writer.write(asset_metadata)

    symbol_map = asset_metadata.symbol
    sessions = calendar.sessions_in_range(start_session,
                                          end_session)

    raw_data.set_index(["date", "symbol"], inplace=True)
    daily_bar_writer.write(
        parse_pricing_and_vol(raw_data, sessions,
                              symbol_map),
        show_progress=show_progress,
    )

    raw_data.reset_index(inplace=True)
    raw_data["symbol"] = \
    raw_data["symbol"].astype("category")
    raw_data["sid"] = raw_data.symbol.cat.codes
    adjustment_writer.write(
        splits=parse_splits(
            raw_data[["sid", "date", "split_ratio"]].loc[raw_
data.split_ratio != 1],
            show_progress=show_progress,
        ),
        dividends=parse_dividends(
            raw_data[["sid", "date", "ex_dividend"]].loc[raw_
data.ex_dividend != 0],
            show_progress=show_progress,
        ),
    )
```

The steps that are involved in this process are as follows:

1. Download all the EOD data.
2. Generate the metadata.
3. Apply the trading calendar.
4. Apply the corporate events.

While Quandl's commercial data source is deeply integrated with Zipline, there are alternative data sources.

Importing data from Yahoo Finance and IEX paid data

The project at `https://github.com/hhatefi/zipline_bundles` provides a Zipline bundle for Yahoo Finance and IEX. The package supports Zipline imports from a Yahoo Finance `.csv` file, Yahoo Finance directly, and from IEX. This book will only focus on directly importing from Yahoo Finance and IEX.

While the package does allow automatic installation, I do not recommend it since it requires an empty `extension.py` file in the `C:\Users\<username>\.zipline\extension.py` directory on Windows or `~/.zipline/extension.py` on Mac/Linux.

The installation steps are as follows:

1. Download the repository from `https://github.com/hhatefi/zipline_bundles`.
2. Merge the repository's `\zipline_bundles-master\lib\extension.py` file with `C:\Users\<username>\.zipline\extension.py` on Windows or `~/.zipline/extension.py` on Mac/Linux. If the latter file does not exist, just copy and paste the file.
3. Edit the start and end dates in the following code:

```
register('yahoo_direct', # bundle's name
         direct_ingester('YAHOO',
                         every_min_bar=False,
                         symbol_list_env='YAHOO_SYM_LST',
# the environment variable holding the comma separated
list of assert names
                         downloader=yahoo.get_
downloader(start_date='2010-01-01',

end_date='2020-01-01'
                         ),
         ),
         calendar_name='NYSE',
)
```

Do the same in the following code:

```
register('iex', # bundle's name
         direct_ingester('IEX Cloud',
                         every_min_bar=False,
                         symbol_list_env='IEX_SYM_LST',
# the environemnt variable holding the comma separated
list of assert names
                         downloader=iex.get_
downloader(start_date='2020-01-01',

end_date='2020-01-05'
                         ),
                         filter_cb=lambda df: df[[cal.
is_session(dt) for dt in df.index]]
         ),
         calendar_name='NYSE',
)
```

The full file should look as follows:

```
#!/usr/bin/env python
# -*- coding: utf-8 -*-

from pathlib import Path
from zipline.data.bundles import register
from zipline.data.bundles.ingester import csv_ingester
# ingester.py need to be placed in zipline.data.bundles

_DEFAULT_PATH = str(Path.home()/'.zipline/csv/yahoo')

register(
    'yahoo_csv',
    csv_ingester('YAHOO',
                 every_min_bar=False,
                 # the price is daily
                 csvdir_env='YAHOO_CSVDIR',
                 csvdir=_DEFAULT_PATH,
                 index_column='Date',
```

```
                   column_mapper={'Open': 'open',
                                  'High': 'high',
                                  'Low': 'low',
                                  'Close': 'close',
                                  'Volume': 'volume',
                                  'Adj Close': 'price',
                   },
    ),
    calendar_name='NYSE',
)

from zipline.data.bundles.ingester import direct_ingester

from zipline.data.bundles import yahoo
register('yahoo_direct', # bundle's name
         direct_ingester('YAHOO',
                         every_min_bar=False,
                         symbol_list_env='YAHOO_SYM_LST',
# the environemnt variable holding the comma separated
list of assert names
                         downloader=yahoo.get_
downloader(start_date='2010-01-01',

end_date='2020-01-01'
                         ),
         ),
         calendar_name='NYSE',
)

from zipline.data.bundles import iex
import trading_calendars as tc

cal=tc.get_calendar('NYSE')
register('iex', # bundle's name
         direct_ingester('IEX Cloud',
                         every_min_bar=False,
```

```
                                symbol_list_env='IEX_SYM_LST', #
the environemnt variable holding the comma separated list
of assert names
                                downloader=iex.get_
downloader(start_date='2020-01-01',

end_date='2020-01-05'
                                ),
                                filter_cb=lambda df: df[[cal.
is_session(dt) for dt in df.index]]
                ),
                calendar_name='NYSE',
)
```

4. Find the location of the `bundles` directory using the following command:

```
python -c "import zipline.data.bundles as bdl;
print(bdl.__path__)"
```

This results in the following output on my computer:

```
['d:\\Anaconda3\\envs\\zipline_env\\lib\\site-packages\\
zipline\\data\\bundles']
```

5. Copy the `Copy \zipline_bundles-master\lib\iex.py`, `\zipline_bundles-master\lib\ingester.py`, and `\zipline_bundles-master\lib\yahoo.py` repository files into your Zipline `bundles` directory; for example, `d:\\Anaconda3\\envs\\zipline_env\\lib\\site-packages\\zipline\\data\\bundles\`.

6. Set the tickers of interest as environmental variables. For example, for Windows, use the following code:

```
    set YAHOO_SYM_LST=GOOG,AAPL,GE,MSFT
    set IEX_SYM_LST=GOOG,AAPL,GE,MSFT
```

For Mac/Linux, use the following code:

```
    export YAHOO_SYM_LST=GOOG,AAPL,GE,MSFT
    export IEX_SYM_LST=GOOG,AAPL,GE,MSFT
```

7. Set an IEX token (it starts with `sk_`), if available, like so on Windows:

```
set IEX_TOKEN=xxx
```

For Mac/Linux, do the following:

```
export IEX_TOKEN=xxx
```

8. Ingest the data:

```
zipline ingest -b yahoo_direct
zipline ingest -b iex
```

This results in the following output in terms of the `yahoo_direct` bundle:

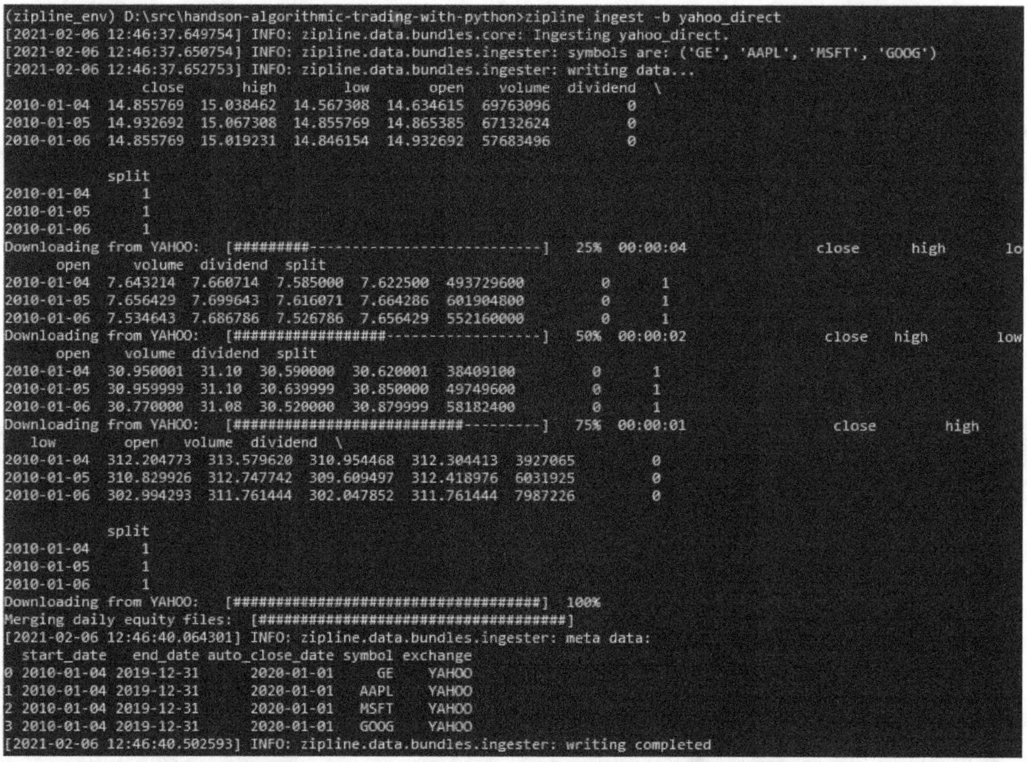

```
(zipline_env) D:\src\handson-algorithmic-trading-with-python>zipline ingest -b yahoo_direct
[2021-02-06 12:46:37.649754] INFO: zipline.data.bundles.core: Ingesting yahoo_direct.
[2021-02-06 12:46:37.650754] INFO: zipline.data.bundles.ingester: symbols are: ('GE', 'AAPL', 'MSFT', 'GOOG')
[2021-02-06 12:46:37.652753] INFO: zipline.data.bundles.ingester: writing data...
                close       high        low       open    volume  dividend  \
2010-01-04  14.855769  15.038462  14.567308  14.634615  69763096         0
2010-01-05  14.932692  15.067308  14.855769  14.865385  67132624         0
2010-01-06  14.855769  15.019231  14.846154  14.932692  57683496         0

           split
2010-01-04     1
2010-01-05     1
2010-01-06     1
Downloading from YAHOO:   [#########---------------------------]   25%  00:00:04                close       high        lo
     open     volume  dividend  split
2010-01-04  7.643214  7.660714  7.585000  7.622500  493729600         0      1
2010-01-05  7.656429  7.699643  7.616071  7.664286  601904800         0      1
2010-01-06  7.534643  7.686786  7.526786  7.656429  552160000         0      1
Downloading from YAHOO:   [##################------------------]   50%  00:00:02                close    high        low
     open     volume  dividend  split
2010-01-04  30.950001  31.10  30.590000  30.620001  38409100         0      1
2010-01-05  30.959999  31.10  30.639999  30.850000  49749600         0      1
2010-01-06  30.770000  31.08  30.520000  30.879999  58182400         0      1
Downloading from YAHOO:   [###########################---------]   75%  00:00:01                close        high
   low         open    volume  dividend  \
2010-01-04  312.204773  313.579620  310.954468  312.304413  3927065         0
2010-01-05  310.829926  312.747742  309.609497  312.418976  6031925         0
2010-01-06  302.994293  311.761444  302.047852  311.761444  7987226         0

           split
2010-01-04     1
2010-01-05     1
2010-01-06     1
Downloading from YAHOO:   [####################################]  100%
Merging daily equity files:  [####################################]
[2021-02-06 12:46:40.064301] INFO: zipline.data.bundles.ingester: meta data:
  start_date   end_date auto_close_date symbol exchange
0 2010-01-04 2019-12-31      2020-01-01     GE    YAHOO
1 2010-01-04 2019-12-31      2020-01-01   AAPL    YAHOO
2 2010-01-04 2019-12-31      2020-01-01   MSFT    YAHOO
3 2010-01-04 2019-12-31      2020-01-01   GOOG    YAHOO
[2021-02-06 12:46:40.502593] INFO: zipline.data.bundles.ingester: writing completed
```

Figure 8.5 – Output of ingesting the yahoo_direct bundle

This also results in the following output, which is for the `iex` bundle:

```
(zipline_env) D:\src\handson-algorithmic-trading-with-python>set IEX_SYM_LST=GOOG,AAPL,GE,MSFT

(zipline_env) D:\src\handson-algorithmic-trading-with-python>zipline ingest -b iex
[2021-02-06 13:06:15.243864] INFO: zipline.data.bundles.core: Ingesting iex.
[2021-02-06 13:06:15.243864] INFO: zipline.data.bundles.ingester: symbols are: ('GOOG', 'AAPL', 'MSFT', 'GE')
[2021-02-06 13:06:15.246865] INFO: zipline.data.bundles.ingester: writing data...
Downloading from IEX Cloud:   [####################################]  100%
Merging daily equity files:  [####################################]
[2021-02-06 13:06:20.014374] INFO: zipline.data.bundles.ingester: meta data:
  start_date   end_date auto_close_date symbol    exchange
0 2020-01-02 2021-02-05      2021-02-06   GOOG  IEX Cloud
1 2020-01-02 2021-02-05      2021-02-06   AAPL  IEX Cloud
2 2020-01-02 2021-02-05      2021-02-06   MSFT  IEX Cloud
3 2020-01-02 2021-02-05      2021-02-06     GE  IEX Cloud
[2021-02-06 13:06:20.509529] INFO: zipline.data.bundles.ingester: writing completed
```

Figure 8.6 – Output of ingesting the iex bundle

Integrating with other data sources, such as a local MySQL database, is similar to the code in `https://github.com/hhatefi/zipline_bundles`. Some such bundles are available on `github.com`.

Structuring Zipline/PyFolio backtesting modules

Typical Zipline backtesting code defines three functions:

- `initialize`: This method is called before any simulated trading happens; it's used to enrich the context object with the definition of tickers and other key trading information. It also enables commission and slippage considerations.
- `handle_data`: This method downloads the market data, calculates the trading signals, and places the trades. This is where you put the actual trading logic on entry/exit positions.
- `analyze`: This method is called to perform trading analytics. In our code, we will use pyfolio's standard analytics. Notice that the `pf.utils.extract_rets_pos_txn_from_zipline(perf)` function returns any returns, positions, and transactions for custom analytics.

Finally, the code defines the **start date** and the **end date** and performs backtesting by calling the `run_algorithm` method. This method returns a comprehensive summary of all the trades to be persisted to a file, which can be analyzed later.

There are a few typical patterns when it comes to Zipline's code, depending on the use case.

Trading happens every day

Let's refer to the handle_data method directly from the run_algorithm method:

```
from zipline import run_algorithm
from zipline.api import order_target_percent, symbol
from datetime import datetime
import pytz
import matplotlib.pyplot as plt
import pandas as pd
import pyfolio as pf
from random import random

def initialize(context):
    pass

def handle_data(context, data):
    pass

def analyze(context, perf):
    returns, positions, transactions = \
    pf.utils.extract_rets_pos_txn_from_zipline(perf)
    pf.create_returns_tear_sheet(returns,
                                 benchmark_rets = None)

start_date = pd.to_datetime('1996-1-1', utc=True)
end_date = pd.to_datetime('2020-12-31', utc=True)

results = run_algorithm(start = start_date, end = end_date,
                        initialize = initialize,
                        analyze = analyze,
                        handle_data = handle_data,
                        capital_base = 10000,
                        data_frequency = 'daily',
                        bundle ='quandl')
```

The handle_data method will be called for every single day between start_date and end_date.

Trading happens on a custom schedule

We omit the references to the `handle_data` method in the `run_algorithm` method. Instead, we set the scheduler in the `initialize` method:

```
from zipline import run_algorithm
from zipline.api import order_target_percent, symbol, set_
commission, schedule_function, date_rules, time_rules from
datetime import datetime
import pytz
import matplotlib.pyplot as plt
import pandas as pd
import pyfolio as pf
from random import random

def initialize(context):
    # definition of the stocks and the trading parameters, e.g.
commission
    schedule_function(handle_data, date_rules.month_end(),
                      time_rules.market_open(hours=1))

def handle_data(context, data):
    pass

def analyze(context, perf):
    returns, positions, transactions = \
    pf.utils.extract_rets_pos_txn_from_zipline(perf)
    pf.create_returns_tear_sheet(returns,
                                 benchmark_rets = None)

start_date = pd.to_datetime('1996-1-1', utc=True)
end_date = pd.to_datetime('2020-12-31', utc=True)

results = run_algorithm(start = start_date, end = end_date,
                        initialize = initialize,
                        analyze = analyze,
                        capital_base = 10000,
                        data_frequency = 'daily',
                        bundle ='quandl')
```

The `handle_data` method will be called for every single `month_end` with the prices 1 hour after the market opens.

We can specify various date rules, as shown here:

date_rules	Description
date_rules.every_day()	Trading is triggered every day.
date_rules.month_end(days_offset=0)	Trading is triggered a given number of days before each month ends.
date_rules.month_start(days_offset=0)	Trading is triggered a given number of days after each month starts.
date_rules.week_end(days_offset=0)	Trading is triggered a given number of days before each week ends.
date_rules.week_start(days_offset=0)	Trading is triggered a given number of days after each week starts.
Custom	It is also trivial to write your own customized date rules.

Figure 8.7 – Table containing various date rules

Similarly, we can specify time rules, as shown here:

time_rules	Description
time_rules.every_minute()	No special time has been chosen.
time_rules.market_close(offset=None, hours=None, minutes=None)	The rule is triggered at a fixed offset before the market closes.
time_rules.market_open(offset=None, hours=None, minutes=None)	The rule is triggered at a fixed offset after the market opens.
Custom	It is also trivial to write your own customized time rules.

Figure 8.8 – Table containing various time rules

We will now learn how to review the key Zipline API reference.

Reviewing the key Zipline API reference

In this section, we will outline the key features from `https://www.zipline.io/appendix.html`.

For backtesting, the most important features are order types, commission models, and slippage models. Let's look at them in more detail.

Types of orders

Zipline supports these types of orders:

Order Type	Description
zipline.api.order(self, asset, amount, limit_price=None, stop_price=None, style=None)	Place an order for a fixed number of shares.
zipline.api.order_value(self, asset, value, limit_price=None, stop_price=None, style=None)	Place an order for a fixed amount of money.
zipline.api.order_percent(self, asset, percent, limit_price=None, stop_price=None, style=None)	Place an order for the specified asset to be owned in a given percentage of the current portfolio's value.
zipline.api.order_target(self, asset, target, limit_price=None, stop_price=None, style=None)	Place an order to adjust a position to the target number of shares.
zipline.api.order_target_value(self, asset, target, limit_price=None, stop_price=None, style=None)	Place an order to adjust a position to the target value of shares.
zipline.api.order_target_percent(self, asset, target, limit_price=None, stop_price=None, style=None)	Place an order to adjust a position to the target percentage of the portfolio's value.

Figure 8.9 – Supported order types

The order-placing logic is typically placed in the `handle_data` method.

The following is an example:

```
def handle_data(context, data):
    price_hist = data.history(context.stock, "close",
                              context.rolling_window, "1d")
    order_target_percent(context.stock, 1.0 if price_hist[-1] >
price_hist.mean() else 0.0)
```

This example places an order so that we own 100% of the stock if the last daily price is above the average of the close prices.

Commission models

Commission is the fee that's charged by a brokerage for selling or buying stocks.

Zipline supports various types of commissions, as shown here:

Commission Type	Description
zipline.finance.commission.PerShare(cost=0.001, min_trade_cost=0.0)	Calculates a transaction commission based on the per share cost.
zipline.finance.commission.PerTrade(cost=0.0)	Calculates a transaction commission based on the per trade cost.
zipline.finance.commission.PerDollar(cost=0.0015)	Calculates a transaction commission based on the per dollar that's transacted.

Figure 8.10 – Supported commission types

This logic is typically placed into the `initialize` method.

The following is an example:

```
def initialize(context):
    context.stock = symbol('AAPL')
    context.rolling_window = 90
    set_commission(PerTrade(cost=5))
```

In this example, we have defined a commission of 5 USD per trade.

Slippage models

Slippage is defined as the difference between the expected price and the executed price.

Zipline offers these slippage models:

Slippage Model	Description
zipline.finance.slippage.FixedSlippage(spread=0.0)	Model assuming a fixed-size spread for all assets.
zipline.finance.slippage.VolumeShareSlippage(volume_limit=0.025, price_impact=0.1)	Model assuming a quadratic function for the percentage of the historical volume.

Figure 8.11 – Supported slippage models

The slippage model should be placed in the `initialize` method.

The following is an example:

```
def initialize(context):
    context.stock = symbol('AAPL')
    context.rolling_window = 90
    set_commission(PerTrade(cost=5))
    set_slippage(VolumeShareSlippage(volume_limit=0.025,
                                      price_impact=0.05))
```

In this example, we have chosen `VolumeShareSlippage` with a limit of `0.025` and a price impact of `0.05`.

Running Zipline backtesting from the command line

For large backtesting jobs, it's preferred to run backtesting from the command line.

The following command runs the backtesting strategy defined in the `job.py` Python script and saves the resulting DataFrame in the `job_results.pickle` pickle file:

```
zipline run -f job.py --start 2016-1-1 --end 2021-1-1 -o job_
results.pickle --no-benchmark
```

For example, you can set up a batch consisting of tens of Zipline command-line jobs to run overnight, with each storing the results in a pickle file for later analysis.

It's a good practice to keep a journal and library of past backtesting pickle files for easy reference.

Introduction to risk management with PyFolio

Having a risk management system is a fundamental part of having a successful algorithmic trading system.

Various risks are involved in algorithmic trading:

- **Market risk**: While all strategies lose money at some point in their life cycle, quantifying risk measures and ensuring there are risk management systems in place can mitigate strategy losses. In some cases, bad risk management can increase trading losses to an extreme and even shut down successful trading firms completely.
- **Regulatory risk**: This is the risk that stems from either accidentally or intentionally violating regulations. It is designed to enforce smooth and fair market functionality. Some well-known examples include *spoofing*, *quote stuffing*, and *banging the close*.
- **Software implementation risk**: Software development is a complex process and sophisticated algorithmic trading strategy systems are especially complex. Even seemingly minor software bugs can lead to malfunctioning algorithmic trading strategies and yield catastrophic outcomes.
- **Operational risk**: This risk comes from deploying and operating these algorithmic trading systems. Operations/trading personnel mistakes can also lead to disastrous outcomes. Perhaps the most well-known error in this category is the fat-finger error, which refers to accidentally sending huge orders and/or at unintentional prices.

The PyFolio library provides extensive market performance and risk reporting functionality.

A typical PyFolio report looks as follows:

Start date	2000-01-03
End date	2017-12-29
Total months	215

	Backtest
Annual return	24.9%
Cumulative returns	5324.2%
Annual volatility	29.9%
Sharpe ratio	0.89
Calmar ratio	0.42
Stability	0.92
Max drawdown	-59.4%
Omega ratio	1.21
Sortino ratio	1.37
Skew	0.41
Kurtosis	7.82
Tail ratio	1.16
Daily value at risk	-3.7%

Worst drawdown periods	Net drawdown in %	Peak date	Valley date	Recovery date	Duration
0	59.37	2000-03-22	2003-03-24	2004-10-14	1192
1	31.34	2015-02-23	2016-09-09	2017-05-09	577
2	25.44	2005-02-16	2005-07-18	2005-10-20	177
3	24.14	2006-01-13	2006-02-09	2006-10-23	202
4	21.45	2012-04-09	2013-07-19	2013-12-03	432

Figure 8.12 – PyFolio's standard output showing the backtesting summary and key risk statistics

The following text aims to explain the key statistics in this report; that is, **Annual volatility**, **Sharpe ratio**, and **drawdown**.

For the purpose of this chapter, let's generate trades and returns from a hypothetical trading strategy.

The following code block generates hypothetical PnLs for a trading strategy with a slight positive bias and hypothetical positions with no bias:

```
dates = pd.date_range('1992-01-01', '2012-10-22')
np.random.seed(1)
pnls = np.random.randint(-990, 1000, size=len(dates))
# slight positive bias
pnls = pnls.cumsum()
positions = np.random.randint(-1, 2, size=len(dates))
positions = positions.cumsum()
strategy_performance = \
pd.DataFrame(index=dates,
             data={'PnL': pnls, 'Position': positions})

strategy_performance
                PnL    Position
1992-01-01       71           0
1992-01-02     -684           0
1992-01-03      258           1
    ...         ...         ...
2012-10-21    32100         -27
2012-10-22    32388         -26
7601 rows × 2 columns
```

Let's review how the PnL varies over the course of 20 years:

```
strategy_performance['PnL'].plot(figsize=(12,6), color='black',
legend='PnL')
```

Here's the output:

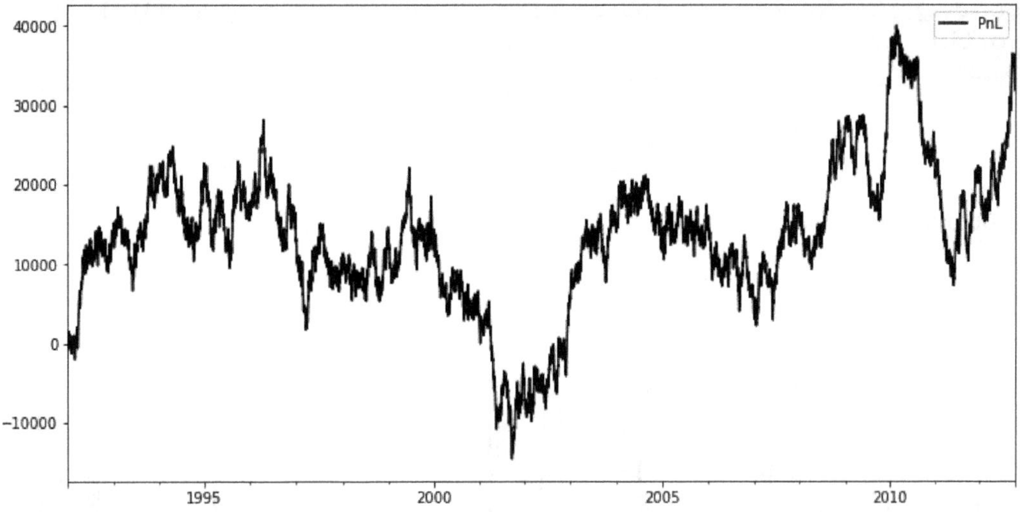

Figure 8.13 – Plot showing the synthetically generated PnLs with a slight positive bias

This plot confirms that the slight positive bias causes the strategy to be profitable in the long run.

Now, let's explore some risk metrics of this hypothetical strategy's performance.

Market volatility, PnL variance, and PnL standard deviation

Market volatility is defined as the standard deviation of prices. Generally, during more volatile market conditions, trading strategy PnLs also undergo increased swings in magnitude. This is because the same positions are susceptible to larger price moves, which means that the PnL moves.

PnL variance is used to measure the magnitude of volatility in the strategy's performance/returns.

The code to compute the PnL's standard deviation is identical to the code that's used to compute the standard deviation of prices (market volatility).

Let's compute the PnL standard deviation over a rolling 20-day period:

```
strategy_performance['PnLStdev'] = strategy_performance['PnL'].
rolling(20).std().fillna(method='backfill')
strategy_performance['PnLStdev'].plot(figsize=(12,6),
                                      color='black',
                                      legend='PnLStdev')
```

The output is as follows:

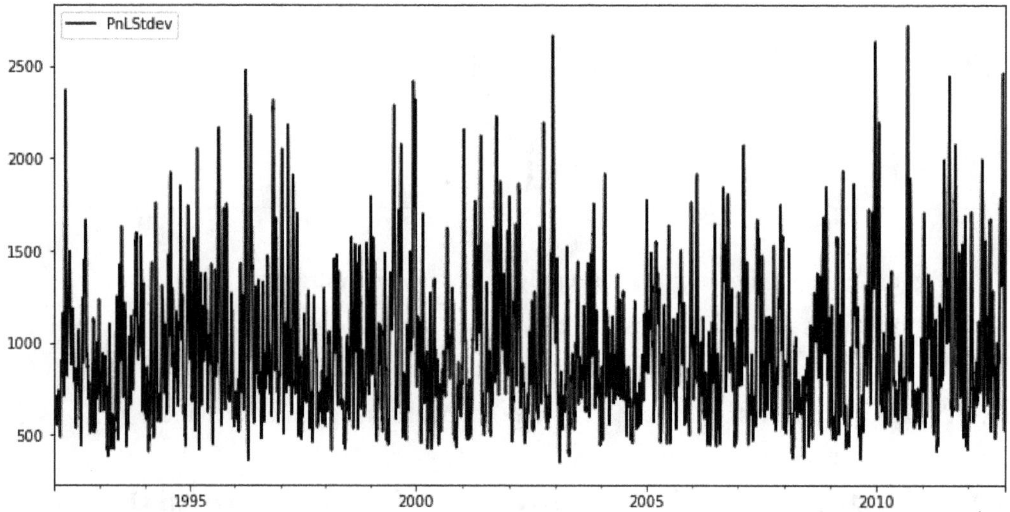

Figure 8.14 – Plot showing PnL standard deviations across a 20-day rolling period

This plot proves that, in this case, there is not a significant pattern – it is a relatively random strategy.

Trade-level Sharpe ratio

The trade-level Sharpe ratio compares average PnLs (strategy returns) relative to PnL standard deviations (strategy volatility). Compared to the standard Sharpe ratio, the Trade Level Sharpe Ratio assumes that the risk-free rate is *0* since we don't roll over positions, so there is no interest charge. This assumption is realistic for intraday or daily trading.

The advantage of this measure is that it's a single number that takes all the relevant risk management factors into account, so we can easily compare the performance of different strategies. Nevertheless, it's important to realize that the Sharpe ratio does not tell the whole story and that it's critical to use it in combination with other risk measures.

The Trade Level Sharpe Ratio is defined as follows:

$$SharpeRatio = \frac{AvgDailyPnL}{DailyPnLStandardDeviation}$$

Let's generate the Sharpe ratio for our strategy's returns. First, we'll generate the daily PnLs:

```
daily_pnl_series = strategy_performance['PnL'].shift(-1) - 
strategy_performance['PnL']
daily_pnl_series.fillna(0, inplace=True)
avg_daily_pnl = daily_pnl_series.mean()
std_daily_pnl = daily_pnl_series.std()
sharpe_ratio = avg_daily_pnl/std_daily_pnl
sharpe_ratio
0.007417596376703097
```

Intuitively, this Sharpe ratio makes sense since the hypothetical strategy's expected daily average performance was set to (1000-990)/2 = $5 and the daily standard deviation of PnLs was set to be roughly $1,000 based on this line:

```
pnls = np.random.randint(-990, 1000, size=len(dates))
# slight positive bias
```

In practice, Sharpe ratios are often annualized so that we can make comparisons between strategies with different horizons fairer. To annualize the Sharpe ratio computed over daily returns, we must multiply it by the square root of 252 (the number of trading dates in a year):

$$AnnualizedSharpeRatio = DailySharpeRatio * \sqrt{252}$$

The code for this is as follows:

```
annualized_sharpe_ratio = sharpe_ratio * np.sqrt(252)
annualized_sharpe_ratio
0.11775069203166105
```

Now, let's interpret the Sharpe ratio:

- A ratio of 3.0 or higher is excellent.
- A ratio > 1.5 is very good.
- A ratio > 1.0 is acceptable.
- A ratio < 1.0 is considered sub-optimal.

We will now look at maximum drawdown.

Maximum drawdown

Maximum drawdown is the peak-to-trough decline in a trading strategy's cumulative PnL over a period of time. In other words, it's the longest streak of losing money compared to the last known maximum cumulative PnL.

This metric quantifies the worst-case decline in a trading account's value based on historical results.

Let's visually find the maximum drawdown in the hypothetical strategy's performance:

```
strategy_performance['PnL'].plot(figsize=(12,6),
                                  color='black',
                                  legend='PnL')
plt.axhline(y=28000, color='darkgrey', linestyle='--',
            label='PeakPnLBeforeDrawdown')
plt.axhline(y=-15000, color='darkgrey', linestyle=':',
            label='TroughPnLAfterDrawdown')
plt.vlines(x='2000', ymin=-15000, ymax=28000,
           label='MaxDrawdown', color='black', linestyle='-.')
plt.legend()
```

Here's the output:

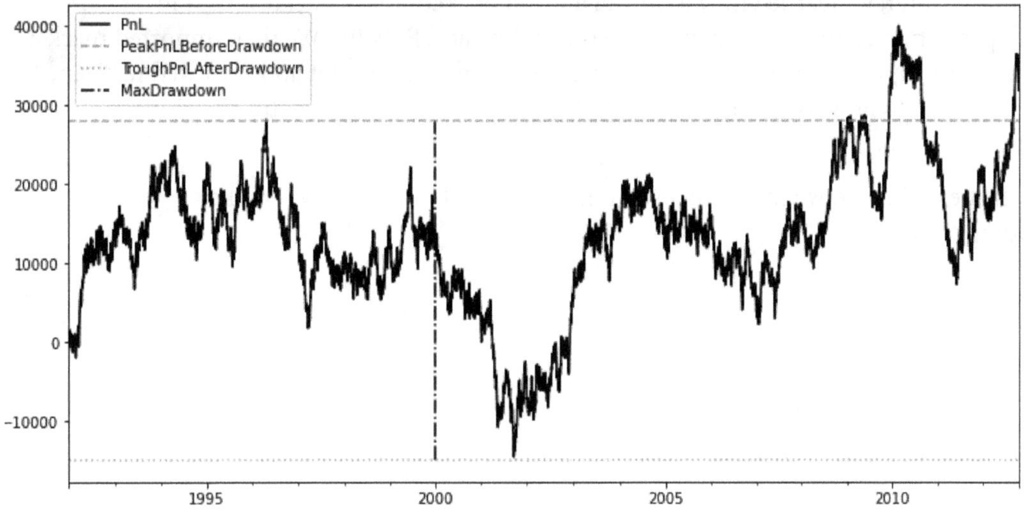

Figure 8.15 – Plot showing the peak and trough PnLs and max drawdown

From this plot, we can assess that the biggest drawdown was $43K for this strategy, from the peak PnL of roughly $28K in 1996 to the trough PnL of roughly -$15K in 2001. If we had started this strategy in 1996, we would have experienced a loss of $43K in our account, which we need to be aware of and prepared for moving forward.

Strategy stop rule – stop loss/maximum loss

Before opening trades, it's important to set a stop loss barrier, which is defined as the maximum number of losses that a strategy or portfolio (which is just a collection of strategies) can take before it is stopped.

The stop loss barrier can be set using historical maximum drawdown values. For our hypothetical strategy, we saw that over the course of 20 years, the maximum drawdown that was achieved was $43K. While historical results are not 100% representative of future results, you might wish to use a $43K stop loss value for this strategy and shut it down if it loses that much money in the future. In practice, setting stop losses is much more complex than described here, but this should help you build some intuition about stop losses.

Once a strategy is stopped, we can decide to shut down the strategy forever or just shut it down for a certain period of time, or even shut it down until certain market conditions change. This decision depends on the strategy's behavior and its risk tolerance.

Summary

In this chapter, we learned how to install and set up a complete backtesting and risk/performance analysis system based on Zipline and PyFolio. We then imported market data into a Zipline/PyFolio backtesting protfolio and structured it and reviewed it. Then, we looked into how to manage risk with PyFolio and make a successful algorithmic trading system.

In the next chapter, we make full use of this setup and introduce several key trading strategies.

9
Fundamental Algorithmic Trading Strategies

This chapter outlines several algorithms profitable on the given stock, given a time window and certain parameters, with the aim of helping you to formulate an idea of how to develop your own trading strategies.

In this chapter, we will discuss the following topics:

- What is an algorithmic trading strategy?
- Learning momentum-based/trend-following strategies
- Learning mean-reversion strategies
- Learning mathematical model-based strategies
- Learning time series prediction-based strategies

Technical requirements

The Python code used in this chapter is available in the `Chapter09/signals_and_strategies.ipynb` notebook in the book's code repository.

What is an algorithmic trading strategy?

Any algorithmic trading strategy should entail the following:

- It should be a model based on an underlying market theory since only then can you find its predictive power. Fitting a model to data with great backtesting results is simple, but usually does not provide sound predictions.
- It should be as simple as possible – the more complex the strategy, the less likely it is to perform well in the long term (overfitting).
- It should restrict the strategy for a well-defined set of financial assets (trading universe) based on the following:

  a) Their returns profile.

  b) Their returns not being correlated.

  c) Their trading patterns – you do not want to trade an illiquid asset; you restrict yourself just to significantly traded assets.
- It should define the relevant financial data:

  a) Frequency: Daily, monthly, intraday, and suchlike

  b) Data source
- It should define the model's parameters.
- It should define their timing, entry, exit rules, and position sizing strategy – for example, we cannot trade more than 10% of the average daily volume; usually, the decision to enter/exit is made by a composition of several indicators.
- It should define the risk levels – how much of a risk a single asset can bear.
- It should define the benchmark used to compare performance against.
- It should define its rebalancing policy – as the markets evolve, the position sizes and risk levels will deviate from their target levels and then it is necessary to adjust the portfolios.

Usually, you have a large library of algorithmic trading strategies, and backtesting will suggest which of these strategies, on which assets, and at what point in time they may generate a profit. You should keep a backtesting journal to keep track of what strategies did or didn't work, on what stock, and during what period.

How do you go about finding a portfolio of stocks to consider for trading? The options are as follows:

- Use ETF/index components – for example, the members of the Dow Jones Industrial Average.
- Use all listed stocks and then restrict the list to the following:

  a) Those stocks that are traded the most

  b) Just non-correlated stocks

  c) Those stocks that are underperforming or overperforming using a returns model, such as the **Fama-French three-factor model**
- You should classify each stock into as many categories as possible:

  a) Value/growth stocks

  b) By industry

Each trading strategy depends on a number of parameters. How do you go about finding the best values for each of them? The possible approaches are as follow:

- A parameter sweep by trying each possible value within the range of possible values for each parameter, but this would require an enormous amount of computing resources.
- Very often, a parameter sweep that involves testing many random samples, instead of all values, from the range of possible values provides a reasonable approximation.

To build a large library of algorithmic trading strategies, you should do the following:

- Subscribe to financial trading blogs.
- Read financial trading books.

The key algorithmic trading strategies can be classified as follows:

- Momentum-based/trend-following strategies
- Mean-reversion strategies
- Mathematical model-based strategies
- Arbitrage strategies
- Market-making strategies
- Index fund rebalancing strategies
- Trading timing optimization strategies (VWAP, TWAP, POV, and so on)

In addition, you yourself should classify all trading strategies depending on the environment where they work best – some strategies work well in volatile markets with strong trends, while others do not.

The following algorithms use the freely accessible Quandl data bundle; thus, the last trading date is January 1, 2018.

You should accumulate many different trading algorithms, list the number of possible parameters, and backtest the stocks on a number of parameters on the universe of stocks (for example, those with an average trading volume of at least *X*) to see which may be profitable. Backtesting should happen in a time window such as the present and near future – for example, the volatility regime.

The best way of reading the following strategies is as follows:

- Identify the signal formula of the strategy and consider it for an entry/exit rule for your own strategy or for a combination with other strategies – some of the most profitable strategies are combinations of existing strategies.
- Consider the frequency of trading – daily trading may not be suitable for all strategies due to the transaction costs.
- Each strategy works for different types of stocks and their market – some work only for trending stocks, some work only for high-volatility stocks, and so on.

Learning momentum-based/trend-following strategies

Momentum-based/trend-following strategies are types of technical analysis strategies. They assume that the near-time future prices will follow an upward or downward trend.

Rolling window mean strategy

This strategy is to own a financial asset if its latest stock price is above the average price over the last *X* days.

In the following example, it works well for Apple stock and a period of 90 days:

```
%matplotlib inline

from zipline import run_algorithm
from zipline.api import order_target_percent, symbol, set_
commission
```

```
from zipline.finance.commission import PerTrade
import pandas as pd
import pyfolio as pf

import warnings
warnings.filterwarnings('ignore')

def initialize(context):
    context.stock = symbol('AAPL')
    context.rolling_window = 90
    set_commission(PerTrade(cost=5))


def handle_data(context, data):
    price_hist = data.history(context.stock, "close",
                              context.rolling_window, "1d")
    order_target_percent(context.stock, 1.0 if price_hist[-1] >
price_hist.mean() else 0.0)

def analyze(context, perf):
    returns, positions, transactions = \
    pf.utils.extract_rets_pos_txn_from_zipline(perf)
    pf.create_returns_tear_sheet(returns,
                                 benchmark_rets = None)

start_date = pd.to_datetime('2000-1-1', utc=True)
end_date = pd.to_datetime('2018-1-1', utc=True)

results = run_algorithm(start = start_date, end = end_date,
                        initialize = initialize,
                        analyze = analyze,
                        handle_data = handle_data,
                        capital_base = 10000,
                        data_frequency = 'daily',
                        bundle ='quandl')
```

The outputs are as follows:

Start date	2000-01-03
End date	2017-12-29
Total months	215
	Backtest
Annual return	24.9%
Cumulative returns	5324.2%
Annual volatility	29.9%
Sharpe ratio	0.89
Calmar ratio	0.42
Stability	0.92
Max drawdown	-59.4%
Omega ratio	1.21
Sortino ratio	1.37
Skew	0.41
Kurtosis	7.82
Tail ratio	1.16
Daily value at risk	-3.7%

Figure 9.1 – Rolling window mean strategy; summary return and risk statistics

When assessing a trading strategy, the preceding statistics are the first step. Each provides a different view on the strategy performance:

- **Sharpe ratio**: This is a measure of excess return versus standard deviation of the excess return. The higher the ratio, the better the algorithm performed on a risk-adjusted basis.
- **Calmar ratio**: This is a measure of the average compounded annual rate of return versus its maximum drawdown. The higher the ratio, the better the algorithm performed on a risk-adjusted basis.

- **Stability**: This is defined as the R-squared value of a linear fit to the cumulative log returns. The higher the number, the higher the trend in the cumulative returns.
- **Omega ratio**: This is defined as the probability weighted ratio of gains versus losses. It is a generalization of the Sharpe ratio, taking into consideration all moments of the distribution. The higher the ratio, the better the algorithm performed on a risk-adjusted basis.
- **Sortino ratio**: This is a variation of the Sharpe ratio – it uses only the standard deviation of the negative portfolio returns (downside risk). The higher the ratio, the better the algorithm performed on a risk-adjusted basis.
- **Tail ratio**: This is defined as the ratio between the right 95% and the left tail 5%. For example, a ratio of 1/3 means that the losses are three times worse than the profits. The higher the number, the better.

In this example, we see that the strategy has a very high stability (.92) over the trading window, which somewhat offsets the high maximum drawdown (-59.4%). The tail ratio is most favorable:

Worst drawdown periods	Net drawdown in %	Peak date	Valley date	Recovery date	Duration
0	59.37	2000-03-22	2003-03-24	2004-10-14	1192
1	31.34	2015-02-23	2016-09-09	2017-05-09	577
2	25.44	2005-02-16	2005-07-18	2005-10-20	177
3	24.14	2006-01-13	2006-02-09	2006-10-23	202
4	21.45	2012-04-09	2013-07-19	2013-12-03	432

Figure 9.2 – Rolling window mean strategy; worst five drawdown periods

While the worst maximum drawdown of 59.37% is certainly not good, if we adjusted the entry/exit strategy rules, we would most likely avoid it. Notice the duration of the drawdown periods – more than 3 years in the maximum drawdown period.

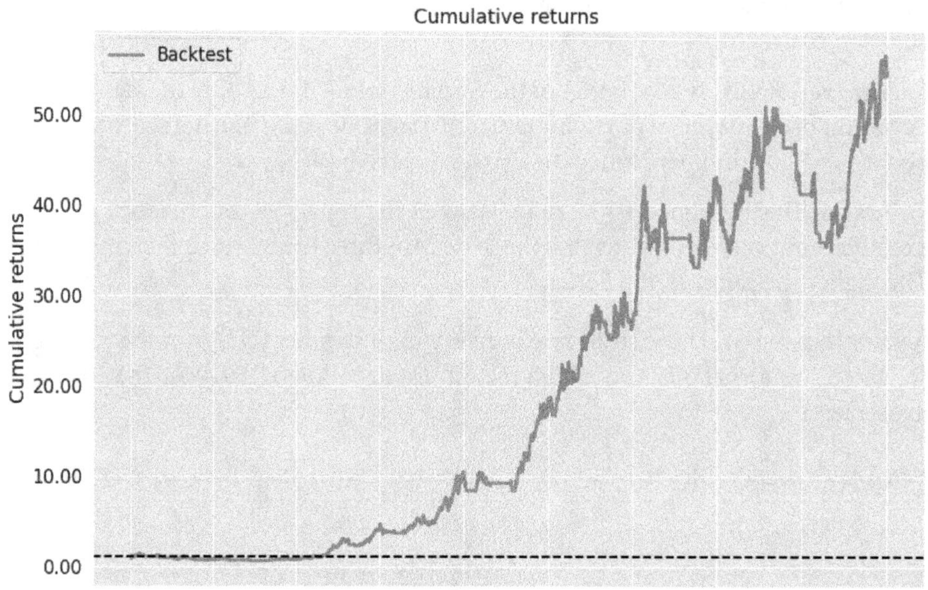

Figure 9.3 – Rolling window mean strategy; cumulative returns over the investment horizon

As the stability measure confirms, we see a positive trend in the cumulative returns over the trading horizon.

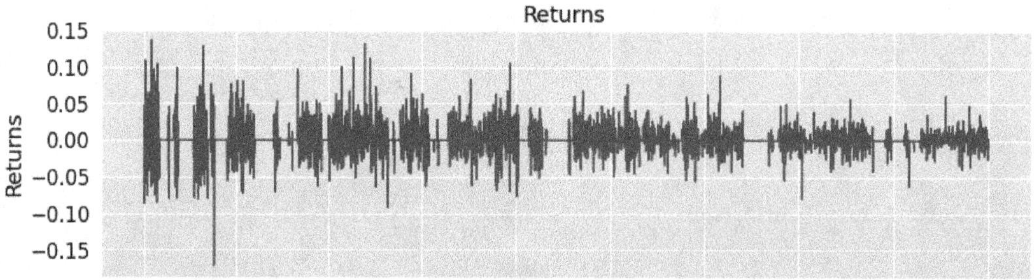

Figure 9.4 – Rolling window mean strategy; returns over the investment horizon

The chart confirms that the returns oscillate widely around zero.

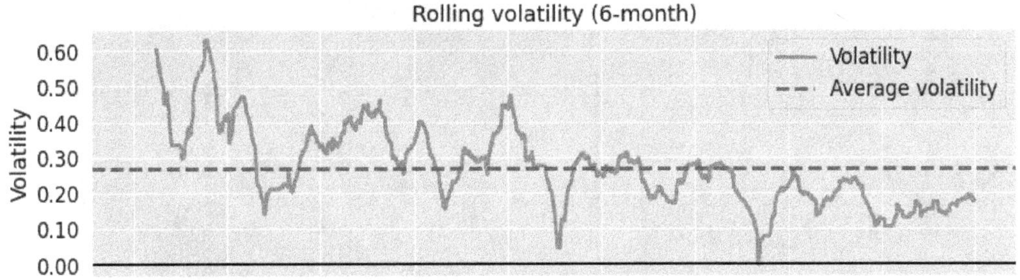

Figure 9.5 – Rolling window mean strategy; 6-month rolling volatility over the investment horizon

This chart illustrates that the strategy's return volatility is decreasing over the time horizon.

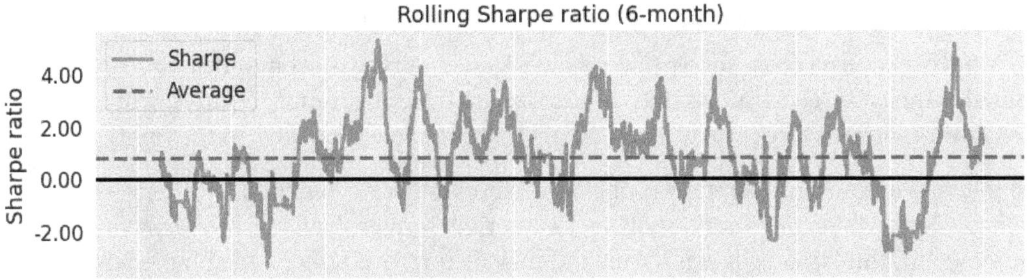

Figure 9.6 – Rolling window mean strategy; 6-month rolling Sharpe ratio over the investment horizon

We see that the maximum Sharpe ratio of the strategy is above 4, with its minimum value below -2. If we reviewed the entry/exit rules, we should be able to improve the strategy's performance.

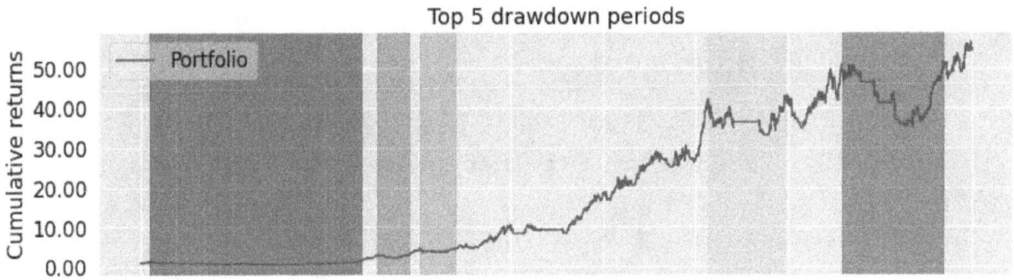

Figure 9.7 – Rolling window mean strategy; top five drawdown periods over the investment horizon

A graphical representation of the maximum drawdown indicates that the periods of maximum drawdown are overly long.

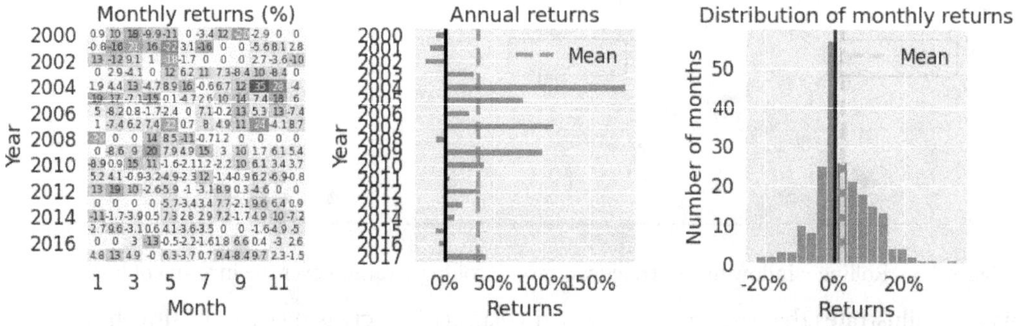

Figure 9.8 – Rolling window mean strategy; monthly returns, annual returns, and the distribution of monthly returns over the investment horizon

The **Monthly returns** chart shows that we have traded during most months. The **Annual returns** bar chart shows that the returns are overwhelmingly positive, while the **Distribution of monthly returns** chart shows that the skew is positive to the right.

The rolling window mean strategy is one of the simplest strategies and is still very profitable for certain combinations of stocks and time frames. Notice that the maximum drawdown for this strategy is significant and may be improved if we added more advanced entry/exit rules.

Simple moving averages strategy

This strategy follows a simple rule: buy the stock if the short-term moving averages rise above the long-term moving averages:

```
%matplotlib inline

from zipline import run_algorithm
from zipline.api import order_target_percent, symbol, set_
commission
from zipline.finance.commission import PerTrade
import pandas as pd
import pyfolio as pf

import warnings
warnings.filterwarnings('ignore')

```

```
def initialize(context):
    context.stock = symbol('AAPL')
    context.rolling_window = 90
    set_commission(PerTrade(cost=5))

def handle_data(context, data):
    price_hist = data.history(context.stock, "close",
                              context.rolling_window, "1d")

    rolling_mean_short_term = \
    price_hist.rolling(window=45, center=False).mean()
    rolling_mean_long_term = \
    price_hist.rolling(window=90, center=False).mean()

    if rolling_mean_short_term[-1] > rolling_mean_long_term[-
1]:
        order_target_percent(context.stock, 1.0)
    elif rolling_mean_short_term[-1] < rolling_mean_long_term[-
1]:
        order_target_percent(context.stock, 0.0)

def analyze(context, perf):
    returns, positions, transactions = \
    pf.utils.extract_rets_pos_txn_from_zipline(perf)
    pf.create_returns_tear_sheet(returns,
                                 benchmark_rets = None)

start_date = pd.to_datetime('2000-1-1', utc=True)
end_date = pd.to_datetime('2018-1-1', utc=True)

results = run_algorithm(start = start_date, end = end_date,
                        initialize = initialize,
                        analyze = analyze,
                        handle_data = handle_data,
                        capital_base = 10000,
                        data_frequency = 'daily',
                        bundle ='quandl')
```

The outputs are as follows:

Start date	2000-01-03
End date	2017-12-29
Total months	215

	Backtest
Annual return	18.0%
Cumulative returns	1847.4%
Annual volatility	32.6%
Sharpe ratio	0.68
Calmar ratio	0.23
Stability	0.91
Max drawdown	-76.8%
Omega ratio	1.17
Sortino ratio	0.96
Skew	-3.14
Kurtosis	95.12
Tail ratio	1.13
Daily value at risk	-4.0%

Figure 9.9 – Simple moving averages strategy; summary return and risk statistics

The statistics show that the strategy is overwhelmingly profitable in the long term (high stability and tail ratios), while the maximum drawdown can be substantial.

Worst drawdown periods	Net drawdown in %	Peak date	Valley date	Recovery date	Duration
0	76.79	2000-03-22	2001-02-28	2005-02-02	1271
1	49.17	2007-12-28	2008-08-04	2009-10-06	463
2	37.37	2015-02-23	2016-05-12	2017-08-08	642
3	27.88	2006-01-13	2006-09-06	2007-04-26	335
4	25.17	2012-09-19	2012-11-15	2014-06-05	447

Figure 9.10 – Simple moving averages strategy; worst five drawdown periods

The worst drawdown periods are rather long – more than 335 days, with some even taking more than 3 years in the worst case.

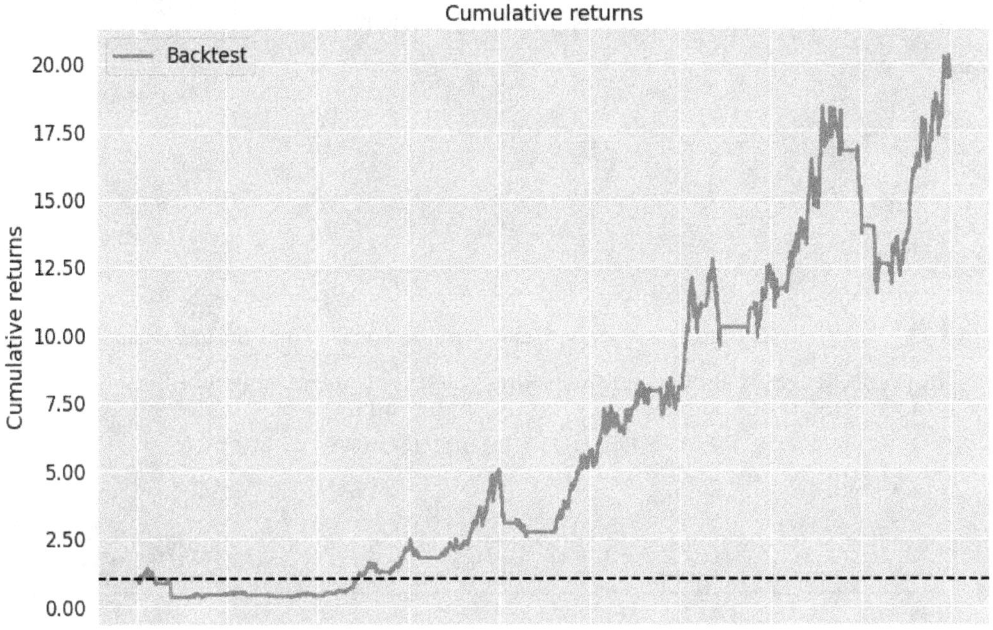

Figure 9.11 – Simple moving averages strategy; cumulative returns over the investment horizon

This chart does, however, confirm that this long-term strategy is profitable – we see the cumulative returns grow consistently after the first drawdown.

Figure 9.12 – Simple moving averages strategy; returns over the investment horizon

The chart illustrates that there was a major negative return event at the very start of the trading window and then the returns oscillate around zero.

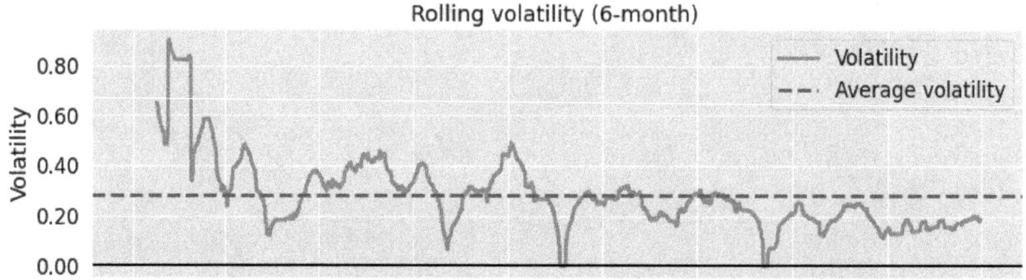

Figure 9.13 – Simple moving averages strategy; 6-month rolling volatility over the investment horizon

The rolling volatility chart shows that the rolling volatility is decreasing with time.

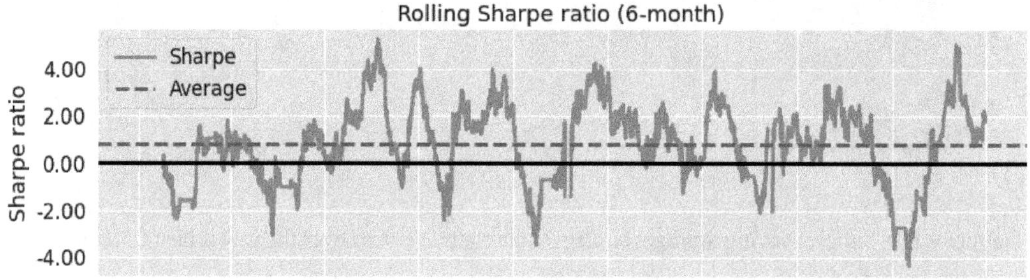

Figure 9.14 – Simple moving averages strategy; 6-month rolling Sharpe ratio over the investment horizon

While the maximum Sharpe ratio was over 4, with the minimum equivalent being below -4, the average Sharpe ratio was 0.68.

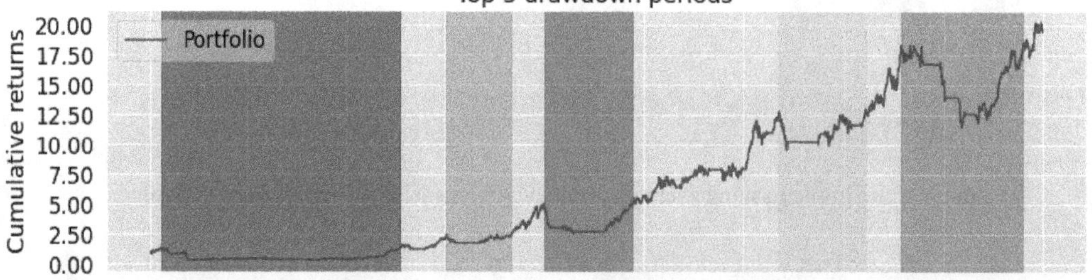

Figure 9.15 – Simple moving averages strategy; top five drawdown periods over the investment horizon

This chart confirms that the maximum drawdown periods were very long.

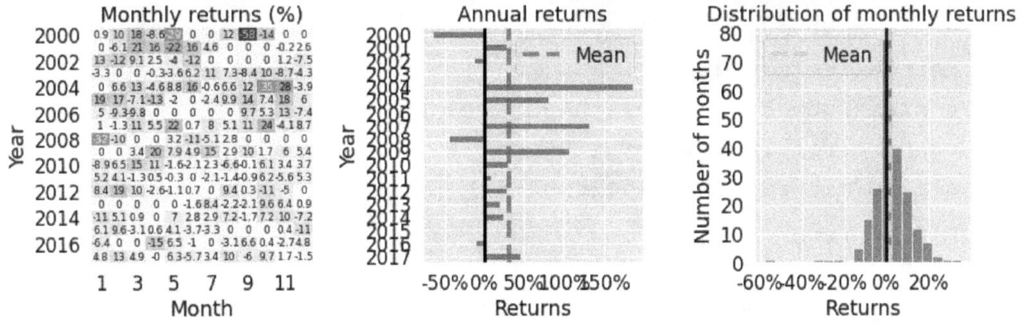

Figure 9.16 – Simple moving averages strategy; monthly returns, annual returns, and the distribution of monthly returns over the investment horizon

The monthly returns table shows that there was no trade across many months. The annual returns were mostly positive. The **Distribution of monthly returns** chart confirms that the skew is negative.

The simple moving averages strategy is less profitable and has a greater maximum drawdown than the rolling window mean strategy. One reason may be that the rolling window for the moving averages is too large.

Exponentially weighted moving averages strategy

This strategy is similar to the previous one, with the exception of using different rolling windows and exponentially weighted moving averages. The results are slightly better than those achieved under the previous strategy.

Some other moving average algorithms use both simple moving averages and exponentially weighted moving averages in the decision rule; for example, if the simple moving average is greater than the exponentially weighted moving average, make a move:

```
%matplotlib inline

from zipline import run_algorithm
from zipline.api import order_target_percent, symbol, set_
commission
from zipline.finance.commission import PerTrade
import pandas as pd
import pyfolio as pf

```

```
import warnings
warnings.filterwarnings('ignore')

def initialize(context):
    context.stock = symbol('AAPL')
    context.rolling_window = 90
    set_commission(PerTrade(cost=5))

def handle_data(context, data):
    price_hist = data.history(context.stock, "close",
                              context.rolling_window, "1d")

    rolling_mean_short_term = \
    price_hist.ewm(span=5, adjust=True,
                   ignore_na=True).mean()
    rolling_mean_long_term = \
    price_hist.ewm(span=30, adjust=True,
                   ignore_na=True).mean()

    if rolling_mean_short_term[-1] > rolling_mean_long_term[-
1]:
        order_target_percent(context.stock, 1.0)
    elif rolling_mean_short_term[-1] < rolling_mean_long_term[-
1]:
        order_target_percent(context.stock, 0.0)

def analyze(context, perf):
    returns, positions, transactions = \
    pf.utils.extract_rets_pos_txn_from_zipline(perf)
    pf.create_returns_tear_sheet(returns,
                                 benchmark_rets = None)

start_date = pd.to_datetime('2000-1-1', utc=True)
end_date = pd.to_datetime('2018-1-1', utc=True)

results = run_algorithm(start = start_date, end = end_date,
                        initialize = initialize,
```

```
analyze = analyze,
handle_data = handle_data,
capital_base = 10000,
data_frequency = 'daily',
bundle ='quandl')
```

The outputs are as follows:

Start date	2000-01-03
End date	2017-12-29
Total months	215
	Backtest
Annual return	20.8%
Cumulative returns	2902.2%
Annual volatility	29.0%
Sharpe ratio	0.80
Calmar ratio	0.48
Stability	0.92
Max drawdown	-43.4%
Omega ratio	1.20
Sortino ratio	1.21
Skew	0.43
Kurtosis	8.91
Tail ratio	1.12
Daily value at risk	-3.6%

Figure 9.17 – Exponentially weighted moving averages strategy; summary return and risk statistics

The results show that the level of maximum drawdown has dropped from the previous strategies, while still keeping very strong stability and tail ratios.

Worst drawdown periods	Net drawdown in %	Peak date	Valley date	Recovery date	Duration
0	43.44	2000-03-22	2001-10-17	2003-07-25	873
1	35.83	2005-02-16	2005-06-27	2005-11-02	186
2	25.53	2008-05-13	2009-02-23	2009-04-23	248
3	25.31	2011-02-16	2011-12-21	2012-02-28	270
4	24.99	2006-11-28	2007-02-27	2007-05-30	132

Figure 9.18 – Exponentially weighted moving averages strategy; worst five drawdown periods

The magnitude of the worst drawdown, as well as its maximum duration in days, is far better than for the previous two strategies.

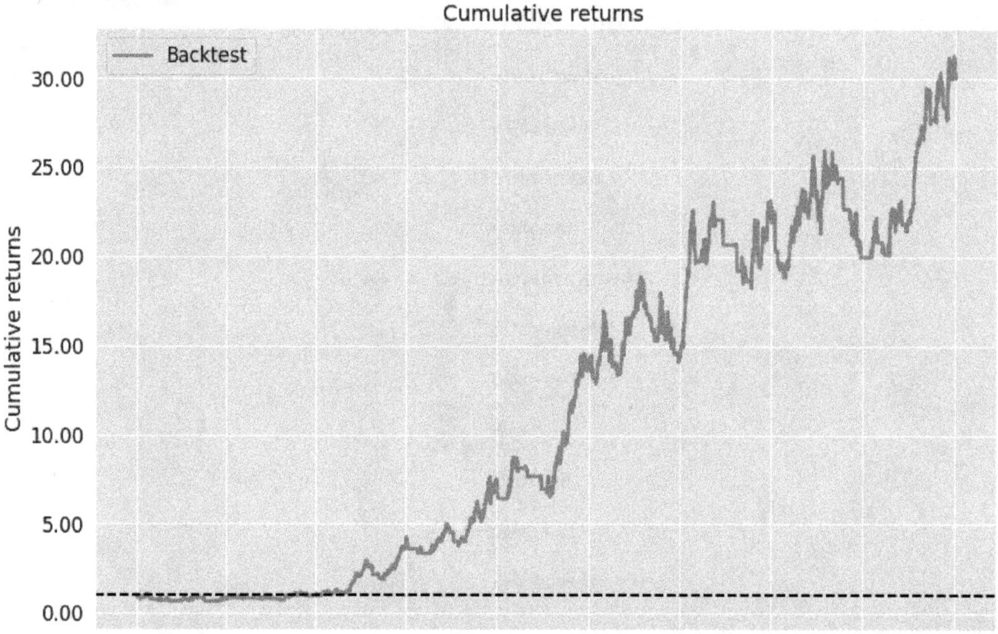

Figure 9.19 – Exponentially weighted moving averages strategy; cumulative returns over the investment horizon

As the stability indicator shows, we see consistent positive cumulative returns.

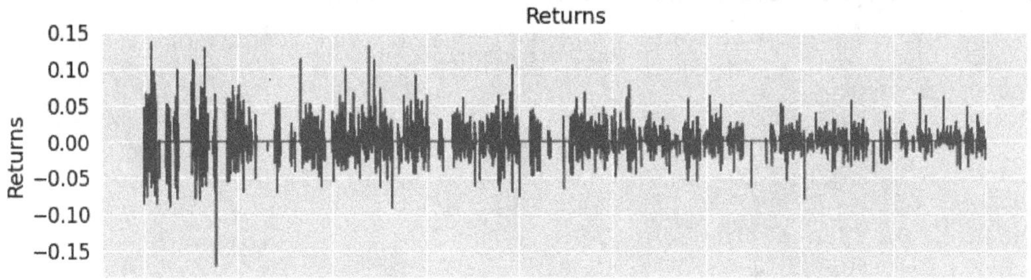

Figure 9.20 – Exponentially weighted moving averages strategy; returns over the investment horizon

The returns oscillate around zero, being more positive than negative.

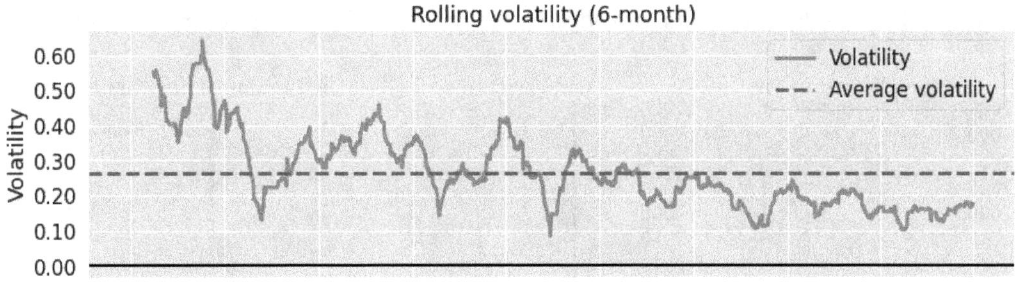

Figure 9.21 – Exponentially weighted moving averages strategy; 6-month rolling volatility over the investment horizon

The rolling volatility is dropping over time.

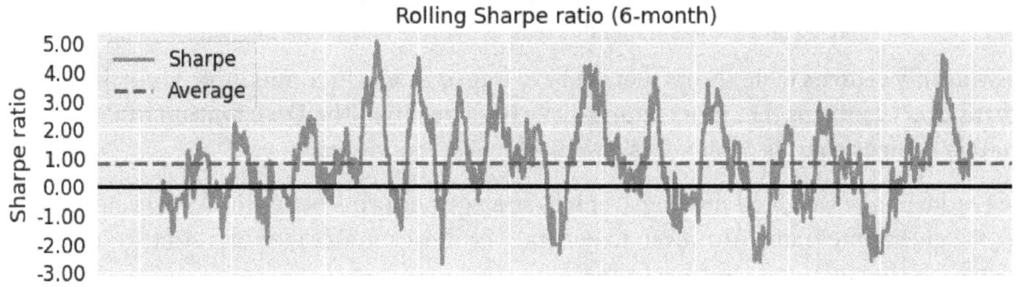

Figure 9.22 – Exponentially weighted moving averages strategy; 6-month rolling Sharpe ratio over the investment horizon

We see that the maximum Sharpe ratio reached almost 5, while the minimum was slightly below -2, which again is better than for the two previous algorithms.

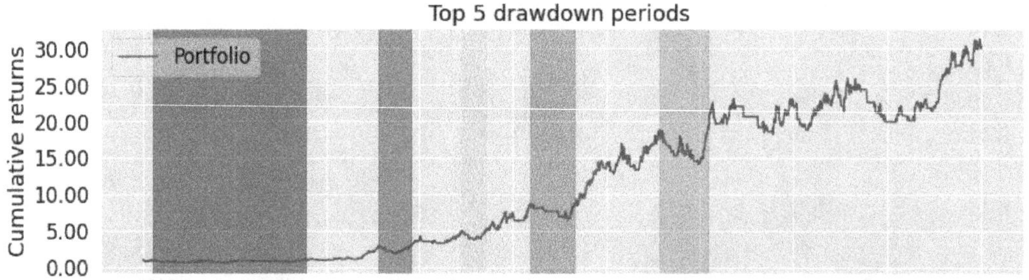

Figure 9.23 – Exponentially weighted moving averages strategy; top five drawdown periods over the investment horizon

Notice that the periods of the worst drawdown are not identical for the last three algorithms.

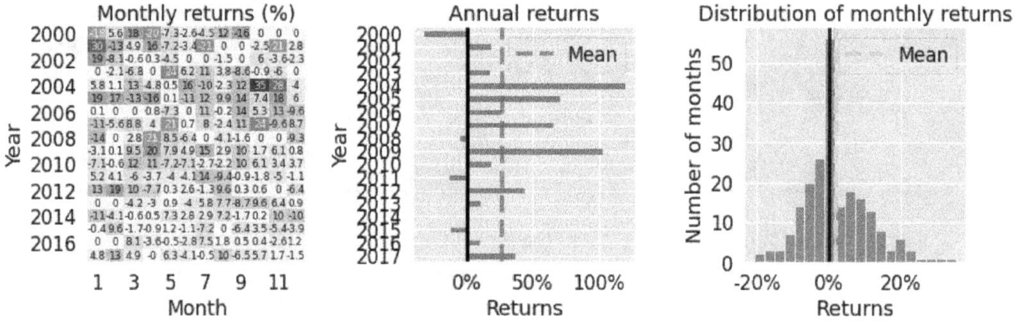

Figure 9.24 – Exponentially weighted moving averages strategy; monthly returns, annual returns, and the distribution of monthly returns over the investment horizon

The **Monthly returns** table shows that we have traded in most months. The **Annual returns** chart confirms that most returns have been positive. The **Distribution of monthly returns** chart is positively skewed, which is a good sign.

The exponentially weighted moving averages strategy performs better for Apple's stock over the given time frame. However, in general, the most suitable averages strategy depends on the stock and the time frame.

RSI strategy

This strategy depends on the `stockstats` package. It is very instructive to read the source code at `https://github.com/intrad/stockstats/blob/master/stockstats.py`.

To install it, use the following command:

```
pip install stockstats
```

The RSI indicator measures the velocity and magnitude of price movements and provides an indicator when a financial asset is oversold or overbought. It is a leading indicator.

It is measured from 0 to 100, with values over 70 indicating overbought, and values below 30 oversold:

```
%matplotlib inline

from zipline import run_algorithm
from zipline.api import order_target_percent, symbol, set_
commission
from zipline.finance.commission import PerTrade
import pandas as pd
import pyfolio as pf
from stockstats import StockDataFrame as sdf

import warnings
warnings.filterwarnings('ignore')

def initialize(context):
    context.stock = symbol('AAPL')
    context.rolling_window = 20
    set_commission(PerTrade(cost=5))

def handle_data(context, data):
    price_hist = data.history(context.stock,
                              ["open", "high",
                               "low","close"],
                              context.rolling_window, "1d")

```

```
    stock=sdf.retype(price_hist)

    rsi = stock.get('rsi_12')

    if rsi[-1] > 90:
        order_target_percent(context.stock, 0.0)
    elif rsi[-1] < 10:
        order_target_percent(context.stock, 1.0)

def analyze(context, perf):
    returns, positions, transactions = \
    pf.utils.extract_rets_pos_txn_from_zipline(perf)
    pf.create_returns_tear_sheet(returns,
                                 benchmark_rets = None)

start_date = pd.to_datetime('2015-1-1', utc=True)
end_date = pd.to_datetime('2018-1-1', utc=True)

results = run_algorithm(start = start_date, end = end_date,
                        initialize = initialize,
                        analyze = analyze,
                        handle_data = handle_data,
                        capital_base = 10000,
                        data_frequency = 'daily',
                        bundle ='quandl')
```

The outputs are as follows:

Start date	2015-01-02
End date	2017-12-29
Total months	35

	Backtest
Annual return	11.0%
Cumulative returns	36.8%
Annual volatility	9.9%
Sharpe ratio	1.11
Calmar ratio	1.04
Stability	0.84
Max drawdown	-10.6%
Omega ratio	1.52
Sortino ratio	2.00
Skew	3.03
Kurtosis	33.05
Tail ratio	1.44
Daily value at risk	-1.2%

Figure 9.25 – RSI strategy; summary return and risk statistics

The first look at the strategy shows an excellent Sharpe ratio, with a very low maximum drawdown and a favorable tail ratio.

Worst drawdown periods	Net drawdown in %	Peak date	Valley date	Recovery date	Duration
0	10.55	2016-10-25	2016-11-14	2017-01-09	55
1	8.29	2016-05-26	2016-06-27	2016-07-27	45
2	5.77	2016-08-15	2016-09-09	2016-09-14	23
3	5.05	2016-05-03	2016-05-12	2016-05-20	14
4	2.92	2016-09-15	2016-09-29	2016-10-10	18

Figure 9.26 – RSI strategy; worst five drawdown periods

The worst drawdown periods were very short – less than 2 months – and not substantial – a maximum drawdown of only -10.55%.

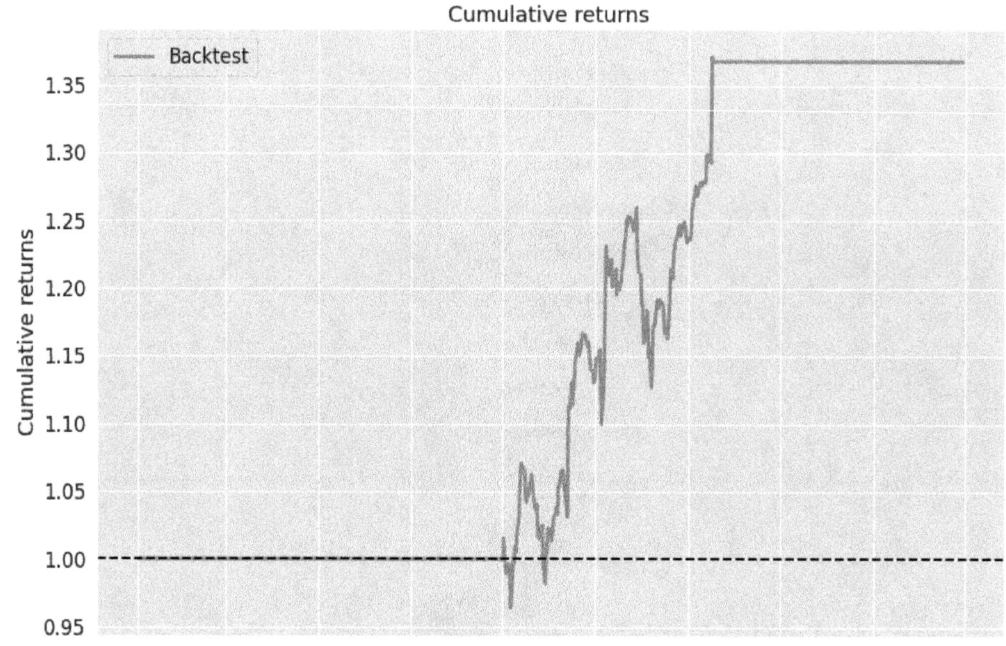

Figure 9.27 – RSI strategy; cumulative returns over the investment horizon

The **Cumulative returns** chart shows that we have not traded across most of the trading horizon and when we did trade, there was a positive trend in the cumulative returns.

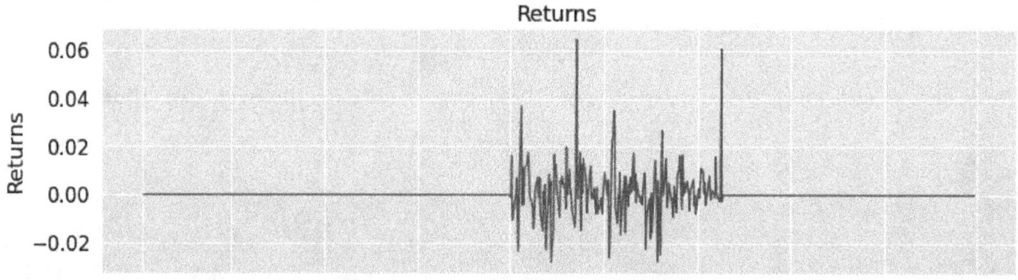

Figure 9.28 – RSI strategy; returns over the investment horizon

We can see that when we traded, the returns were more likely to be positive than negative.

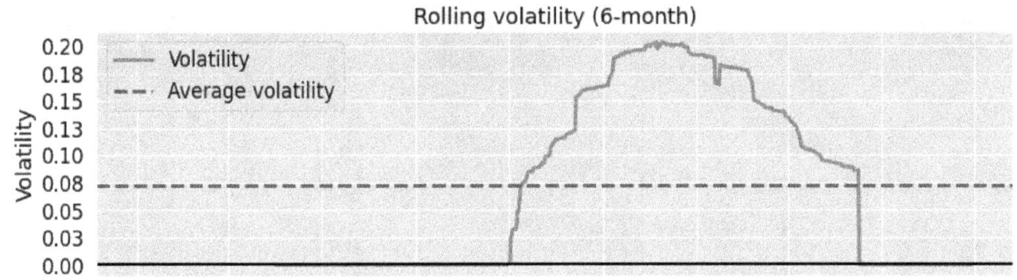

Figure 9.29 – RSI strategy; 6-month rolling volatility over the investment horizon

Notice that the maximum rolling volatility of 0.2 is far lower than for the previous strategies.

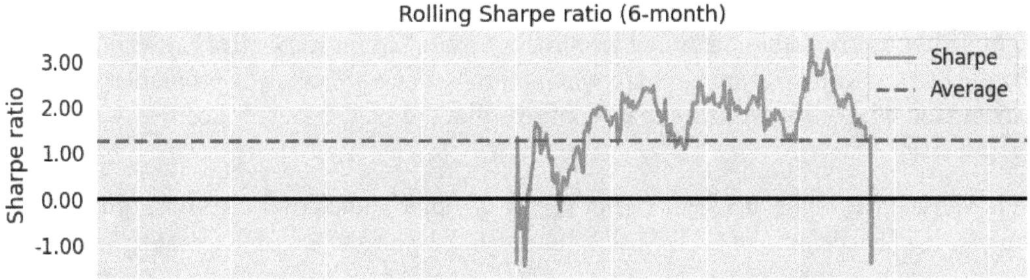

Figure 9.30 – RSI strategy; 6-month rolling Sharpe ratio over the investment horizon

We can see that Sharpe's ratio has consistently been over 1, with its maximum value over 3 and its minimum value below -1.

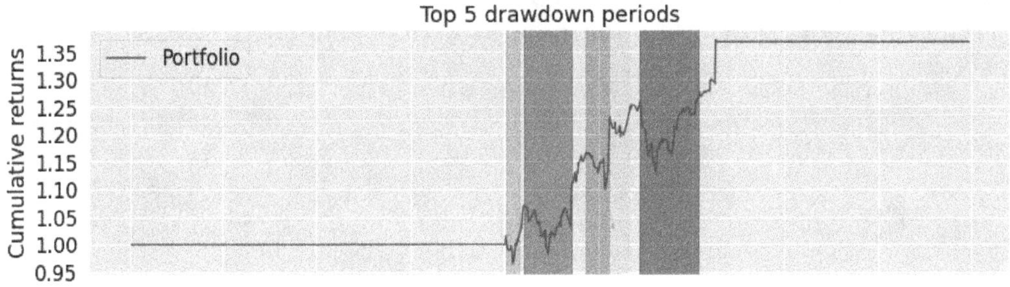

Figure 9.31 – RSI strategy; top five drawdown periods over the investment horizon

The chart illustrates short and insignificant drawdown periods.

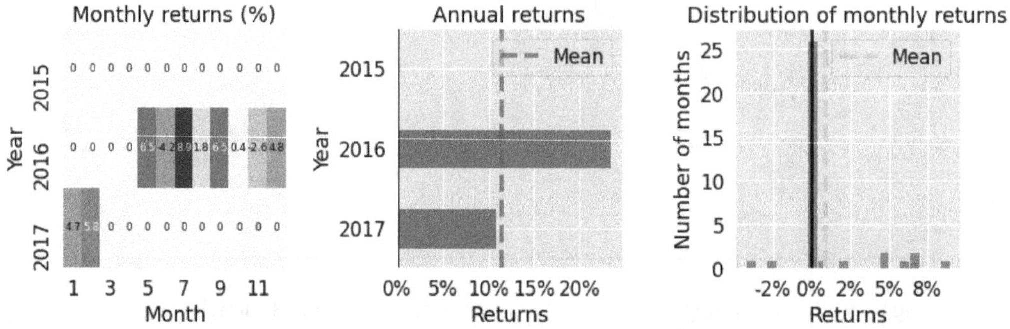

Figure 9.32 – RSI strategy; monthly returns, annual returns, and the distribution of monthly returns over the investment horizon

The **Monthly returns** table states that we have not traded in most months. However, according to the **Annual returns** chart, when we traded, we were hugely profitable. The **Distribution of monthly returns** chart confirms that the skew is hugely positive, with a large kurtosis.

The RSI strategy is highly performant in the case of Apple's stock over the given time frame, with a Sharpe ratio of 1.11. Notice, however, that the success of the strategy depends largely on the very strict entry/exit rules, meaning we are not trading in certain months at all.

MACD crossover strategy

Moving Average Convergence Divergence (**MACD**) is a lagging, trend-following momentum indicator reflecting the relationship between two moving averages of stock prices.

The strategy depends on two statistics, the MACD and the MACD signal line:

- The MACD is defined as the difference between the 12-day exponential moving average and the 26-day exponential moving average.
- The MACD signal line is then defined as the 9-day exponential moving average of the MACD.

The MACD crossover strategy is defined as follows:

- A bullish crossover happens when the MACD line turns upward and crosses beyond the MACD signal line.
- A bearish crossover happens when the MACD line turns downward and crosses under the MACD signal line.

Consequently, this strategy is best suited for volatile, highly traded markets:

```
%matplotlib inline

from zipline import run_algorithm
from zipline.api import order_target_percent, symbol, set_
commission
from zipline.finance.commission import PerTrade
import pandas as pd
import pyfolio as pf
from stockstats import StockDataFrame as sdf

import warnings
warnings.filterwarnings('ignore')

def initialize(context):
    context.stock = symbol('AAPL')
    context.rolling_window = 20
    set_commission(PerTrade(cost=5))

def handle_data(context, data):
    price_hist = data.history(context.stock,
                              ["open","high",
                               "low","close"],
```

```
                                context.rolling_window, "1d")

    stock=sdf.retype(price_hist)

    signal = stock['macds']
    macd   = stock['macd']

    if macd[-1] > signal[-1] and macd[-2] <= signal[-2]:
        order_target_percent(context.stock, 1.0)
    elif macd[-1] < signal[-1] and macd[-2] >= signal[-2]:
        order_target_percent(context.stock, 0.0)

def analyze(context, perf):
    returns, positions, transactions = \
    pf.utils.extract_rets_pos_txn_from_zipline(perf)
    pf.create_returns_tear_sheet(returns,
                                   benchmark_rets = None)

start_date = pd.to_datetime('2015-1-1', utc=True)
end_date = pd.to_datetime('2018-1-1', utc=True)

results = run_algorithm(start = start_date, end = end_date,
                        initialize = initialize,
                        analyze = analyze,
                        handle_data = handle_data,
                        capital_base = 10000,
                        data_frequency = 'daily',
                        bundle ='quandl')
```

The outputs are as follows:

Start date	2015-01-02
End date	2017-12-29
Total months	35
	Backtest
Annual return	10.0%
Cumulative returns	33.0%
Annual volatility	15.2%
Sharpe ratio	0.70
Calmar ratio	0.42
Stability	0.41
Max drawdown	-24.0%
Omega ratio	1.19
Sortino ratio	1.00
Skew	-0.33
Kurtosis	10.99
Tail ratio	1.00
Daily value at risk	-1.9%

Figure 9.33 – MACD crossover strategy; summary return and risk statistics

The tail ratio illustrates that the top gains and losses are roughly of the same magnitude. The very low stability indicates that there is no strong trend in cumulative returns.

Worst drawdown periods	Net drawdown in %	Peak date	Valley date	Recovery date	Duration
0	23.97	2015-02-23	2016-02-23	2017-02-15	518
1	7.07	2017-05-12	2017-06-29	2017-10-16	112
2	3.96	2017-11-09	2017-12-27	NaT	NaN
3	3.48	2015-01-26	2015-01-27	2015-01-28	3
4	2.83	2017-04-04	2017-04-28	2017-05-05	24

Figure 9.34 – MACD crossover strategy; worst five drawdown periods

Apart from the worst drawdown period, the other periods were shorter than 6 months, with a net drawdown lower than 10%.

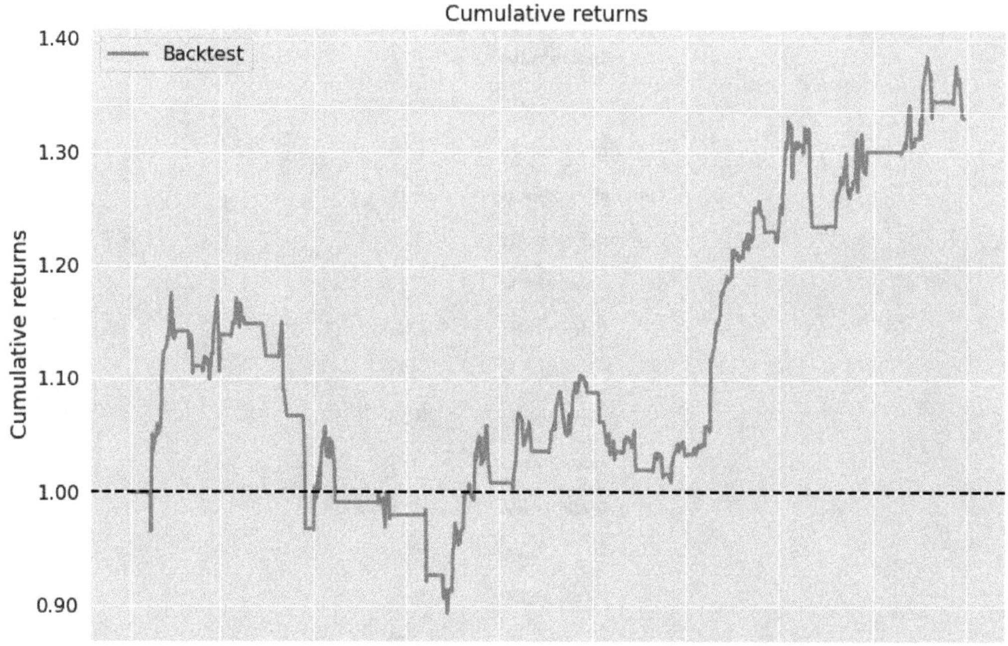

Figure 9.35 – MACD crossover strategy; cumulative returns over the investment horizon

The **Cumulative returns** chart confirms the low stability indicator value.

The following is the **Returns** chart:

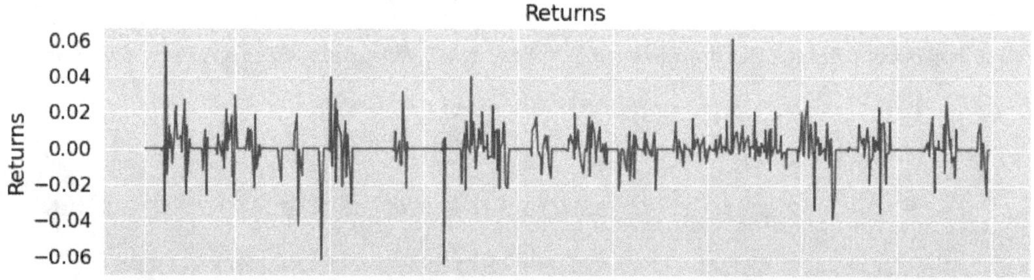

Figure 9.36 – MACD crossover strategy; returns over the investment horizon

The **Returns** chart shows that returns oscillated widely around zero, with a few outliers.

The following is the **Rolling volatility** chart:

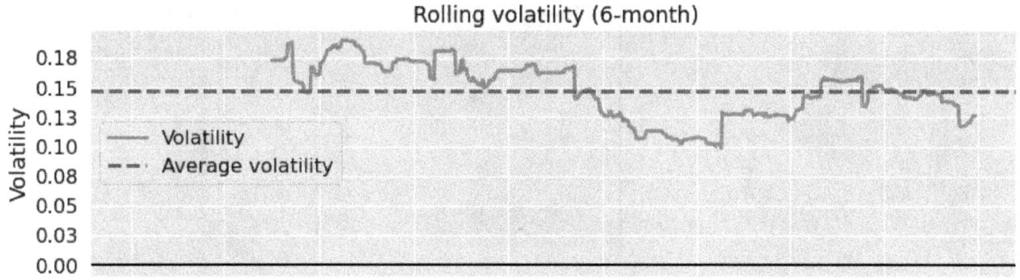

Figure 9.37 – MACD crossover strategy; 6-month rolling volatility over the investment horizon

The rolling volatility has been oscillating around 0.15.

The following is the rolling Sharpe ratio chart:

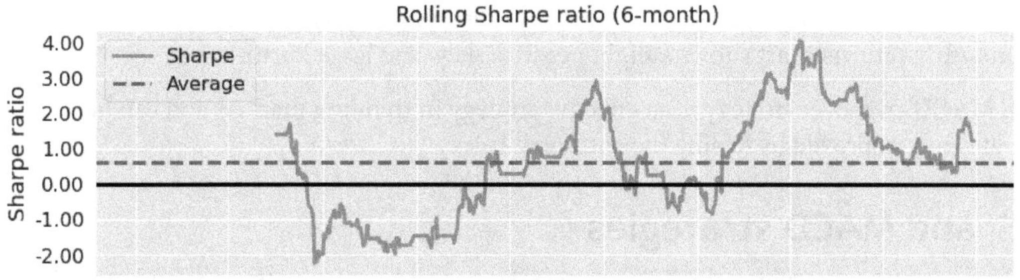

Figure 9.38 – MACD crossover strategy; 6-month rolling Sharpe ratio over the investment horizon

The maximum rolling Sharpe ratio of about 4, with a minimum ratio of -2, is largely favorable.

The following is the top five drawdown periods chart:

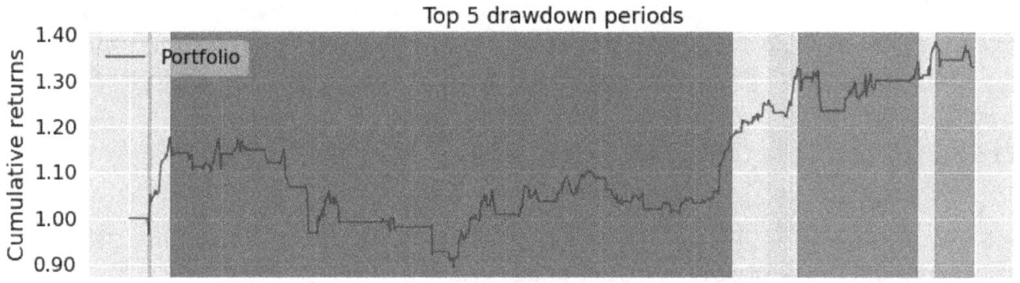

Figure 9.39 – MACD crossover strategy; top five drawdown periods over the investment horizon

We see that the worst two drawdown periods have been rather long.

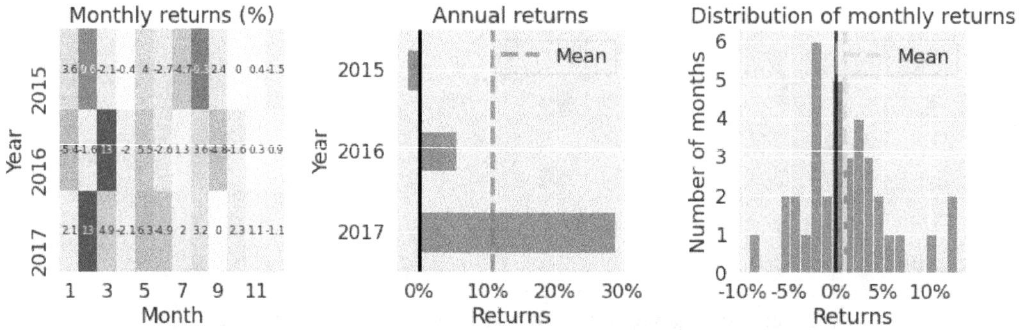

Figure 9.40 – MACD crossover strategy; monthly returns, annual returns, and the distribution of monthly returns over the investment horizon

The **Monthly returns** table confirms that we have traded across most months. The **Annual returns** chart indicates that the most profitable year was 2017. The **Distribution of monthly returns** chart shows a slight negative skew and large kurtosis.

The MACD crossover strategy is an effective strategy in trending markets and can be significantly improved by raising the entry/exit rules.

RSI and MACD strategies

In this strategy, we combine the RSI and MACD strategies and own the stock if both RSI and MACD criteria provide a signal to buy.

Using multiple criteria provides a more complete view of the market (note that we generalize the RSI threshold values to 50):

```
%matplotlib inline

from zipline import run_algorithm
from zipline.api import order_target_percent, symbol, set_commission
from zipline.finance.commission import PerTrade
import pandas as pd
import pyfolio as pf
from stockstats import StockDataFrame as sdf

import warnings
```

```
warnings.filterwarnings('ignore')

def initialize(context):
    context.stock = symbol('MSFT')
    context.rolling_window = 20
    set_commission(PerTrade(cost=5))

def handle_data(context, data):
    price_hist = data.history(context.stock,
                              ["open", "high",
                               "low","close"],
                              context.rolling_window, "1d")

    stock=sdf.retype(price_hist)

    rsi = stock.get('rsi_12')

    signal = stock['macds']
    macd   = stock['macd']

    if rsi[-1] < 50 and macd[-1] > signal[-1] and macd[-2] <=
signal[-2]:
        order_target_percent(context.stock, 1.0)
    elif rsi[-1] > 50 and macd[-1] < signal[-1] and macd[-2] >=
signal[-2]:
        order_target_percent(context.stock, 0.0)

def analyze(context, perf):
    returns, positions, transactions = \
    pf.utils.extract_rets_pos_txn_from_zipline(perf)
    pf.create_returns_tear_sheet(returns,
                                 benchmark_rets = None)

start_date = pd.to_datetime('2015-1-1', utc=True)
end_date = pd.to_datetime('2018-1-1', utc=True)
```

```
results = run_algorithm(start = start_date, end = end_date,
                        initialize = initialize,
                        analyze = analyze,
                        handle_data = handle_data,
                        capital_base = 10000,
                        data_frequency = 'daily',
                        bundle ='quandl')
```

The outputs are as follows:

Start date	2015-01-02
End date	2017-12-29
Total months	35
	Backtest
Annual return	18.7%
Cumulative returns	67.2%
Annual volatility	14.3%
Sharpe ratio	1.27
Calmar ratio	1.81
Stability	0.84
Max drawdown	-10.4%
Omega ratio	1.59
Sortino ratio	2.52
Skew	4.33
Kurtosis	47.86
Tail ratio	1.39
Daily value at risk	-1.7%

Figure 9.41 – RSI and MACD strategies; summary return and risk statistics

The high stability value, with a high tail ratio and excellent Sharpe ratio, as well as a low maximum drawdown, indicates that the strategy is excellent.

The following is the worst five drawdown periods chart:

Worst drawdown periods	Net drawdown in %	Peak date	Valley date	Recovery date	Duration
0	10.36	2016-01-29	2016-02-09	2016-03-31	45
1	8.61	2016-05-31	2016-06-27	2016-07-12	31
2	8.61	2015-02-23	2015-04-02	2015-04-24	45
3	5.91	2015-04-28	2015-05-06	2015-10-01	113
4	4.34	2016-04-01	2016-05-23	2016-05-27	41

Figure 9.42 – RSI and MACD strategies; worst five drawdown periods

We see that the worst drawdown periods were short – less than 4 months – with the worst net drawdown of -10.36%.

The following is the **Cumulative returns** chart:

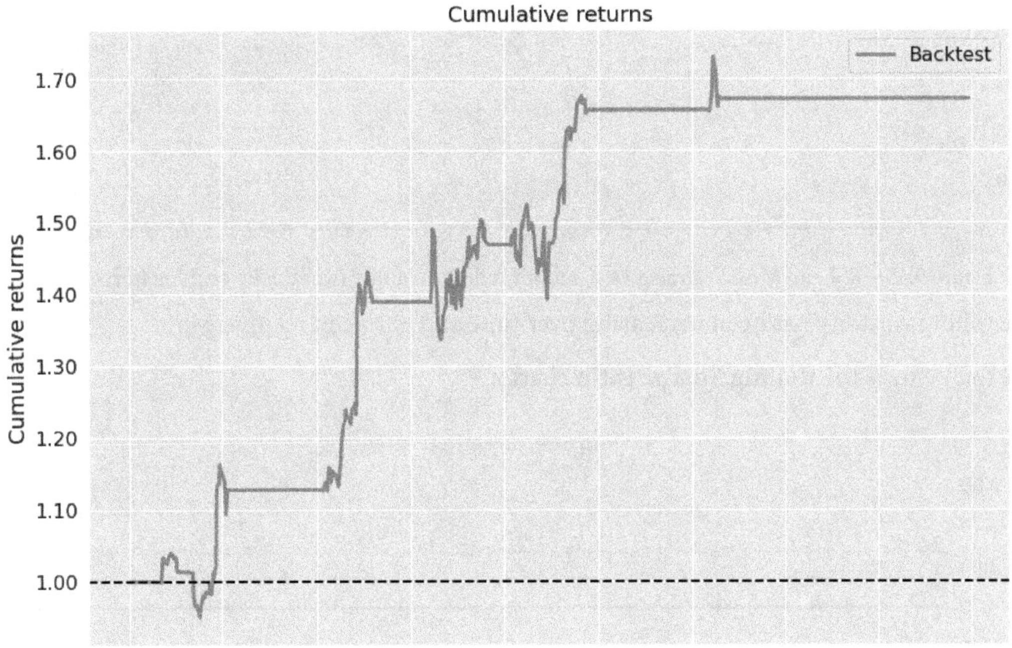

Figure 9.43 – RSI and MACD strategies; cumulative returns over the investment horizon

The high stability value is favorable. Notice the horizontal lines in the chart; these indicate that we have not traded.

The following is the **Returns** chart:

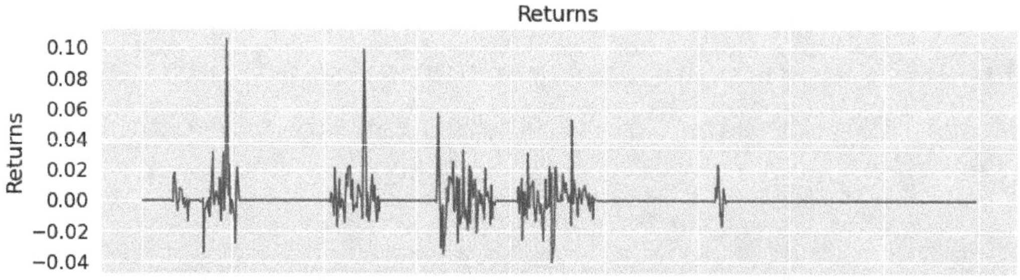

Figure 9.44 – RSI and MACD strategies; returns over the investment horizon

The **Returns** chart shows that when we traded, the positive returns outweighed the negative ones.

The following is the **Rolling volatility** chart:

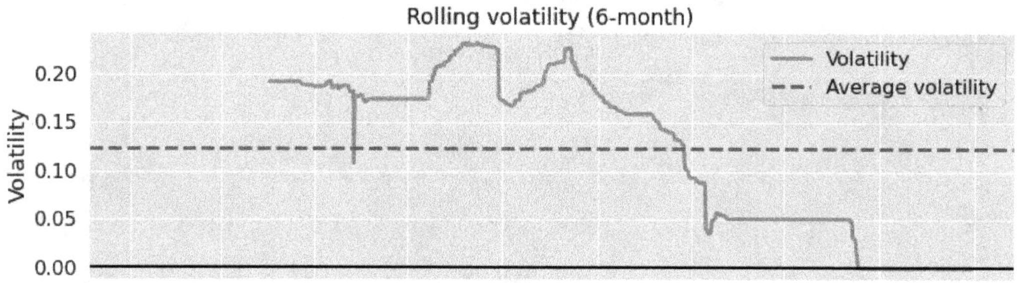

Figure 9.45 – RSI and MACD strategies; 6-month rolling volatility over the investment horizon

The rolling volatility has been decreasing over time and has been relatively low.

The following is the **Rolling Sharpe ratio** chart:

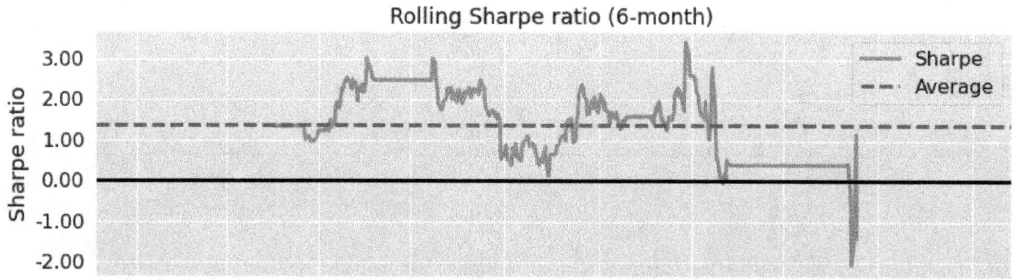

Figure 9.46 – RSI and MACD strategies; 6-month rolling Sharpe ratio over the investment horizon

The maximum rolling Sharpe ratio was over 3, with a minimum of below -2 and an average above 1.0 indicative of a very good result.

The following is the **Top 5 drawdown periods** chart:

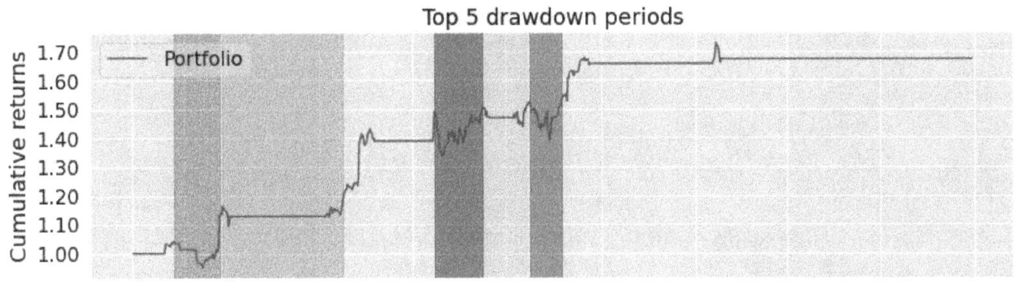

Figure 9.47 – RSI and MACD strategies; top five drawdown periods over the investment horizon

We see that the drawdown periods were short and not significant.

The following are the **Monthly returns**, **Annual returns**, and **Distribution of monthly returns** charts:

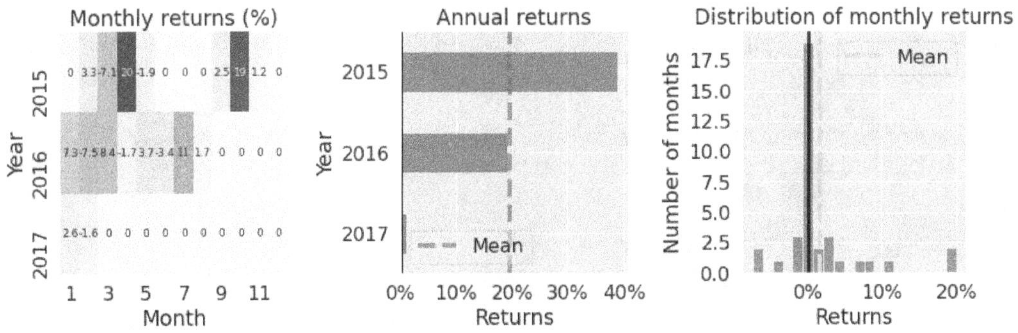

Figure 9.48 – RSI and MACD strategies; monthly returns, annual returns, and the distribution of monthly returns over the investment horizon

The **Monthly returns** table confirms we have not traded in most months. However, according to the **Annual returns** chart, when we did trade, it was hugely profitable. The **Distribution of monthly returns** chart is positive, with high kurtosis.

The RSI and MACD strategy, as a combination of two strategies, demonstrates excellent performance, with a Sharpe ratio of 1.27 and a maximum drawdown of -10.4%. Notice that it does not trigger any trading in some months.

Triple exponential average strategy

The **Triple Exponential Average** (**TRIX**) indicator is an oscillator oscillating around the zero line. A positive value indicates an overbought market, whereas a negative value is indicative of an oversold market:

```
%matplotlib inline

from zipline import run_algorithm
from zipline.api import order_target_percent, symbol, set_
commission
from zipline.finance.commission import PerTrade
import pandas as pd
import pyfolio as pf
from stockstats import StockDataFrame as sdf

import warnings
warnings.filterwarnings('ignore')

def initialize(context):
    context.stock = symbol('MSFT')
    context.rolling_window = 20
    set_commission(PerTrade(cost=5))

def handle_data(context, data):
    price_hist = data.history(context.stock,
                              ["open","high",
                               "low","close"],
                              context.rolling_window, "1d")

    stock=sdf.retype(price_hist)

    trix = stock.get('trix')

    if trix[-1] > 0 and trix[-2] < 0:
        order_target_percent(context.stock, 0.0)
    elif trix[-1] < 0 and trix[-2] > 0:
        order_target_percent(context.stock, 1.0)
```

```
def analyze(context, perf):
    returns, positions, transactions = \
    pf.utils.extract_rets_pos_txn_from_zipline(perf)
    pf.create_returns_tear_sheet(returns,
                                 benchmark_rets = None)

start_date = pd.to_datetime('2015-1-1', utc=True)
end_date = pd.to_datetime('2018-1-1', utc=True)

results = run_algorithm(start = start_date, end = end_date,
                        initialize = initialize,
                        analyze = analyze,
                        handle_data = handle_data,
                        capital_base = 10000,
                        data_frequency = 'daily',
                        bundle ='quandl')
```

The outputs are as follows:

Start date	2015-01-02
End date	2017-12-29
Total months	35
	Backtest
Annual return	10.6%
Cumulative returns	35.1%
Annual volatility	17.6%
Sharpe ratio	0.66
Calmar ratio	0.68
Stability	0.74
Max drawdown	-15.6%
Omega ratio	1.20
Sortino ratio	0.97
Skew	0.04
Kurtosis	19.96
Tail ratio	1.19
Daily value at risk	-2.2%

Figure 9.49 – TRIX strategy; summary return and risk statistics

The high tail ratio with an above average stability suggests, in general, a profitable strategy.

The following is the worst five drawdown periods chart:

Worst drawdown periods	Net drawdown in %	Peak date	Valley date	Recovery date	Duration
0	15.57	2015-01-08	2015-04-02	2015-10-02	192
1	14.25	2015-12-29	2016-06-27	2017-10-05	463
2	3.70	2015-11-06	2015-11-13	2015-12-01	18
3	3.49	2015-12-16	2015-12-18	2015-12-29	10
4	3.24	2015-12-04	2015-12-11	2015-12-16	9

Figure 9.50 – TRIX strategy; worst five drawdown periods

The second worst drawdown period was over a year. The worst net drawdown was -15.57%.

The following is the **Cumulative returns** chart:

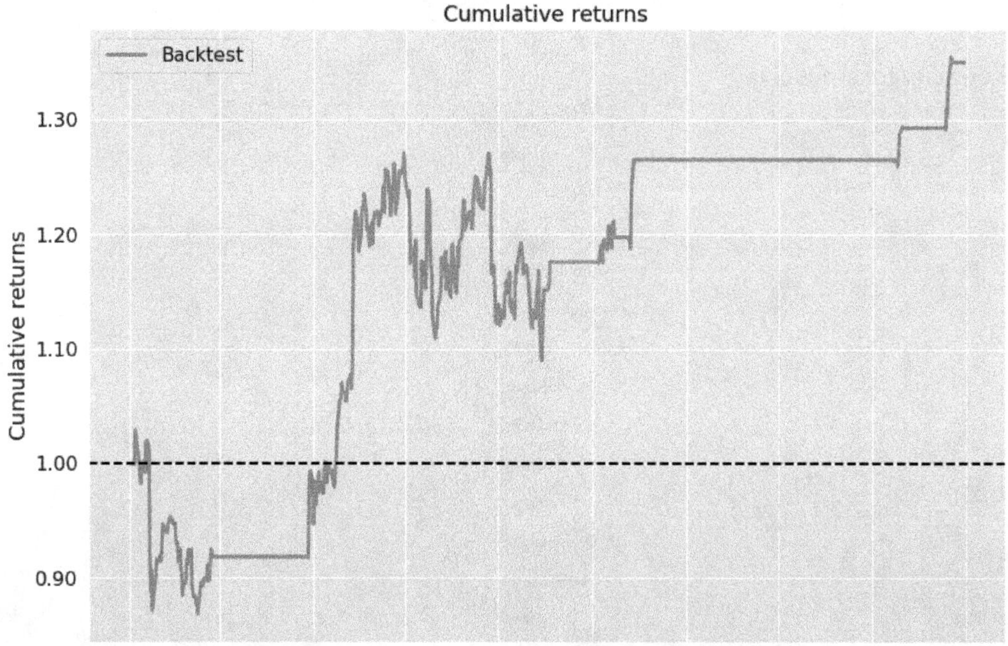

Figure 9.51 – TRIX strategy; cumulative returns over the investment horizon

The **Cumulative returns** chart indicates that we have not traded in many months (the horizontal line) and that there is a long-term positive trend, as confirmed by the high stability value.

The following is the **Returns** chart:

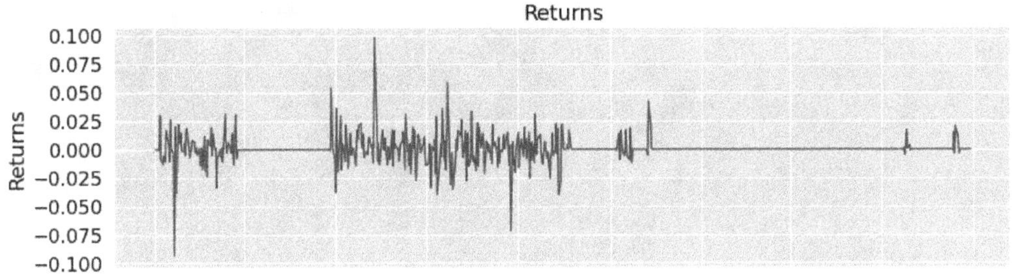

Figure 9.52 – TRIX strategy; returns over the investment horizon

This chart suggests that when we traded, we were more likely to reach a positive return.

The following is the **Rolling volatility** chart:

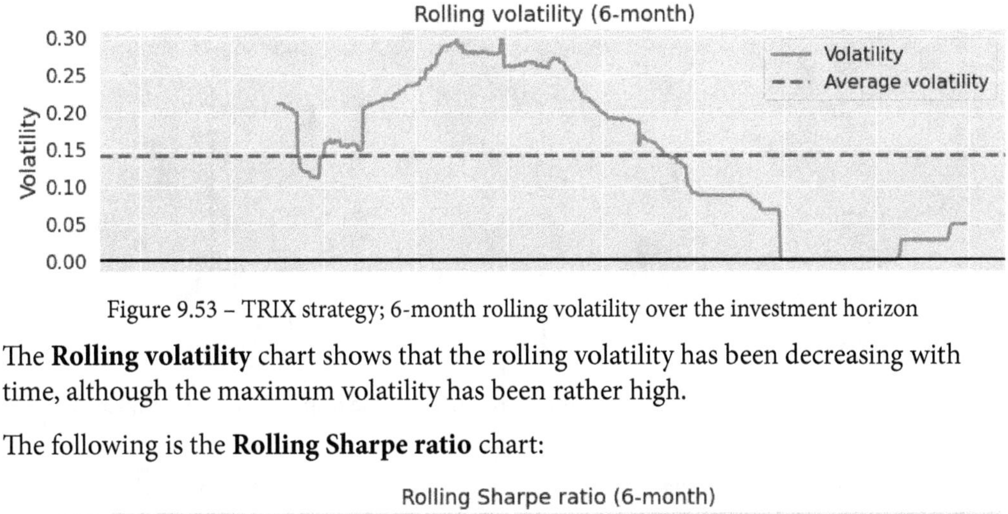

Figure 9.53 – TRIX strategy; 6-month rolling volatility over the investment horizon

The **Rolling volatility** chart shows that the rolling volatility has been decreasing with time, although the maximum volatility has been rather high.

The following is the **Rolling Sharpe ratio** chart:

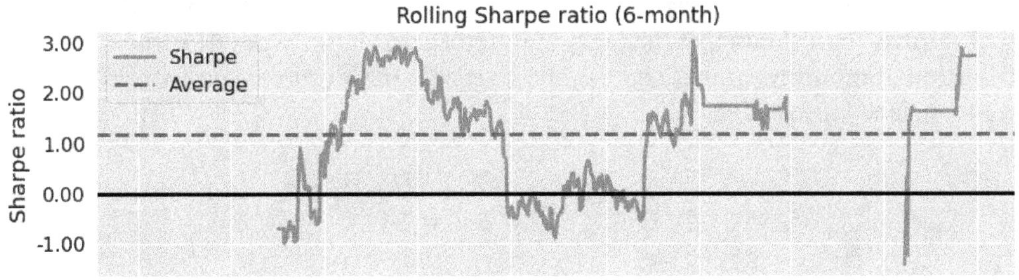

Figure 9.54 – TRIX strategy; 6-month rolling Sharpe ratio over the investment horizon

The rolling Sharpe ratio has been more likely to be positive than negative, with its maximum value in the region of 3 and a minimum value slightly below -1.

The following is the top five drawdown periods chart:

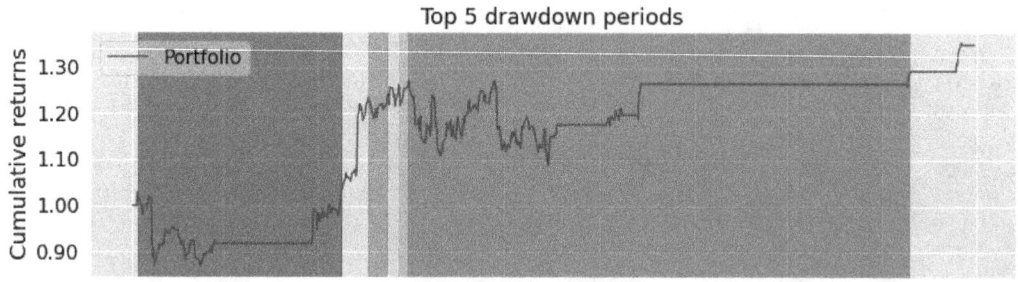

Figure 9.55 – TRIX strategy; top five drawdown periods over the investment horizon

The top five drawdown periods confirm that the worst drawdown periods have been long.

The following are the **Monthly returns**, **Annual returns**, and **Distribution of monthly returns** charts:

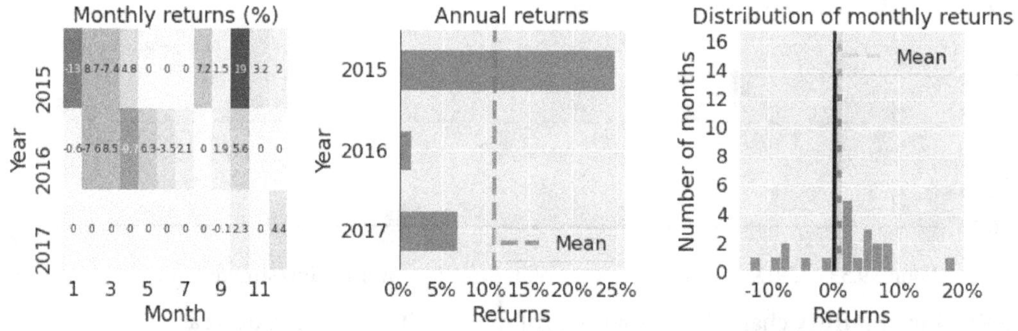

Figure 9.56 – TRIX strategy; monthly returns, annual returns, and the distribution of monthly returns over the investment horizon

The **Monthly returns** table confirms that we have not traded in many months. The **Annual returns** chart shows that the maximum return was in the year 2015. The **Distribution of monthly returns** chart shows a very slightly positive skew with a somewhat large kurtosis.

The TRIX strategy's performance for some stocks, such as Apple, is very bad over the given time frame. For other stocks such as Microsoft, included in the preceding report, performance is excellent for certain years.

Williams R% strategy

This strategy was developed by Larry Williams, and the William R% oscillates from 0 to -100. The `stockstats` library has implemented the values from 0 to +100.

The values above -20 indicate that the security has been overbought, while values below -80 indicate that the security has been oversold.

This strategy is hugely successful for Microsoft's stock, while not so much for Apple's stock:

```
%matplotlib inline

from zipline import run_algorithm
from zipline.api import order_target_percent, symbol, set_
commission
from zipline.finance.commission import PerTrade
import pandas as pd
import pyfolio as pf
from stockstats import StockDataFrame as sdf

import warnings
warnings.filterwarnings('ignore')

def initialize(context):
    context.stock = symbol('MSFT')
    context.rolling_window = 20
    set_commission(PerTrade(cost=5))

def handle_data(context, data):
    price_hist = data.history(context.stock,
                              ["open", "high",
                               "low","close"],
                              context.rolling_window, "1d")

```

```
    stock=sdf.retype(price_hist)

    wr = stock.get('wr_6')

    if wr[-1] < 10:
        order_target_percent(context.stock, 0.0)
    elif wr[-1] > 90:
        order_target_percent(context.stock, 1.0)

def analyze(context, perf):
    returns, positions, transactions = \
    pf.utils.extract_rets_pos_txn_from_zipline(perf)
    pf.create_returns_tear_sheet(returns,
                                 benchmark_rets = None)

start_date = pd.to_datetime('2015-1-1', utc=True)
end_date = pd.to_datetime('2018-1-1', utc=True)

results = run_algorithm(start = start_date, end = end_date,
                        initialize = initialize,
                        analyze = analyze,
                        handle_data = handle_data,
                        capital_base = 10000,
                        data_frequency = 'daily',
                        bundle ='quandl')
```

The outputs are as follows:

Start date	2015-01-02
End date	2017-12-29
Total months	35

	Backtest
Annual return	18.8%
Cumulative returns	67.4%
Annual volatility	11.7%
Sharpe ratio	1.53
Calmar ratio	1.88
Stability	0.98
Max drawdown	-10.0%
Omega ratio	1.71
Sortino ratio	2.72
Skew	1.50
Kurtosis	16.37
Tail ratio	1.96
Daily value at risk	-1.4%

Figure 9.57 – Williams R% strategy; summary return and risk statistics

The summary statistics show an excellent strategy – high stability confirms consistency in the returns, with a large tail ratio, a very low maximum drawdown, and a solid Sharpe ratio.

The following is the worst five drawdown periods chart:

Worst drawdown periods	Net drawdown in %	Peak date	Valley date	Recovery date	Duration
0	10.00	2015-05-27	2015-08-25	2015-10-02	93
1	4.97	2016-01-14	2016-01-21	2016-01-29	12
2	3.99	2015-01-28	2015-01-30	2015-02-05	7
3	2.56	2015-02-05	2015-03-12	2015-03-18	30
4	2.52	2015-03-20	2015-04-02	2015-04-06	12

Figure 9.58 – Williams R% strategy; worst five drawdown periods

Apart from the worst drawdown period lasting about 3 months with a net drawdown of -10%, the other periods were insignificant in both duration and magnitude.

The following is the **Cumulative returns** chart:

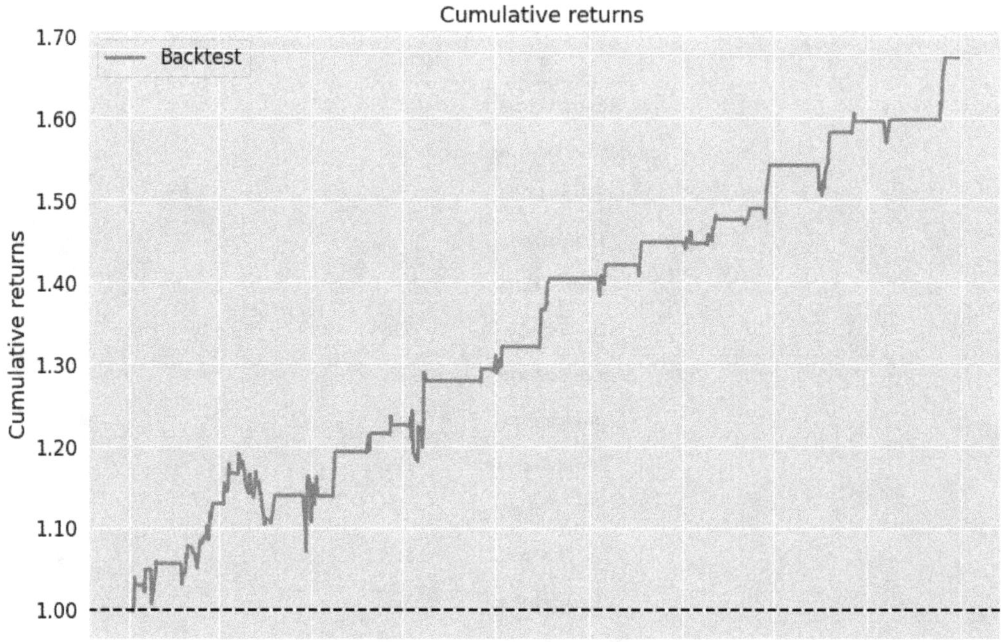

Figure 9.59 – Williams R% strategy; cumulative returns over the investment horizon

This chart confirms the high stability value of the strategy – the cumulative returns are growing at a steady rate.

The following is the **Returns** chart:

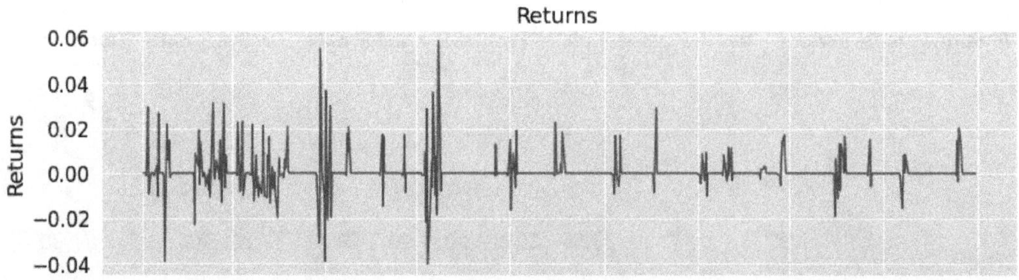

Figure 9.60 – Williams R% strategy; returns over the investment horizon

The **Returns** chart indicates that whenever we traded, it was more profitable than not.

The following is the **Rolling volatility** chart:

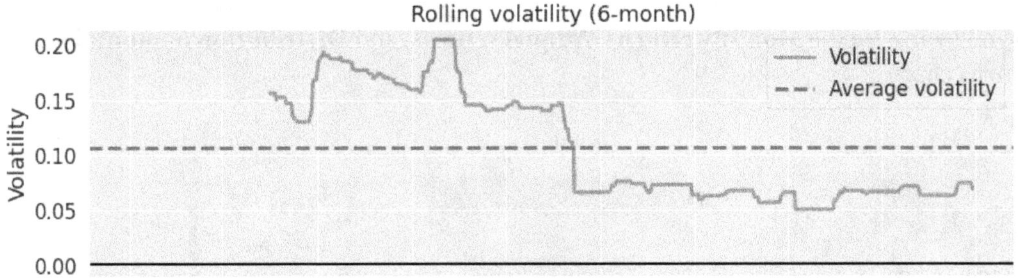

Figure 9.61 – Williams R% strategy; 6-month rolling volatility over the investment horizon

The **Rolling volatility** chart shows a decreasing value of rolling volatility over time.

The following is the **Rolling Sharpe ratio** chart:

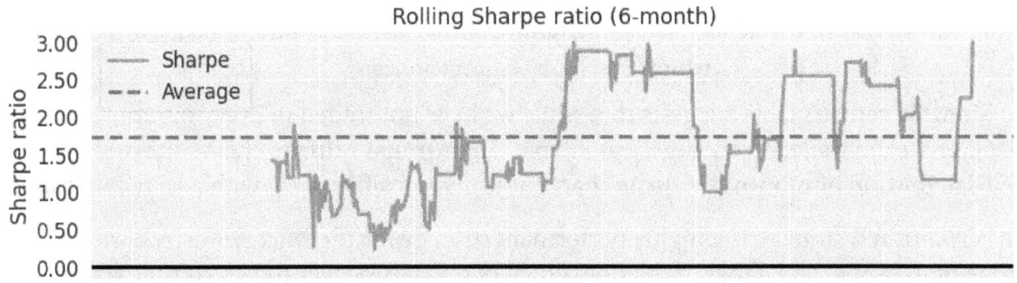

Figure 9.62 – Williams R% strategy; 6-month rolling Sharpe ratio over the investment horizon

The **Rolling Sharpe ratio** chart confirms that the Sharpe ratio has been positive over the trading horizon, with a maximum value of 3.0.

The following is the top five drawdown periods chart:

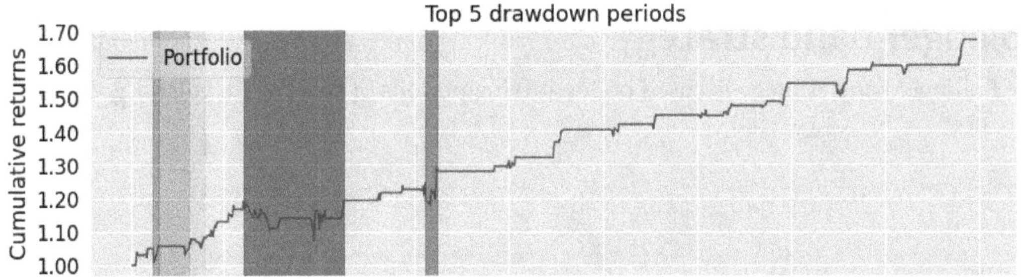

Figure 9.63 – Williams R% strategy; top five drawdown periods over the investment horizon

The **Top 5 drawdown periods** chart shows that apart from one period, the other worst drawdown periods were not significant.

The following are the **Monthly returns**, **Annual returns**, and **Distribution of monthly returns** charts:

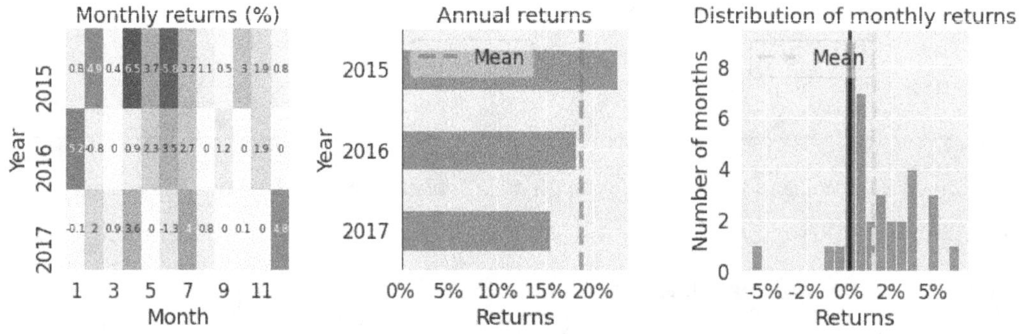

Figure 9.64 – Williams R% strategy; monthly returns, annual returns, and the distribution of monthly returns over the investment horizon

The **Monthly returns** table suggests that while we have not traded in every month, whenever we did trade, it was largely profitable. The **Annual returns** chart confirms this. The **Distribution of monthly returns** chart confirms a positive skew with a large kurtosis.

The Williams R% strategy is a highly performant strategy for the Microsoft stock with a Sharpe ratio of 1.53 and a maximum drawdown of only -10% over the given time frame.

Learning mean-reversion strategies

Mean-reversion strategies are based on the assumption that some statistics will revert to their long-term mean values.

Bollinger band strategy

The Bollinger band strategy is based on identifying periods of short-term volatility.

It depends on three lines:

- *The middle band line* is the simple moving average, usually 20-50 days.
- *The upper band* is the 2 standard deviations above the middle base line.
- *The lower band* is the 2 standard deviations below the middle base line.

One way of creating trading signals from Bollinger bands is to define the overbought and oversold market state:

- The market is overbought when the price of the financial asset rises above the upper band and so is due for a pullback.
- The market is oversold when the price of the financial asset drops below the lower band and so is due to bounce back.

This is a mean-reversion strategy, meaning that long term, the price should remain within the lower and upper bands. It works best for low-volatility stocks:

```
%matplotlib inline

from zipline import run_algorithm
from zipline.api import order_target_percent, symbol, set_
commission
from zipline.finance.commission import PerTrade
import pandas as pd
import pyfolio as pf

import warnings
warnings.filterwarnings('ignore')

def initialize(context):
    context.stock = symbol('DG')
    context.rolling_window = 20
    set_commission(PerTrade(cost=5))

def handle_data(context, data):
    price_hist = data.history(context.stock, "close",
                              context.rolling_window, "1d")

```

```
    middle_base_line = price_hist.mean()
    std_line =  price_hist.std()
    lower_band = middle_base_line - 2 * std_line
    upper_band = middle_base_line + 2 * std_line

    if price_hist[-1] < lower_band:
        order_target_percent(context.stock, 1.0)
    elif price_hist[-1] > upper_band:
        order_target_percent(context.stock, 0.0)

def analyze(context, perf):
    returns, positions, transactions = \
    pf.utils.extract_rets_pos_txn_from_zipline(perf)
    pf.create_returns_tear_sheet(returns,
                                             benchmark_rets = None)

start_date = pd.to_datetime('2000-1-1', utc=True)
end_date = pd.to_datetime('2018-1-1', utc=True)

results = run_algorithm(start = start_date, end = end_date,
                        initialize = initialize,
                        analyze = analyze,
                        handle_data = handle_data,
                        capital_base = 10000,
                        data_frequency = 'daily',
                        bundle ='quandl')
```

The outputs are as follows:

Start date	2000-01-03
End date	2017-12-29
Total months	215
	Backtest
Annual return	6.6%
Cumulative returns	215.2%
Annual volatility	11.4%
Sharpe ratio	0.62
Calmar ratio	0.24
Stability	0.76
Max drawdown	-27.3%
Omega ratio	1.31
Sortino ratio	0.93
Skew	-1.58
Kurtosis	107.60
Tail ratio	1.42
Daily value at risk	-1.4%

Figure 9.65 – Bollinger band strategy; summary return and risk statistics

The summary statistics do show that the stability is solid, with the tail ratio favorable. However, the max drawdown is a substantial -27.3%.

The following is the worst five drawdown periods chart:

Worst drawdown periods	Net drawdown in %	Peak date	Valley date	Recovery date	Duration
0	27.29	2016-08-24	2016-10-05	NaT	NaN
1	25.47	2015-08-19	2015-11-13	2016-05-26	202
2	11.70	2011-06-21	2011-08-04	2011-08-30	51
3	11.11	2010-08-04	2011-02-14	2011-06-09	222
4	7.93	2012-08-07	2012-08-29	2012-09-21	34

Figure 9.66 – Bollinger band strategy; worst five drawdown periods

The duration of the worst drawdown periods is substantial. Maybe we should tweak the entry/exit rules to avoid entering the trades in these periods.

The following is the **Cumulative returns** chart:

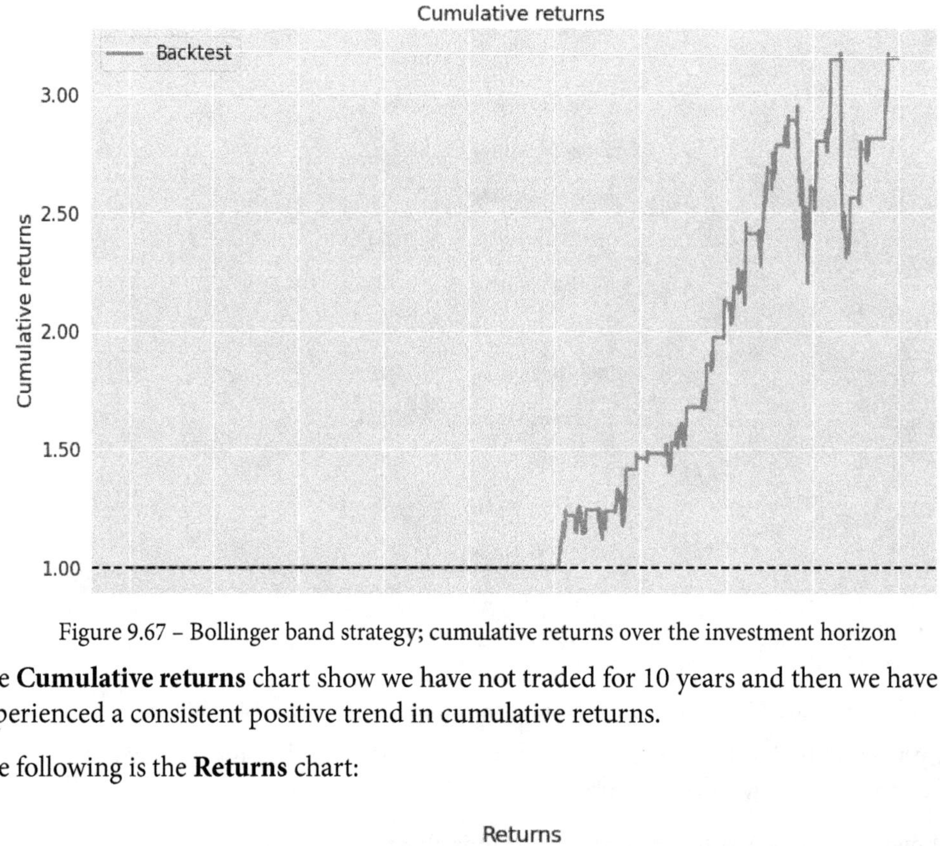

Figure 9.67 – Bollinger band strategy; cumulative returns over the investment horizon

The **Cumulative returns** chart show we have not traded for 10 years and then we have experienced a consistent positive trend in cumulative returns.

The following is the **Returns** chart:

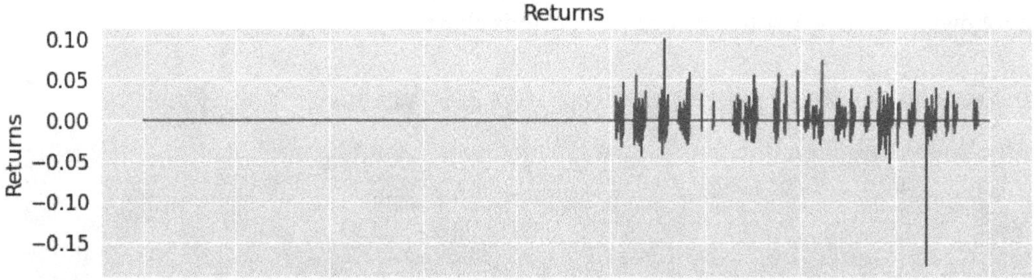

Figure 9.68 – Bollinger band strategy; returns over the investment horizon

The **Returns** chart shows that the positive returns have outweighed the negative ones.

The following is the **Rolling volatility** chart:

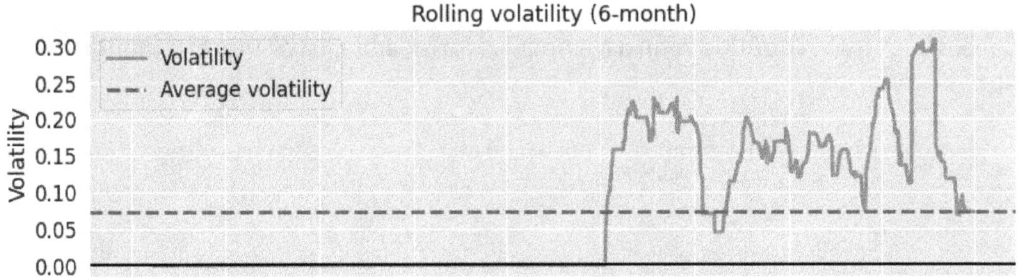

Figure 9.69 – Bollinger band strategy; 6-month rolling volatility over the investment horizon

The **Rolling volatility** chart suggests that the strategy has substantial volatility.

The following is the **Rolling Sharpe ratio** chart:

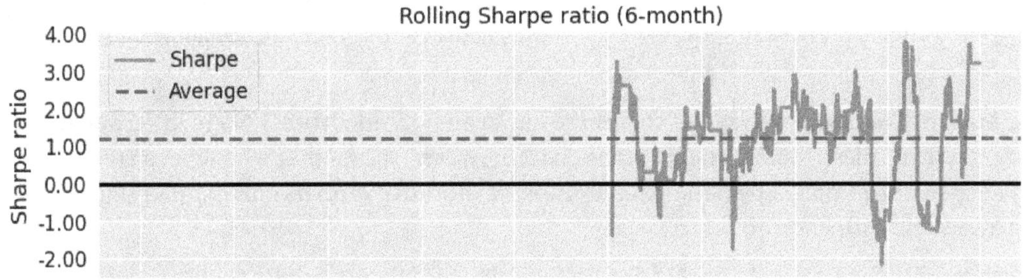

Figure 9.70 – Bollinger band strategy; 6-month rolling Sharpe ratio over the investment horizon

The **Rolling Sharpe ratio** chart shows that the rolling Sharpe ratio fluctuates widely with a max value of close to 4 and a minimum below -2, but on average it is positive.

The following is the **Top 5 drawdown periods** chart:

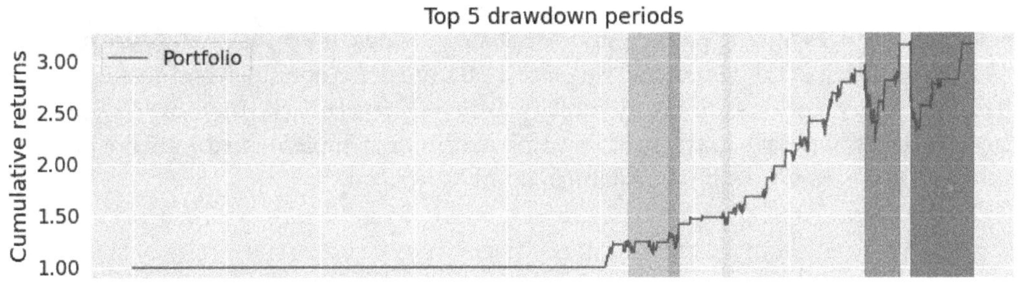

Figure 9.71 – Bollinger band strategy; top five drawdown periods over the investment horizon

The **Top 5 drawdown periods** chart confirms the drawdown periods duration has been substantial.

The following are the **Monthly returns**, **Annual returns**, and **Distribution of monthly returns** charts:

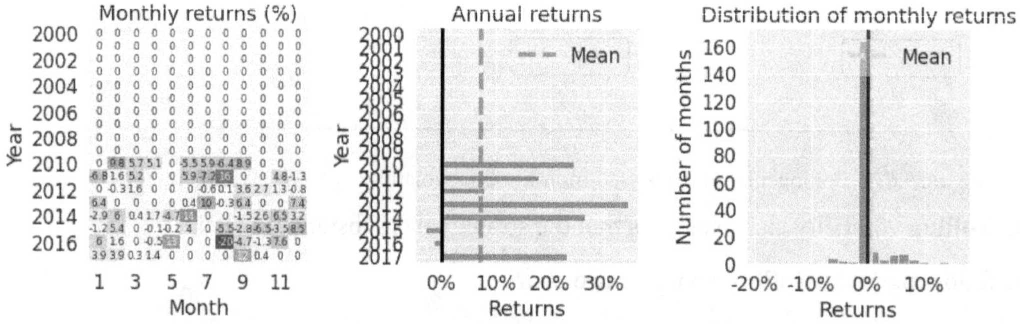

Figure 9.72 – Bollinger band strategy; monthly returns, annual returns, and the distribution of monthly returns over the investment horizon

The **Monthly returns** table shows that there has been no trade from 2000 to 2010 due to our entry/exit rules. The **Annual returns** chart, however, shows that whenever a trade did happen, it was profitable. The **Distribution of monthly returns** chart shows slight negative skew with enormous kurtosis.

The Bollinger band strategy is a suitable strategy for oscillating stocks. Here, we applied it to the stock of **Dollar General** (**DG**) Corp.

Pairs trading strategy

This strategy became very popular some time ago and ever since, has been overused, so is barely profitable nowadays.

This strategy involves finding pairs of stocks that are moving closely together, or are highly co-integrated. Then, at the same time, we place a `BUY` order for one stock and a `SELL` order for the other stock, assuming their relationship will revert back. There are a wide range of varieties of tweaks in terms of how this algorithm is implemented – are the prices log prices? Do we trade only if the relationships are very strong?

For simplicity, we have chosen the **Pepsi Cola** (**PEP**) and **Coca-Cola** (**KO**) stocks. Another choice could be **Citibank** (**C**) and **Goldman Sachs** (**GS**). We have two conditions: first, the p-value of cointegration has to be very strong, and then the z-score has to be very strong:

```
%matplotlib inline

from zipline import run_algorithm
from zipline.api import order_target_percent, symbol, set_
commission
from zipline.finance.commission import PerTrade
import pandas as pd
import pyfolio as pf
import numpy as np
import statsmodels.api as sm
from statsmodels.tsa.stattools import coint


import warnings
warnings.filterwarnings('ignore')

def initialize(context):
    context.stock_x = symbol('PEP')
    context.stock_y = symbol('KO')
    context.rolling_window = 500
    set_commission(PerTrade(cost=5))
    context.i = 0

def handle_data(context, data):
    context.i += 1
    if context.i < context.rolling_window:
        return

    try:
        x_price = data.history(context.stock_x, "close",
                                context.rolling_window,"1d")
        x = np.log(x_price)
```

```
        y_price = data.history(context.stock_y, "close",
                               context.rolling_window,"1d")
        y = np.log(y_price)

        _, p_value, _  = coint(x, y)
        if p_value < .9:
            return

        slope, intercept = sm.OLS(y, sm.add_constant(x,
prepend=True)).fit().params

        spread = y - (slope * x + intercept)
        zscore = (\
        spread[-1] - spread.mean()) / spread.std()

        if -1 < zscore < 1:
            return

        side = np.copysign(0.5, zscore)
        order_target_percent(context.stock_y,
                             -side * 100 / y_price[-1])
        order_target_percent(context.stock_x,
                             side * slope*100/x_price[-1])
    except:
        pass

def analyze(context, perf):
    returns, positions, transactions = \
    pf.utils.extract_rets_pos_txn_from_zipline(perf)
    pf.create_returns_tear_sheet(returns,
                                 benchmark_rets = None)

start_date = pd.to_datetime('2015-1-1', utc=True)
end_date = pd.to_datetime('2018-01-01', utc=True)
```

```
results = run_algorithm(start = start_date, end = end_date,
                        initialize = initialize,
                        analyze = analyze,
                        handle_data = handle_data,
                        capital_base = 10000,
                        data_frequency = 'daily',
                        bundle ='quandl')
```

The outputs are as follows:

Start date	2015-01-02
End date	2017-12-29
Total months	35
	Backtest
Annual return	1.8%
Cumulative returns	5.4%
Annual volatility	4.3%
Sharpe ratio	0.43
Calmar ratio	0.30
Stability	0.57
Max drawdown	-5.8%
Omega ratio	1.14
Sortino ratio	0.61
Skew	-0.29
Kurtosis	14.23
Tail ratio	1.23
Daily value at risk	-0.5%

Figure 9.73 – Pairs trading strategy; summary return and risk statistics

While the Sharpe ratio is very low, the max drawdown is also very low. The stability is average.

The following is the worst five drawdown periods chart:

Worst drawdown periods	Net drawdown in %	Peak date	Valley date	Recovery date	Duration
0	5.81	2017-11-14	2017-12-12	NaT	NaN
1	3.59	2017-09-13	2017-09-27	2017-10-17	25
2	2.89	2017-06-06	2017-07-07	2017-07-27	38
3	2.44	2017-03-02	2017-03-24	2017-05-04	46
4	1.67	2017-07-28	2017-08-22	2017-09-05	28

Figure 9.74 – Pairs trading strategy; worst five drawdown periods

The worst five drawdown periods table shows that the max drawdown was negligible and very short.

The following is the **Cumulative returns** chart:

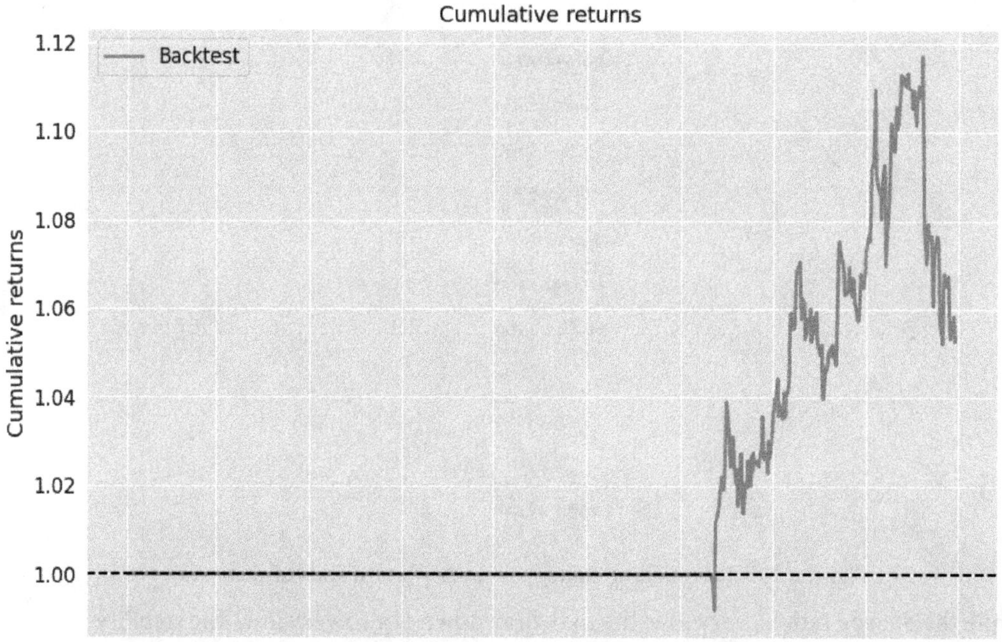

Figure 9.75 – Pairs trading strategy; cumulative returns over the investment horizon

The **Cumulative returns** chart indicates that we have not traded for 2 years and then were hugely profitable until the last period.

The following is the **Returns** chart:

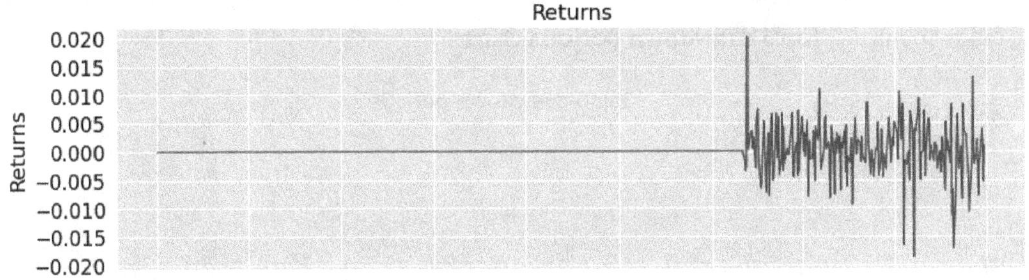

Figure 9.76 – Pairs trading strategy; returns over the investment horizon

The **Returns** chart shows that the returns have been more positive than negative for the trading period except for the last period.

The following is the **Rolling volatility** chart:

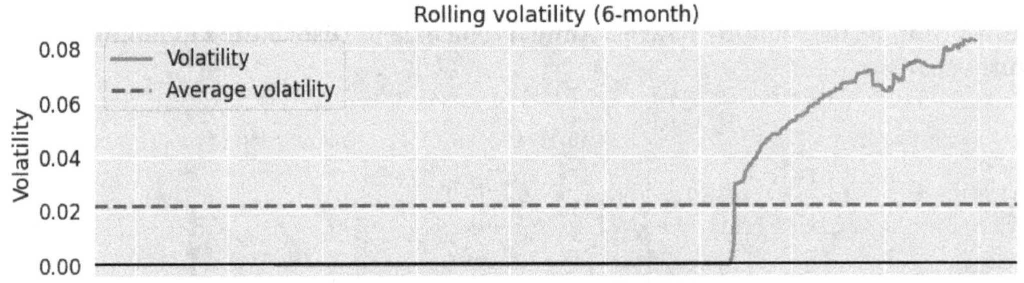

Figure 9.77 – Pairs trading strategy; 6-month rolling volatility over the investment horizon

The **Rolling volatility** chart shows an ever-increasing volatility though the volatility magnitude is not significant.

The following is the **Rolling Sharpe ratio** chart:

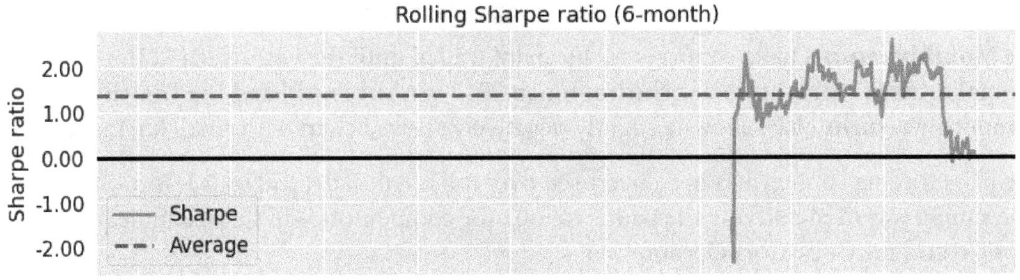

Figure 9.78 – Pairs trading strategy; 6-month rolling Sharpe ratio over the investment horizon

The **Rolling Sharpe ratio** chart shows that if we improved our exit rule and exited earlier, our Sharpe ratio would higher than 1.

The following is the **Top 5 drawdown periods** chart:

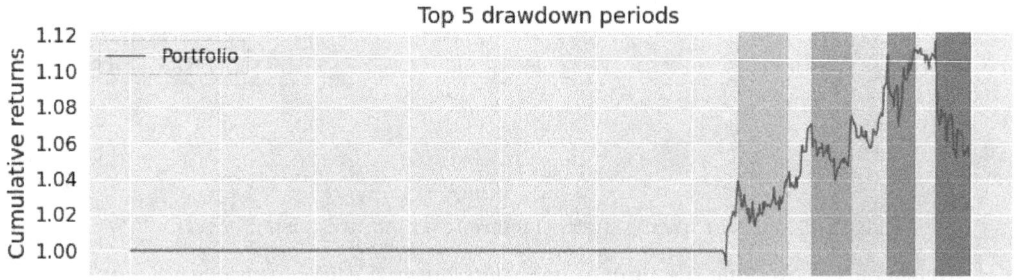

Figure 9.79 – Pairs trading strategy; top five drawdown periods over the investment horizon

The **Top 5 drawdown periods** chart tells us the same story – the last period was the cause of why this backtesting result is not as successful as it could have been.

The following are the **Monthly returns**, **Annual returns**, and **Distribution of monthly returns** charts:

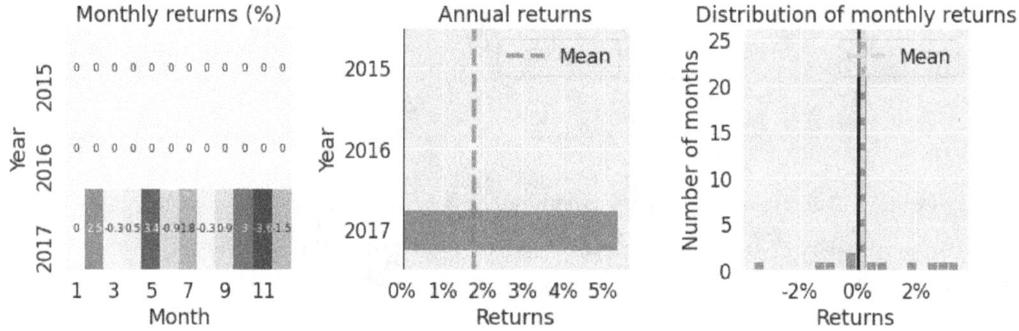

Figure 9.80 – Pairs trading strategy; monthly returns, annual returns, and the distribution of monthly returns over the investment horizon

The **Monthly returns** table confirms we have not traded until the year of 2017. The **Annual returns** chart shows that the trading in 2017 was successful and the **Distribution of monthly returns** chart shows a slightly negatively skewed chart with small kurtosis.

The pairs trading strategy has been overused over the last decade, and so is less profitable. One simple way of identifying the pair is to look for competitors – in this example, PepsiCo and the Coca-Cola Corporation.

Learning mathematical model-based strategies

We will now look at the various mathematical model-based strategies in the following sections.

Minimization of the portfolio volatility strategy with monthly trading

The objective of this strategy is to minimize portfolio volatility. It has been inspired by `https://github.com/letianzj/QuantResearch/tree/master/backtest`.

In the following example, the portfolio consists of all stocks in the *Dow Jones Industrial Average* index.

The key success factors of the strategy are the following:

- The stock universe – perhaps a portfolio of global index ETFs would fare better.
- The rolling window – we go back 200 days.
- The frequency of trades – the following algorithm uses monthly trading – notice the construct.

The code is as follows:

```
%matplotlib inline

from zipline import run_algorithm
from zipline.api import order_target_percent, symbol, set_
commission, schedule_function, date_rules, time_rules
from zipline.finance.commission import PerTrade
import pandas as pd
import pyfolio as pf
from scipy.optimize import minimize
import numpy as np

import warnings
warnings.filterwarnings('ignore')

def initialize(context):
```

```
    context.stocks = [symbol('DIS'), symbol('WMT'),
                      symbol('DOW'), symbol('CRM'),
                      symbol('NKE'), symbol('HD'),
                      symbol('V'), symbol('MSFT'),
                      symbol('MMM'), symbol('CSCO'),
                      symbol('KO'), symbol('AAPL'),
                      symbol('HON'), symbol('JNJ'),
                      symbol('TRV'), symbol('PG'),
                      symbol('CVX'), symbol('VZ'),
                      symbol('CAT'), symbol('BA'),
                      symbol('AMGN'), symbol('IBM'),
                      symbol('AXP'), symbol('JPM'),
                      symbol('WBA'), symbol('MCD'),
                      symbol('MRK'), symbol('GS'),
                      symbol('UNH'), symbol('INTC')]
    context.rolling_window = 200
    set_commission(PerTrade(cost=5))
    schedule_function(handle_data,
                      date_rules.month_end(),
                      time_rules.market_open(hours=1))

def minimum_vol_obj(wo, cov):
    w = wo.reshape(-1, 1)
    sig_p = np.sqrt(np.matmul(w.T,
                              np.matmul(cov, w)))[0, 0]
    return sig_p

def handle_data(context, data):
    n_stocks = len(context.stocks)
    prices = None

    for i in range(n_stocks):
        price_history = \
        data.history(context.stocks[i], "close",
                     context.rolling_window, "1d")

```

```
        price = np.array(price_history)
        if prices is None:
            prices = price
        else:
            prices = np.c_[prices, price]

    rets = prices[1:,:]/prices[0:-1, :]-1.0
    mu = np.mean(rets, axis=0)
    cov = np.cov(rets.T)

    w0 = np.ones(n_stocks) / n_stocks

    cons = ({'type': 'eq',
             'fun': lambda w: np.sum(w) - 1.0},
            {'type': 'ineq', 'fun': lambda w: w})
    TOL = 1e-12
    res = minimize(minimum_vol_obj, w0, args=cov,
                   method='SLSQP', constraints=cons,
                   tol=TOL, options={'disp': False})

    if not res.success:
        return;

    w = res.x

    for i in range(n_stocks):
        order_target_percent(context.stocks[i], w[i])

def analyze(context, perf):
    returns, positions, transactions = \
    pf.utils.extract_rets_pos_txn_from_zipline(perf)
    pf.create_returns_tear_sheet(returns,
                                 benchmark_rets = None)

start_date = pd.to_datetime('2010-1-1', utc=True)
end_date = pd.to_datetime('2018-1-1', utc=True)
```

```
results = run_algorithm(start = start_date, end = end_date,
                        initialize = initialize,
                        analyze = analyze,
                        capital_base = 10000,
                        data_frequency = 'daily'
                        bundle ='quandl')
```

The outputs are as follows:

Start date	2010-01-04
End date	2017-12-29
Total months	95
	Backtest
Annual return	9.7%
Cumulative returns	109.6%
Annual volatility	10.6%
Sharpe ratio	0.93
Calmar ratio	0.53
Stability	0.91
Max drawdown	-18.2%
Omega ratio	1.18
Sortino ratio	1.36
Skew	-0.08
Kurtosis	2.98
Tail ratio	1.04
Daily value at risk	-1.3%

Figure 9.81 – Minimization of the portfolio volatility strategy; summary return and risk statistics

The results are positive – see the strong stability of `0.91` while the tail ratio is just over 1.

Notice the results are including the transaction costs and they would be much worse if we traded daily. Always experiment with the optimal trading frequency.

The following is the worst five drawdown periods chart:

Worst drawdown periods	Net drawdown in %	Peak date	Valley date	Recovery date	Duration
0	18.22	2014-11-28	2015-08-25	2016-07-11	422
1	9.97	2011-07-07	2011-08-10	2011-10-27	81
2	8.56	2013-11-25	2014-02-03	2014-03-31	91
3	8.15	2010-11-04	2011-03-16	2011-04-26	124
4	7.23	2012-10-18	2012-11-15	2013-01-25	72

Figure 9.82 – Minimization of the portfolio volatility strategy; worst five drawdown periods

The worst drawdown period was over a year with the net drawdown of -18.22%. The magnitude of the net drawdown for the other worst periods is below -10%.

The following is the **Cumulative returns** chart:

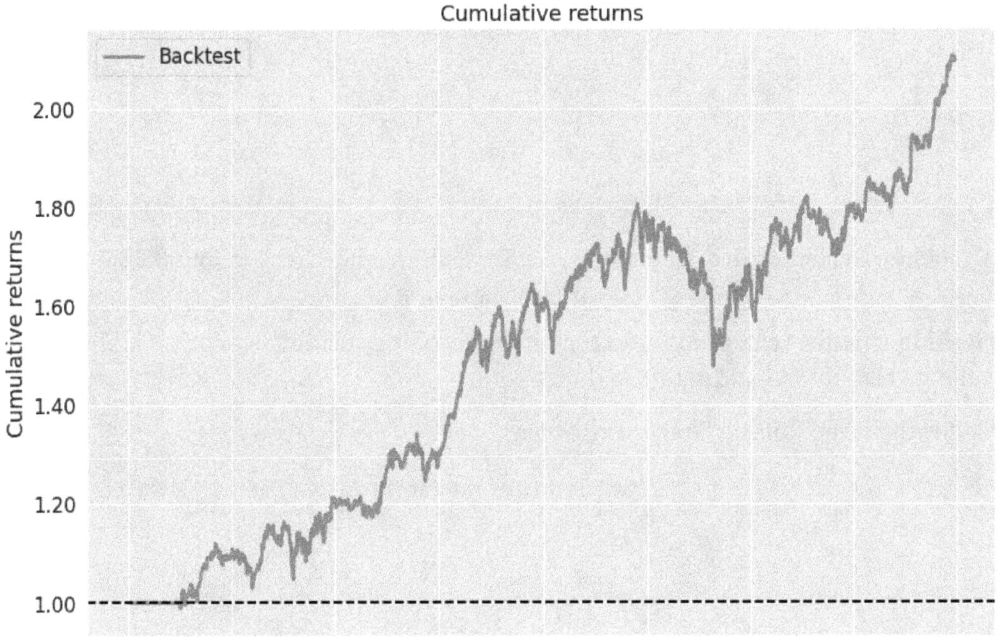

Figure 9.83 – Minimization of the portfolio volatility strategy; cumulative returns over the investment horizon

We see that the cumulative returns are consistently growing, which is expected given the stability of 0.91.

The following is the **Returns** chart:

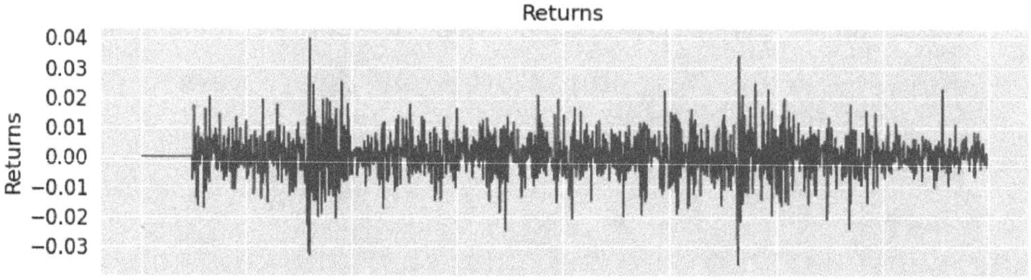

Figure 9.84 – Minimization of the portfolio volatility strategy; returns over the investment horizon

The **Returns** chart shows the returns' oscillation around zero within the interval `-0.3` to `0.04`.

The following is the **Rolling volatility** chart:

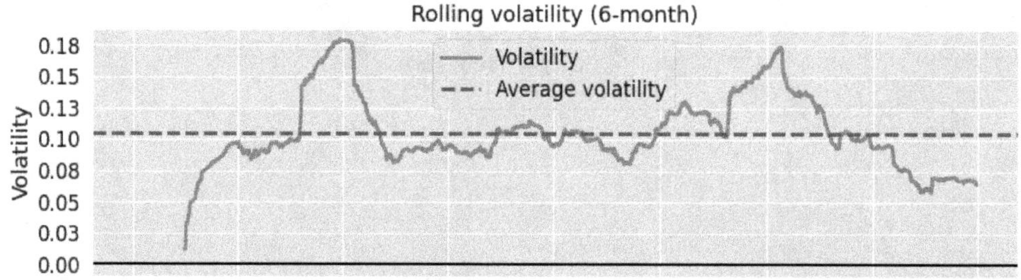

Figure 9.85 – Minimization of the portfolio volatility strategy; 6-month rolling volatility over the investment horizon

The **Rolling volatility** chart illustrates that the max rolling volatility was `0.18` and that the rolling volatility was cycling around `0.1`.

The following is the **Rolling Sharpe ratio** chart:

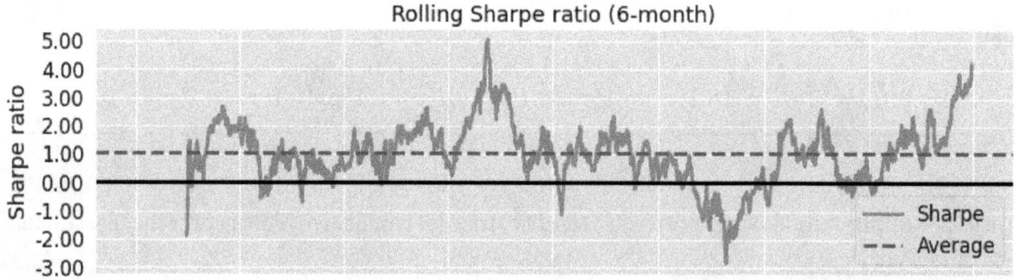

Figure 9.86 – Minimization of the portfolio volatility strategy; 6-month rolling Sharpe ratio over the investment horizon

The **Rolling Sharpe ratio** chart shows the maximum rolling Sharpe ratio of `5.0` with the minimum slightly above `-3.0`.

The following is the **Top 5 drawdown periods** chart:

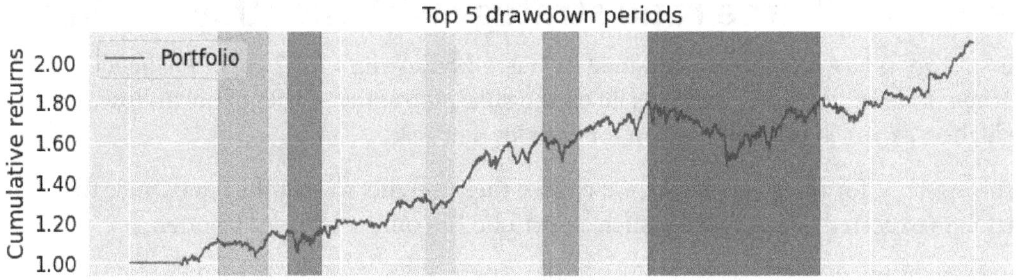

Figure 9.87 – Minimization of the portfolio volatility strategy; top five drawdown periods over the investment horizon

The **Top 5 drawdown periods** chart confirms that if we avoided the worst drawdown period by smarter choice of entry/exit rules, we would have dramatically improved the strategy's performance.

The following are the **Monthly returns**, **Annual returns**, and **Distribution of monthly returns** charts:

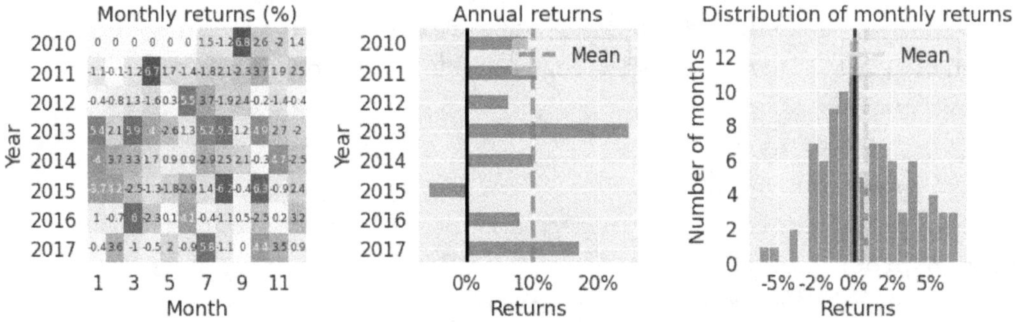

Figure 9.88 – Minimization of the portfolio volatility strategy; monthly returns, annual returns, and the distribution of monthly returns over the investment horizon

The **Monthly returns** table illustrates that we have not traded for the first few months of 2010. The **Annual returns** chart shows that the strategy has been profitable every year, but 2015. The **Distribution of monthly returns** chart draws a slightly negatively skewed strategy with small kurtosis.

Minimization of the portfolio volatility strategy is usually only profitable for non-daily trading. In this example, we used monthly trading and achieved a Sharpe ratio of 0.93, with a maximum drawdown of -18.2%.

Maximum Sharpe ratio strategy with monthly trading

This strategy is based on ideas contained in Harry Markowitz's 1952 paper *Portfolio Selection*. In brief, the best portfolios lie on the *efficient frontier* – a set of portfolios with the highest expected portfolio return for each level of risk.

In this strategy, for the given stocks, we choose their weights so that they maximize the portfolio's expected Sharpe ratio – such a portfolio lies on the efficient frontier.

We use the `PyPortfolioOpt` Python library. To install it, either use the book's `conda` environment or the following command:

```
pip install PyPortfolioOpt


%matplotlib inline

from zipline import run_algorithm
from zipline.api import order_target_percent, symbols, set_
commission, schedule_function, date_rules, time_rules
from zipline.finance.commission import PerTrade
import pandas as pd
import pyfolio as pf
import numpy as np
from pypfopt.efficient_frontier import EfficientFrontier
from pypfopt import risk_models
from pypfopt import expected_returns

import warnings
warnings.filterwarnings('ignore')

def initialize(context):
    context.stocks = \
    symbols('DIS','WMT','DOW','CRM','NKE','HD','V','MSFT',
            'MMM','CSCO','KO','AAPL','HON','JNJ','TRV',
```

```
                 'PG','CVX','VZ','CAT','BA','AMGN','IBM','AXP',
                 'JPM','WBA','MCD','MRK','GS','UNH','INTC')
    context.rolling_window = 252
    set_commission(PerTrade(cost=5))
    schedule_function(handle_data, date_rules.month_end(),
                      time_rules.market_open(hours=1))

def handle_data(context, data):
    prices_history = data.history(context.stocks, "close",
                                  context.rolling_window,
                                  "1d")
    avg_returns = \
    expected_returns.mean_historical_return(prices_history)
    cov_mat = risk_models.sample_cov(prices_history)

    efficient_frontier = EfficientFrontier(avg_returns,
                                           cov_mat)
    weights = efficient_frontier.max_sharpe()
    cleaned_weights = efficient_frontier.clean_weights()

    for stock in context.stocks:
        order_target_percent(stock, cleaned_weights[stock])

def analyze(context, perf):
    returns, positions, transactions = \
    pf.utils.extract_rets_pos_txn_from_zipline(perf)
    pf.create_returns_tear_sheet(returns,
                                 benchmark_rets = None)

start_date = pd.to_datetime('2010-1-1', utc=True)
end_date = pd.to_datetime('2018-1-1', utc=True)

results = run_algorithm(start = start_date, end = end_date,
                        initialize = initialize,
                        analyze = analyze,
                        capital_base = 10000,
```

```
                    data_frequency = 'daily',
                    bundle ='quandl')
```

The outputs are as follows:

Start date	2010-01-04
End date	2017-12-29
Total months	95
	Backtest
Annual return	12.4%
Cumulative returns	153.5%
Annual volatility	17.0%
Sharpe ratio	0.77
Calmar ratio	0.58
Stability	0.76
Max drawdown	-21.1%
Omega ratio	1.15
Sortino ratio	1.15
Skew	0.48
Kurtosis	7.23
Tail ratio	1.01
Daily value at risk	-2.1%

Figure 9.89 – Maximum Sharpe ratio strategy; summary return and risk statistics

The strategy shows solid stability of `0.76` with the tail ratio close to 1 (`1.01`). However, the annual volatility of this strategy is very high (`17.0%`).

The following is the worst five drawdown periods chart:

Worst drawdown periods	Net drawdown in %	Peak date	Valley date	Recovery date	Duration
0	21.14	2015-10-27	2017-02-02	2017-11-30	548
1	14.52	2011-07-07	2011-08-08	2012-03-19	183
2	13.53	2012-04-09	2012-05-18	2012-08-24	100
3	13.42	2015-02-24	2015-08-25	2015-10-27	176
4	11.06	2010-04-23	2010-05-20	2010-06-17	40

Figure 9.90 – Maximum Sharpe ratio strategy; worst five drawdown periods

The worst drawdown period lasted over 2 years and had a magnitude of net drawdown of -21.14%. If we tweaked the entry/exit rules to avoid this drawdown period, the results would have been dramatically better.

The following is the **Cumulative returns** chart:

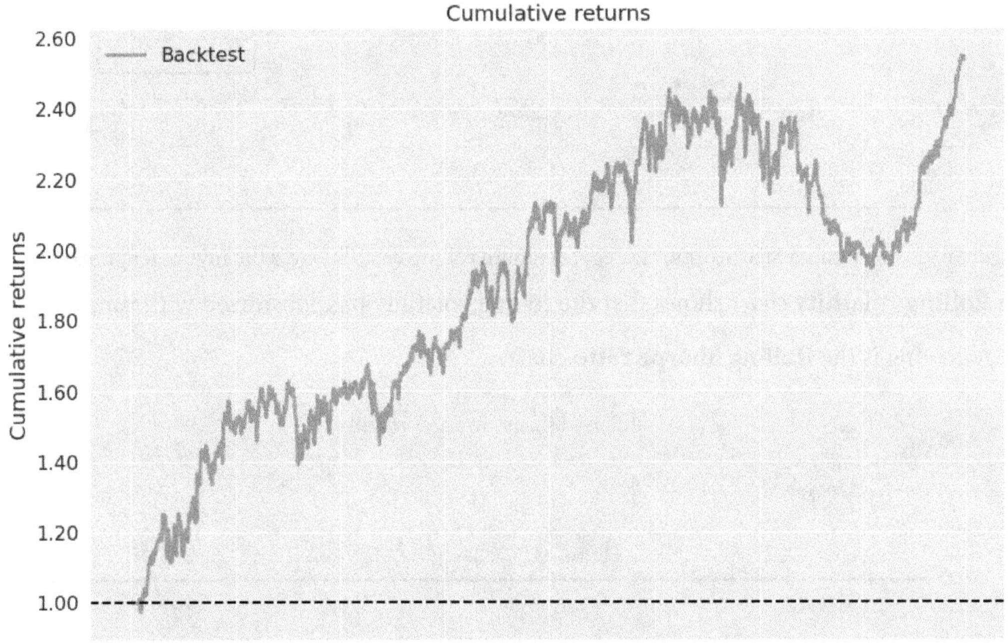

Figure 9.91 – Maximum Sharpe ratio strategy; cumulative returns over the investment horizon

The **Cumulative returns** chart shows positive stability.

The following is the **Returns** chart:

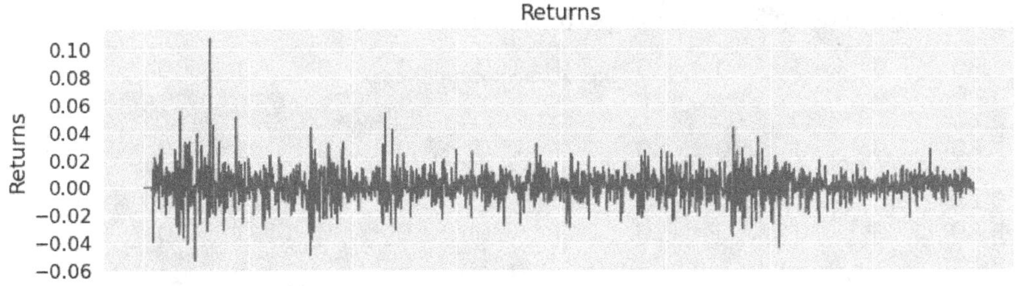

Figure 9.92 – Maximum Sharpe ratio strategy; returns over the investment horizon

The **Returns** chart show that the strategy was highly successful at the very beginning of the investment horizon.

The following is the **Rolling volatility** chart:

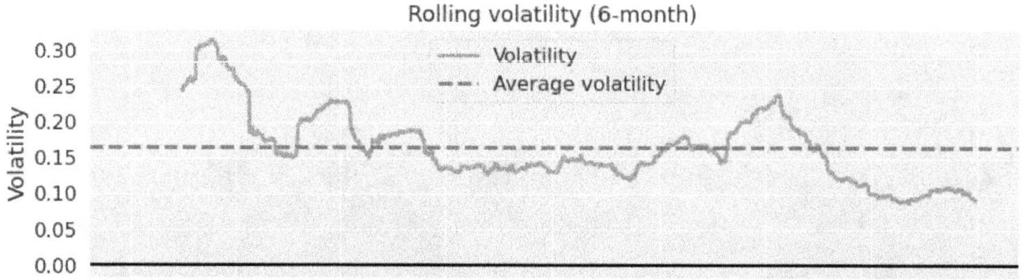

Figure 9.93 – Maximum Sharpe ratio strategy; 6-month rolling volatility over the investment horizon

The **Rolling volatility** chart shows that the rolling volatility has subsidized with time.

The following is the **Rolling Sharpe ratio** chart:

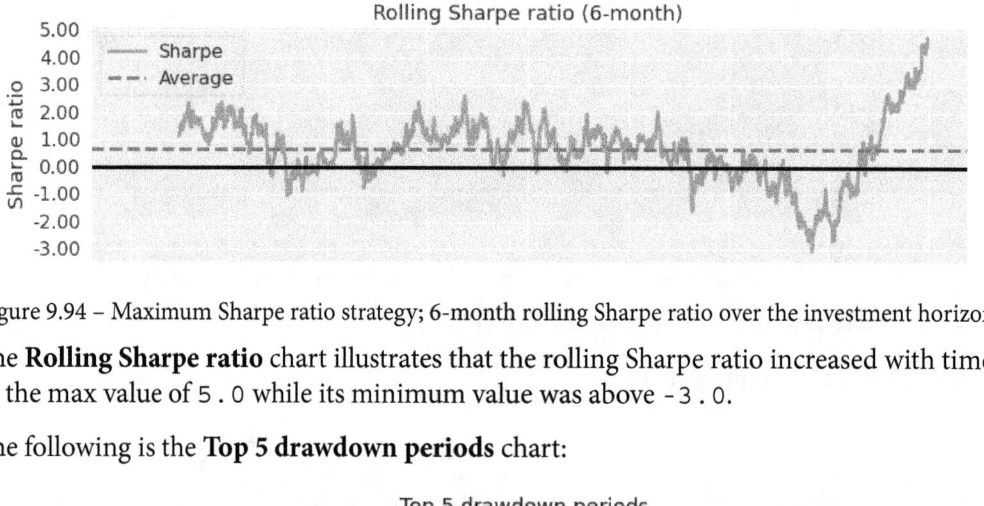

Figure 9.94 – Maximum Sharpe ratio strategy; 6-month rolling Sharpe ratio over the investment horizon

The **Rolling Sharpe ratio** chart illustrates that the rolling Sharpe ratio increased with time to the max value of `5.0` while its minimum value was above `-3.0`.

The following is the **Top 5 drawdown periods** chart:

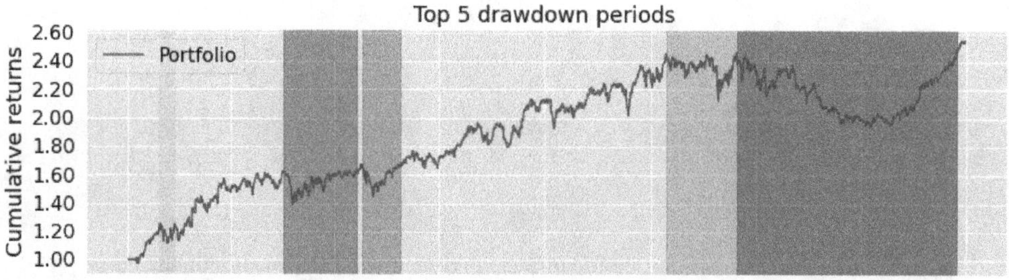

Figure 9.95 – Maximum Sharpe ratio strategy; top five drawdown periods over the investment horizon

The **Top 5 drawdown periods** chart shows that the maximum drawdown periods have been long.

The following are the **Monthly returns**, **Annual returns**, and **Distribution of monthly returns** charts:

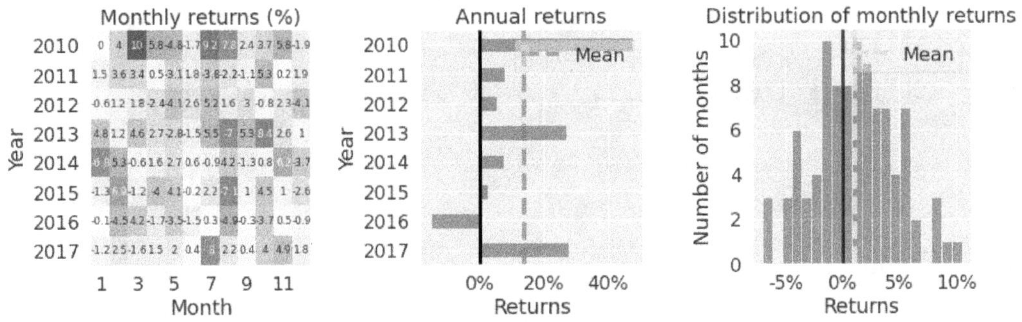

Figure 9.96 – Maximum Sharpe ratio strategy; monthly returns, annual returns, and the distribution of monthly returns over the investment horizon

The **Monthly returns** table proves that we have traded virtually in every month. The **Annual returns** chart shows that the annual returns have been positive for every year but 2016. The **Distribution of monthly returns** chart is positively skewed with minor kurtosis.

The maximum Sharpe ratio strategy is again usually only profitable for non-daily trading.

Learning time series prediction-based strategies

Time series prediction-based strategies depend on having a precise estimate of stock prices at some time in the future, along with their corresponding confidence intervals. A calculation of the estimates is usually very time-consuming.

The simple trading rule then incorporates the relationship between the last known price and the future price, or its lower/upper confidence interval value.

More complex trading rules incorporate decisions based on the trend component and seasonality components.

SARIMAX strategy

This strategy is based on the most elementary rule: own the stock if the current price is lower than the predicted price in 7 days:

```
%matplotlib inline

from zipline import run_algorithm
from zipline.api import order_target_percent, symbol, set_
commission
from zipline.finance.commission import PerTrade
import pandas as pd
import pyfolio as pf
import pmdarima as pm

import warnings
warnings.filterwarnings('ignore')

def initialize(context):
    context.stock = symbol('AAPL')
    context.rolling_window = 90
    set_commission(PerTrade(cost=5))


def handle_data(context, data):
    price_hist = data.history(context.stock, "close",
                              context.rolling_window, "1d")
    try:
        model = pm.auto_arima(price_hist, seasonal=True)
        forecasts = model.predict(7)
        order_target_percent(context.stock, 1.0 if price_hist[-
1] < forecasts[-1] else 0.0)
    except:
        pass

def analyze(context, perf):
    returns, positions, transactions = \
    pf.utils.extract_rets_pos_txn_from_zipline(perf)
```

```
    pf.create_returns_tear_sheet(returns,
                                 benchmark_rets = None)

start_date = pd.to_datetime('2017-1-1', utc=True)
end_date = pd.to_datetime('2018-1-1', utc=True)

results = run_algorithm(start = start_date, end = end_date,
                        initialize = initialize,
                        analyze = analyze,
                        handle_data = handle_data,
                        capital_base = 10000,
                        data_frequency = 'daily',
                        bundle ='quandl')
```

The outputs are as follows:

Start date	2017-01-03
End date	2017-12-29
Total months	11
	Backtest
Annual return	9.3%
Cumulative returns	9.3%
Annual volatility	9.3%
Sharpe ratio	1.01
Calmar ratio	1.22
Stability	0.25
Max drawdown	-7.7%
Omega ratio	1.36
Sortino ratio	1.45
Skew	-1.09
Kurtosis	15.97
Tail ratio	1.95
Daily value at risk	-1.1%

Figure 9.97 – SARIMAX strategy; summary return and risk statistics

Over the trading horizon, the strategy exhibited a high tail ratio of `1.95` with a very low stability of `0.25`. The max drawdown of `-7.7%` is excellent.

The following is the worst five drawdown periods chart:

Worst drawdown periods	Net drawdown in %	Peak date	Valley date	Recovery date	Duration
0	7.67	2017-05-12	2017-06-15	NaT	NaN
1	2.83	2017-04-04	2017-04-19	2017-05-01	20
2	1.15	2017-03-20	2017-03-21	2017-03-28	7
3	0.84	2017-01-11	2017-02-07	2017-02-13	24
4	0.80	2017-03-01	2017-03-09	2017-03-15	11

Figure 9.98 – SARIMAX strategy; worst five drawdown periods

The worst drawdown periods have displayed the magnitude of net drawdown below -10%.

The following is the **Cumulative returns** chart:

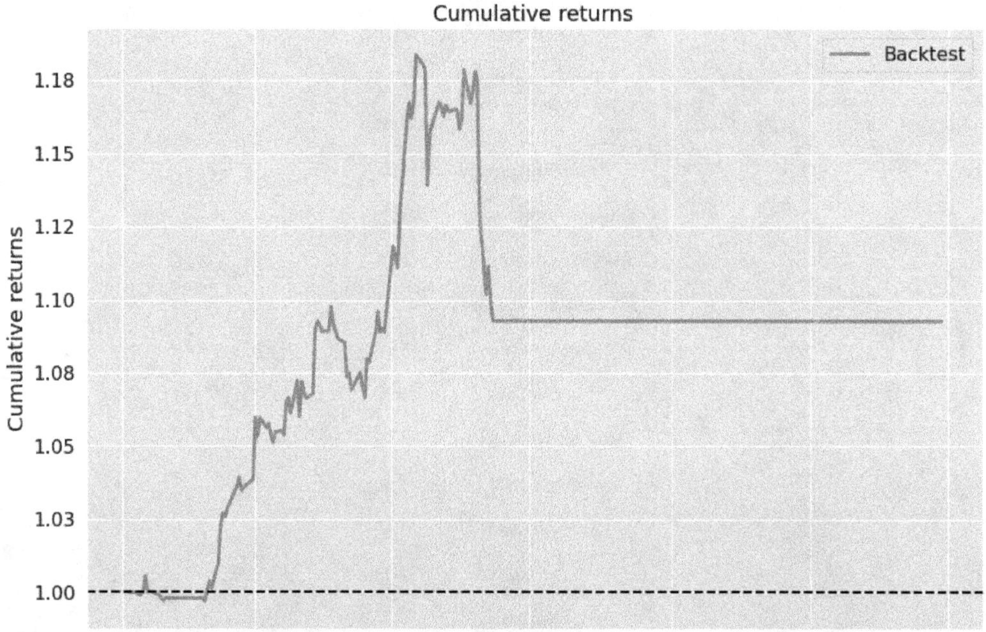

Figure 9.99 – SARIMAX strategy; cumulative returns over the investment horizon

The **Cumulative returns** chart proves that we have traded only in the first half of the trading horizon.

The following is the **Returns** chart:

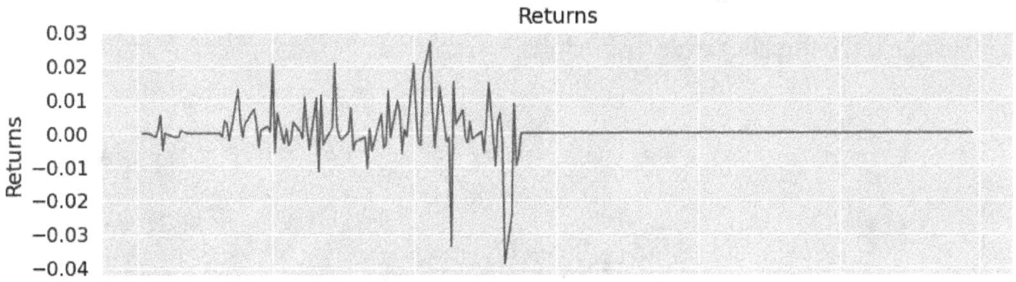

Figure 9.100 – SARIMAX strategy; returns over the investment horizon

The **Returns** chart shows that the magnitude of returns swing has been larger than with other strategies.

The following is the **Rolling volatility** chart:

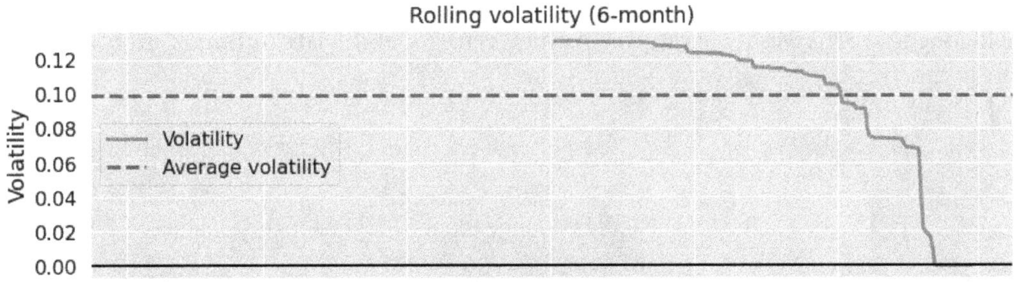

Figure 9.101 – SARIMAX strategy; 6-month rolling volatility over the investment horizon

The **Rolling volatility** chart shows that the rolling volatility has decreased with time.

The following is the **Rolling Sharpe ratio** chart:

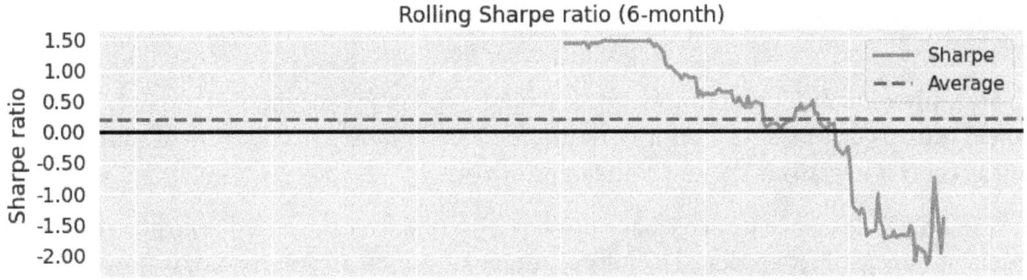

Figure 9.102 – SARIMAX strategy; 6-month rolling Sharpe ratio over the investment horizon

The **Rolling Sharpe ratio** chart shows that the Sharpe ratio in the first half of the trading horizon was excellent and then started to decrease.

The following is the **Top 5 drawdown periods** chart:

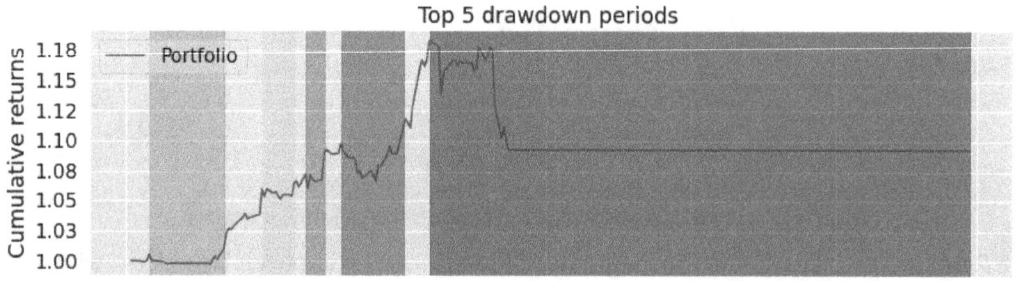

Figure 9.103 – SARIMAX strategy; top five drawdown periods over the investment horizon

The **Top 5 drawdown periods** chart demonstrates that the worst drawdown period was the entire second half of the trading window.

The following are the **Monthly returns**, **Annual returns**, and **Distribution of monthly returns** charts:

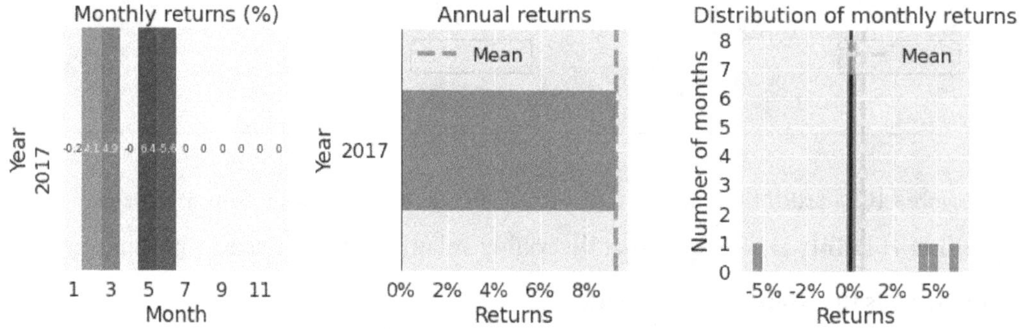

Figure 9.104 – Monthly returns, annual returns, and the distribution of monthly returns over the investment horizon

The **Monthly returns** table confirms we have not traded in the second half of 2017. The **Annual returns** chart shows a positive return for 2017 and the **Distribution of monthly returns** chart is negatively skewed with large kurtosis.

The SARIMAX strategy entry rule has not been triggered over the tested time horizon on a frequent basis. Still, it produced a Sharpe ratio of 1.01, with a maximum drawdown of -7.7%.

Prophet strategy

This strategy is based on the prediction confidence intervals, and so is more robust than the previous one. In addition, Prophet predictions are more robust to frequent changes than SARIMAX. The backtesting results are all identical, but the prediction algorithms are significantly better.

We only buy the stock if the last price is below the lower value of the confidence interval (we anticipate that the stock price will go up) and sell the stock if the last price is above the upper value of the predicted confidence interval (we anticipate that the stock price will go down):

```
%matplotlib inline

from zipline import run_algorithm
from zipline.api import order_target_percent, symbol, set_
commission
from zipline.finance.commission import PerTrade
import pandas as pd
import pyfolio as pf
from fbprophet import Prophet
import logging

logging.getLogger('fbprophet').setLevel(logging.WARNING)

import warnings
warnings.filterwarnings('ignore')

def initialize(context):
    context.stock = symbol('AAPL')
    context.rolling_window = 90
    set_commission(PerTrade(cost=5))


def handle_data(context, data):
    price_hist = data.history(context.stock, "close",
                              context.rolling_window, "1d")

    price_df = pd.DataFrame({'y' : price_hist}).rename_
```

```
axis('ds').reset_index()
    price_df['ds'] = price_df['ds'].dt.tz_convert(None)

    model = Prophet()
    model.fit(price_df)
    df_forecast = model.make_future_dataframe(periods=7,
                                              freq='D')
    df_forecast = model.predict(df_forecast)

    last_price=price_hist[-1]
    forecast_lower=df_forecast['yhat_lower'].iloc[-1]
    forecast_upper=df_forecast['yhat_upper'].iloc[-1]

    if last_price < forecast_lower:
        order_target_percent(context.stock, 1.0)
    elif last_price > forecast_upper:
        order_target_percent(context.stock, 0.0)

def analyze(context, perf):
    returns, positions, transactions = \
    pf.utils.extract_rets_pos_txn_from_zipline(perf)
    pf.create_returns_tear_sheet(returns,
                                 benchmark_rets = None)

start_date = pd.to_datetime('2017-1-1', utc=True)
end_date = pd.to_datetime('2018-1-1', utc=True)

results = run_algorithm(start = start_date, end = end_date,
                        initialize = initialize,
                        analyze = analyze,
                        handle_data = handle_data,
                        capital_base = 10000,
                        data_frequency = 'daily',
                        bundle ='quandl')
```

The outputs are as follows:

Start date	2017-01-03
End date	2017-12-29
Total months	11
	Backtest
Annual return	19.4%
Cumulative returns	19.3%
Annual volatility	15.5%
Sharpe ratio	1.22
Calmar ratio	2.23
Stability	0.35
Max drawdown	-8.7%
Omega ratio	1.33
Sortino ratio	2.03
Skew	1.07
Kurtosis	9.47
Tail ratio	1.37
Daily value at risk	-1.9%

Figure 9.105 – Prophet strategy; summary return and risk statistics

In comparison with the SARIMAX strategy, the Prophet strategy shows far better results – tail ratio of `1.37`, Sharpe ratio of `1.22`, and max drawdown of `-8.7%`.

The following is the worst five drawdown periods chart:

Worst drawdown periods	Net drawdown in %	Peak date	Valley date	Recovery date	Duration
0	8.70	2017-04-04	2017-06-16	2017-08-15	96
1	8.18	2017-09-01	2017-09-25	2017-10-30	42
2	3.40	2017-11-24	2017-12-06	NaT	NaN
3	2.91	2017-11-10	2017-11-15	2017-11-22	9
4	2.70	2017-08-15	2017-08-21	2017-08-29	11

Figure 9.106 – Prophet strategy; worst five drawdown periods

The worst five drawdown periods confirms that the magnitude of the worst net drawdown was below 10%.

The following is the **Cumulative returns** chart:

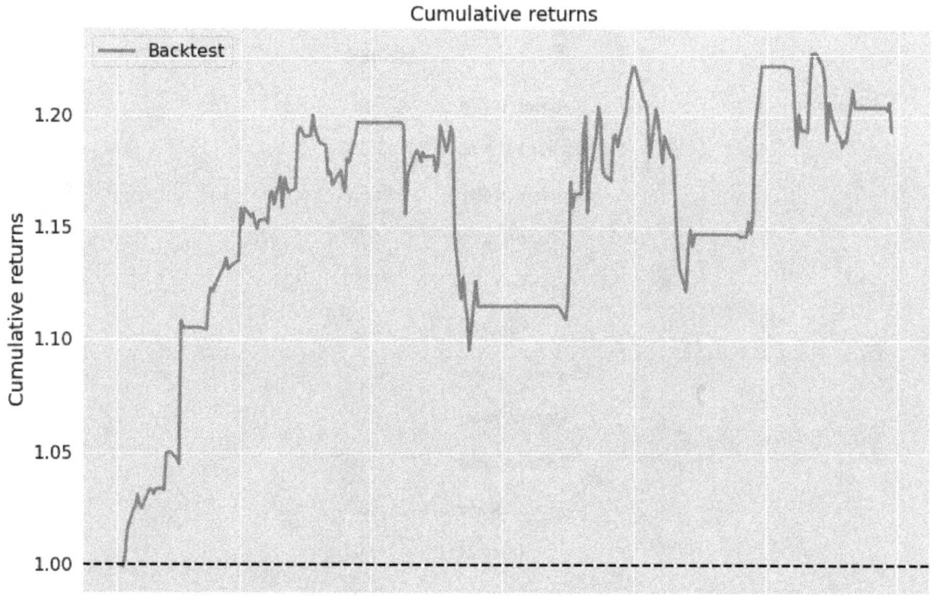

Figure 9.107 – Prophet strategy; cumulative returns over the investment horizon

The **Cumulative returns** chart shows that while we have not traded in certain periods of time, the entry/exit rules have been more robust than in the SARIMAX strategy – compare both the **Cumulative returns** charts.

The following is the **Returns** chart:

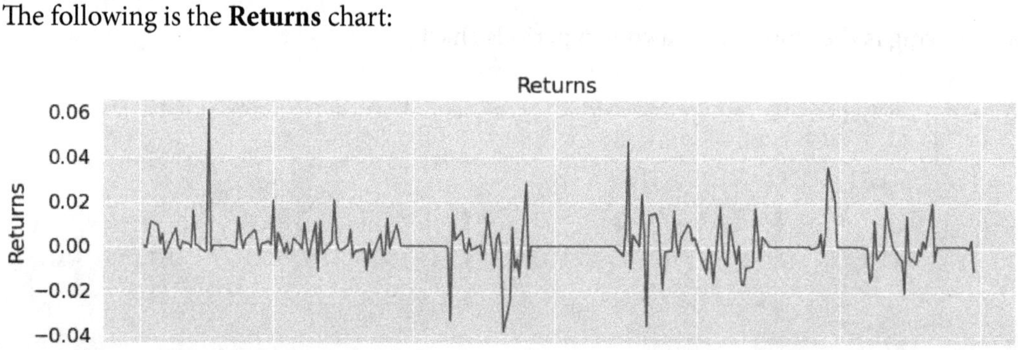

Figure 9.108 – Prophet strategy; returns over the investment horizon

The **Returns** chart suggests that the positive returns outweighed the negative returns.

The following is the **Rolling volatility** chart:

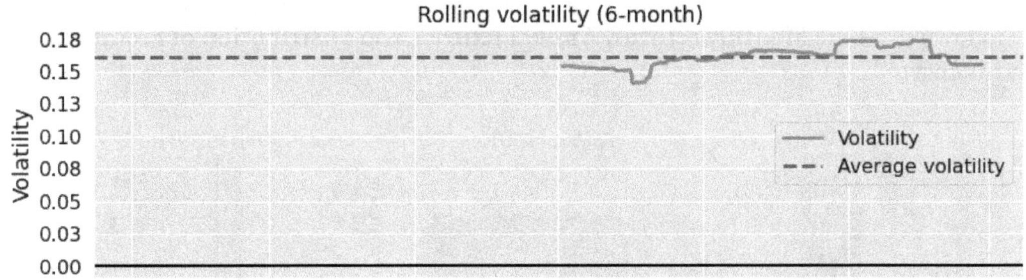

Figure 9.109 – Prophet strategy; 6-month rolling volatility over the investment horizon

The **Rolling volatility** chart shows virtually constant rolling volatility – this is the hallmark of the Prophet strategy.

The following is the **Rolling Sharpe ratio** chart:

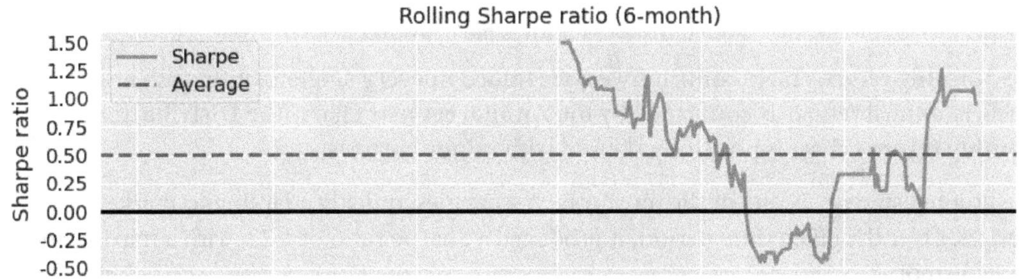

Figure 9.110 – Prophet strategy; 6-month rolling Sharpe ratio over the investment horizon

The **Rolling Sharpe ratio** chart shows that the max rolling Sharpe ratio was between `-.50` and `1.5`.

The following is the **Top 5 drawdown periods** chart:

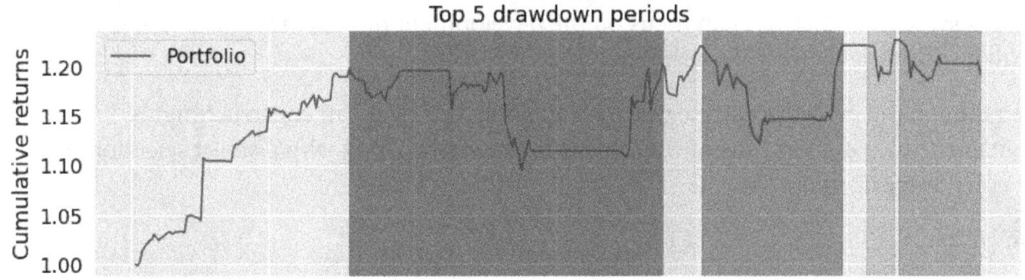

Figure 9.111 – Prophet strategy; top five drawdown periods over the investment horizon

The **Top 5 drawdown periods** chart shows that even though the drawdown periods were substantial, the algorithm was able to deal with them well.

The following are the **Monthly returns**, **Annual returns**, and **Distribution of monthly returns** charts:

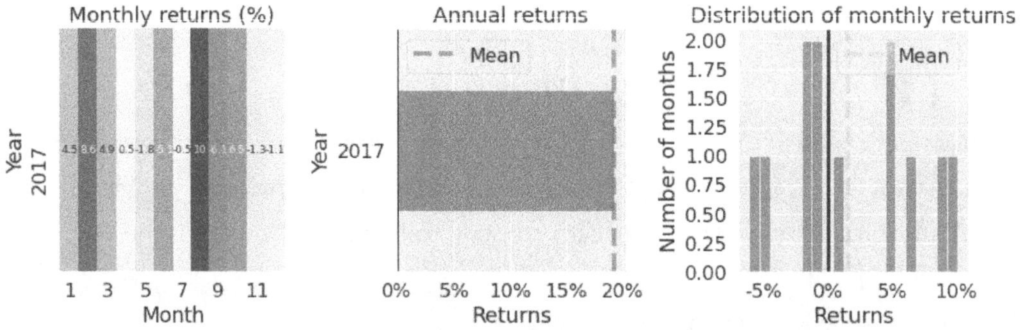

Figure 9.112 – Prophet strategy; monthly returns, annual returns, and the distribution of monthly returns over the investment horizon

The **Monthly returns** table confirms we have traded in every single month, with an excellent annual return as confirmed by the **Annual returns** chart. The **Distribution of monthly returns** chart is positively skewed with minor kurtosis.

The Prophet strategy is one of the most robust strategies, quickly adapting to market changes. Over the given time period, it produced a Sharpe ratio of 1.22, with a maximum drawdown of -8.7.

Summary

In this chapter, we have learned that an algorithmic trading strategy is defined by a model, entry/leave rules, position limits, and further key properties. We have demonstrated how easy it is in Zipline and PyFolio to set up a complete backtesting and risk analysis/position analysis system, so that you can focus on the development of your strategies, rather than wasting your time on the infrastructure.

Even though the preceding strategies are well published, you can construct highly profitable strategies by means of combining them wisely, along with a smart selection of the entry and exit rules.

Bon voyage!

Appendix A How to Setup a Python Environment

This book's GitHub repository (`http://github.com/PacktPublishing/Hands-On-Financial-Trading-with-Python/`) contains Jupyter notebooks that will help you replicate the output shown here.

The environment was created by manually choosing compatible versions of all the included packages.

Technical requirements

The code in this book can run on Windows, Mac, or Linux operating systems.

Initial setup

To set up the Python environment, follow these steps:

1. Download and install Anaconda Python from `https://www.anaconda.com/products/individual` if you do not have it installed yet.
2. `git clone` the repository:

```
git clone XXXXX
```

3. Change the current directory to the cloned GitHub repository.
4. Run the following code:

```
conda env create -f handson-algorithmic-trading-with-
python\environment.yml -n handson-algorithmic-trading-
with-python
```

5. Change the active environment:

```
conda activate handson-algorithmic-trading-with-python
```

6. Set the global environmental variables for market access:

Variable Name	Description	URL of where to obtain the free token
IEX_TOKEN	IEX Market Data	https://iexcloud.io/
MarketStack_Access_Key	MarketStack Access Key	https://marketstack.com/
QUANDL_API_KEY	Quandl API Key	https://www.quandl.com/

Figure 1 – Table of various variable names and where to obtain free token

7. Using Window's Control Panel, set the system environment:

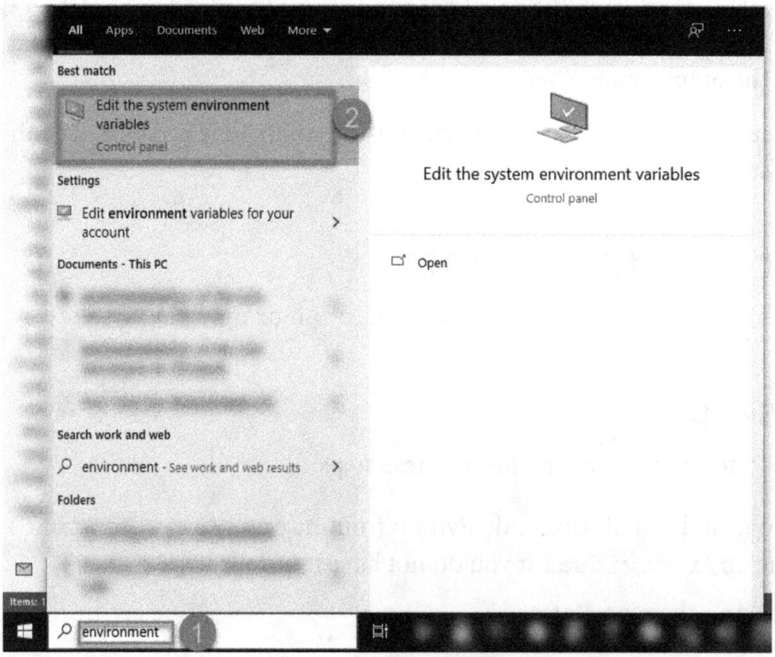

Figure 2 – How to find the Environment dialog in MS Windows

Then, choose **Edit the system environment variables**:

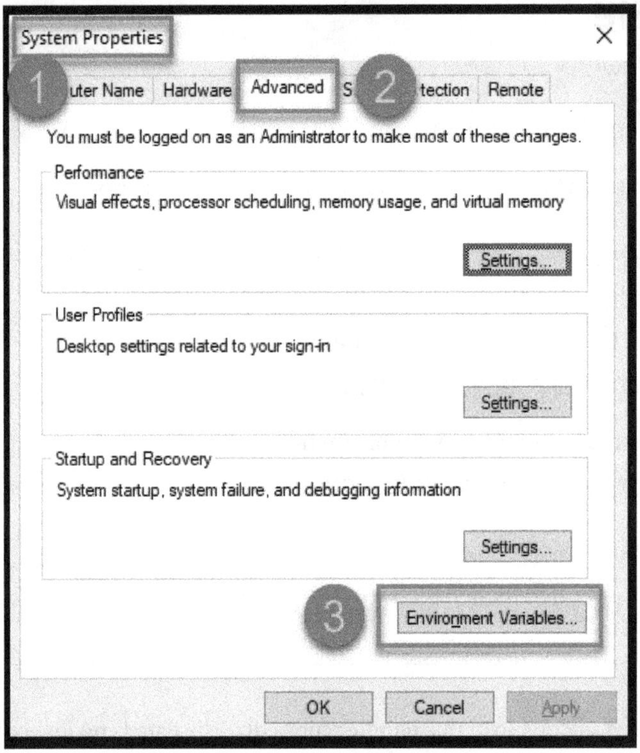

Figure 3 – The steps for setting up a MS Windows environmental variable

Then, specify the variable in the **Environment Variables ...** dialog.

On Mac/Linux, add the following command to `~/.bash_profile` for user-based operations or `~/.bashrc` for non-login interactive shells:

```
Export QUANDL_API_KEY=xxxx
```

Close the Command Prompt so that the global environmental variables can be activated.

8. Proceed with the **Download the Complimentary Quandl Data Bundle** and **Once Installed Setup** stages.

> **Note:**
>
> The `environment.yml` file was generated using the `conda env export > environmenmt.yml` command after one of the packages' meta files was fixed due to a typo.

Downloading the complimentary Quandl data bundle

The steps are as follows:

1. Change the active environment:

```
conda activate handson-algorithmic-trading-with-python
```

2. Set the `QUANDL_API_KEY` value if you have not set it up yet via Window's Control Panel or by using `.bash_profile` or `.bashrc`.

   For Windows, use the following command:

```
SET QUANDL_API_KEY=XXXXXXXX
```

   For Mac/Linux, use the following command:

```
export QUANDL_API_KEY=XXXXXXXX
```

3. Ingest the data:

```
zipline ingest -b quandl
```

> **Note**
> You don't need to download this bundle repeatedly. The data is no longer being updated.

Once you have set up the environment, follow these steps:

1. Change the current directory to the cloned GitHub repository.
2. Change the active environment:

```
conda activate handson-algorithmic-trading-with-python
```

3. Launch Jupyter Lab, like so:

```
jupyter lab
```

Other Books You May Enjoy

If you enjoyed this book, you may be interested in these other books by Packt:

Python Algorithmic Trading Cookbook

Pushpak Dagade

ISBN: 978-1-83898-935-4

- Use Python to set up connectivity with brokers
- Handle and manipulate time series data using Python
- Fetch a list of exchanges, segments, financial instruments, and historical data to interact with the real market
- Understand, fetch, and calculate various types of candles and use them to compute and plot diverse types of technical indicators
- Develop and improve the performance of algorithmic trading strategies
- Perform backtesting and paper trading on algorithmic trading strategies
- Implement real trading in the live hours of stock markets

Python for Finance Cookbook

Eryk Lewinson

ISBN: 978-1-78961-851-8

- Download and preprocess financial data from different sources
- Backtest the performance of automatic trading strategies in a real-world setting
- Estimate financial econometrics models in Python and interpret their results
- Use Monte Carlo simulations for a variety of tasks such as derivatives valuation and risk assessment
- Improve the performance of financial models with the latest Python libraries
- Apply machine learning and deep learning techniques to solve different financial problems
- Understand the different approaches used to model financial time series data

Packt is searching for authors like you

If you're interested in becoming an author for Packt, please visit `authors.packtpub.com` and apply today. We have worked with thousands of developers and tech professionals, just like you, to help them share their insight with the global tech community. You can make a general application, apply for a specific hot topic that we are recruiting an author for, or submit your own idea.

Leave a review - let other readers know what you think

Please share your thoughts on this book with others by leaving a review on the site that you bought it from. If you purchased the book from Amazon, please leave us an honest review on this book's Amazon page. This is vital so that other potential readers can see and use your unbiased opinion to make purchasing decisions, we can understand what our customers think about our products, and our authors can see your feedback on the title that they have worked with Packt to create. It will only take a few minutes of your time, but is valuable to other potential customers, our authors, and Packt. Thank you!

Index

Symbols

A

E

F

N

O

P

Q

R

Printed in the USA
CPSIA information can be obtained
at www.ICGtesting.com
LVHW081926191123
764380LV00022B/115

9 781838 982881